诸子百家智慧故事
Wisdom of Ancient Chinese Sages

WISDOM of HAN FEIZI

韩非子
智慧故事

主编　陶黎铭　张英

中文作者　姚萱

英文作者　潘智丹

英文审订　汪榕培

Editors-in-Chief *Tao Liming*　*Zhang Ying*
Chinese by　*Yao Xuan*
English by　*Pan Zhidan*
Revised by　*Wang Rongpei*

上海外语教育出版社
外教社 SHANGHAI FOREIGN LANGUAGE EDUCATION PRESS

图书在版编目（CIP）数据

韩非子智慧故事：汉英对照／姚萱著，潘智丹译.
—上海：上海外语教育出版社，2010
（诸子百家智慧故事丛书）
ISBN 978-7-5446-1941-7

I.①韩…　II.①姚…　②潘…　III.①韩非（前280～前233）
—哲学思想—通俗读物　IV.①B226.5-49

中国版本图书馆CIP数据核字（2010）第140540号

出版发行： 上海外语教育出版社
　　　　　　（上海外国语大学内）　邮编：200083
电　　话： 021-65425300（总机）
电子邮箱： bookinfo@sflep.com.cn
网　　址： http://www.sflep.com.cn　http://www.sflep.com
责任编辑： 梁瀚杰

印　　刷： 上海叶大印务发展有限公司
开　　本： 890×1240　1/32　印张9.25　字数283千字
版　　次： 2010年12月第1版　2010年12月第1次印刷
印　　数： 3 100册

书　　号： ISBN 978-7-5446-1941-7 / B · 0011
定　　价： 37.00元

本版图书如有印装质量问题，可向本社调换

前　言

　　2000 多年前的春秋战国时代，是中国各种思想流派百花齐放的时期，涌现了孔子、孟子、老子、庄子、墨子、荀子、孙子、韩非子等思想家、哲学家，他们开创了儒、道、墨、法等各具特色、影响深远的思想派别，后世称为"诸子百家"。"诸子百家智慧故事"是一套介绍先秦诸子经典的汉英对照系列丛书，将先秦诸子的生平事迹、哲学思想、格言警句、哲理寓言以及与他们有关的历史故事串联成启迪智慧的短小故事，既能满足中国读者的普及型阅读需求，又照顾到国外读者的文化特点，让大家在轻松愉快的阅读氛围中走近春秋战国时代"百家争鸣"的先哲们。

　　为了让世界更好地了解中国的经典文化，"诸子百家智慧故事"在编写上突出了以下三个特点：

　　轻松阅读——本系列每本书中文不过七八万字，每个故事就是一个相对独立的阅读单位，仅几百字的内容十分钟就能读完，在当今信息爆炸的快节奏时代，这种文本便于读者随时取出翻阅。

　　经济阅读——中国的文字特别是古文字常常是外国人阅读中国经典的障碍，本丛书采取汉英双语对照，中文是浅显易懂的白话体，配以通顺晓畅的英语译文，读者无须钻研艰深的典籍，就能了解先哲的智慧。

　　趣味阅读——本丛书通过一个个短小生动的故事以及古意盎然的插图，为读者深入浅出地解读诸子经典。

　　先秦诸子经典是中国的宝贵精神财富，至今在中国乃至全世界都有广泛的影响。希望本丛书能够引起广大中外读者对先秦诸子百家的兴趣，并能通过书中的故事体会到博大精深的中国智慧。

编者

Preface

Over two millennia ago, China experienced a boom of ideas and philosophies in the form of "100 Schools of Thought". Confucius, Mencius, Laozi, Zhuangzi, Mozi, Xunzi, Han Feizi, Sun Tzu ... These are the stellar names behind the philosophical schools like Confucianism, Taoism, Mohism, Legalism, etc. in the Spring and Autumn Period and the Warring States Period (from 770 BC to 221 BC). The classics of these ancient sages contain great wisdom and have exerted profound influence on Chinese history and thought. While the classics themselves may seem difficult to understand today, you can find lucid and accessible explanations of the ancient philosophies in the books of *Wisdom of Ancient Chinese Sages*. With the help of a collection of short and interesting stories, you can get to know the lives and thoughts of the ancient sages, the axioms and allegories they employed to illustrate their ideas, and some facts about the historical era they lived in.

With the aim of presenting the ancient Chinese classics to the world audience, *Wisdom of Ancient Chinese Sages* boasts three advantages:

Easiness — Each book in the series is comprised of only a few dozen stories, each of which has no more than 2,000 words and can be glanced through in a 10-minute coffee break. Even in your busy life, you can always snatch some time to enjoy a story of wisdom and gain some spiritual nourishment.

Efficiency — The classics may seem a little obscure today since they are written in the ancient Chinese. In this Chinese-English version of *Wisdom of Ancient Chinese Sages*, however, the classics are rendered in simple, everyday English. Without having to tax your brains, you can readily comprehend the profound wisdom of the ancient sages.

Attractiveness — With all the short but lively stories accompanied by beautiful illustrations, *Wisdom of Ancient Chinese Sages* explains to you the ancient philosophical ideas in a friendly and agreeable way.

The ancient philosophical classics in the "100 Schools of Thought" are an important spiritual heritage of China and impose great cultural reverberations beyond the Chinese borders. We hope that the series may let the readers develop an interest in the ancient Chinese sages and their philosophies, and appreciate the quintessential Chinese wisdom that may prove useful in present day.

Editors

目录

Contents

韩非子生平
The Life of Han Feizi

韩非 是我国战国时期(公元前475年～前221年)著名的哲学家、散文家，是法家学说的集大成者。关于他的生平事迹，历史记载流传下来的不多。我们今天对他一生事迹的了解，主要依据西汉司马迁的《史记·老庄申韩列传》。

韩非是战国末期韩国人。其生年不详，研究者多推断在公元前280年左右，卒年为公元前233年(秦始皇十四年)。他出身于韩国君主之家，《史记·老庄申韩列传》说他是"韩之诸公子"，即韩君的妾所生的儿子。注意到韩非这个出身，颇有助于我们理解其学说。可以想见，韩非显贵的地位和接近权力中心的生活环境对他思想和学说的形成是十分重要的。他生长于深宫之中，不可能与广大民众甚至中下层官吏声气相通，这就决定了他的学说与同时代的儒家、墨家、农家的学说不同，不具备显而易见的平民色彩，其服务的唯一对象只能是君王，所思所想也不外是维护君王地位的稳固和权势的独尊。因为他是韩国君主的庶子，故以国名"韩"为氏，其名为"非"。当时的人都有名有字，韩非的字则没有传下来。韩非是先秦诸子之一，后人又尊称他为"韩子"、"韩非子"。

韩非有口吃结巴的毛病，因此不善于辩论言谈，但他却很会撰文著书。心理学上把这种现象称为"补偿反应"，就好比盲人往往听觉特别灵敏。在当时，有识之士要想实施自己的学说大多得靠说服打动君王，像韩非这样天资聪颖、见解深刻、思想敏锐的人，却偏偏要遭受"不能道说"之苦，可以想见，这种生理上的压抑长期得不到有效的释放和排遣，恐怕是会在某种程度上对其学说的构建有所影响的。

韩非从小喜好"刑名法术"之学，即刑名与法术结合所构成的学问。"刑名法术"之学是讲治国要用法律，法律的制定要有一定的规范，有明确的是非标准，该赏则赏，当罚就罚，不避亲私；君主驾驭、控制臣下，要有一套权术计谋。这种观点的宣传者主要是法家，其渊源一般追溯到"黄老"，即黄帝和老子。到韩非求学的时代，当时还注重刑名之学而又有一定影响的人物，只有儒家的别派传人荀子（约公元前313～前230年）。荀子继承了儒家思想，但他能打破门户之见，对各家学派的思想精华兼收并蓄，其中也包括法家思想中的积极因素。因此，从小喜爱刑名之学的韩非便慕名前往拜师，成了荀子的门徒。与他同窗的还有一位著名的人物，那就是李斯。韩非和李斯两人后来都成为法家的代表人物。李斯出身于楚国平民，可以说是实践家；韩非出身于韩国宗室，可以说是理论家。在才华上，韩非比李斯要高出一头，李斯也自认为比不上韩非。在当时战国纷争的时代，韩非作为韩国人，又是君主的儿子，因此学成之后便返回故土，以期报效祖国。而李斯在跟随荀子学习治理国家的办法之后，急于施展自己的政治才华，他认为秦王打算吞并天下，霸气十足，在秦国自己一定能大展身手，于是投奔了秦王，果然得到秦王的重用。

在战国七雄中，韩国是最弱的一个国家。韩非目睹当时的韩国积贫积弱，出于爱国心，他多次向韩王安上书，希望韩王安能变法图强，但其主张始终得不到采纳。当时韩国当道的大臣结党营私，苟且偷安，极力排挤主张革新、要求推行法治的"智术之士"。在这种政治条件下，韩非只好退出政治斗争的名利场，回到书斋，以著书立说来宣扬自己的政治主张。他根据历史上治国的经验教训和现实的社会状况，写出了《孤愤》、《五蠹》、《内外储说》、《说林》、《说难》等文章，洋洋十万余言。

韩非的主张在韩国得不到重视，但《孤愤》和《五蠹》等名篇却传入了秦国。秦王嬴政，即后来的秦始皇，一心想成就统一天下的霸业，读了韩非的文章后喜欢极了，因为韩非的法家思想和建立中央集权政治的主张与秦王称霸的想法不谋而合。他感叹道："哎呀！真是厉害啊！我如果能见到这些文章的作者并且同他促膝交谈，即使死掉也没什么可遗憾的了！"李斯告诉他，这些文章的作者是韩非，这人现在就在韩国，秦王大喜过望。他急于实现自己的称霸野心，认为韩非一定能帮助他尽快完成统一大业。为了早日见到这位旷世奇才，秦王甚至不惜以发动一场战争的代价，发兵加紧攻打韩国，以武力相逼，促使韩王就范。韩王安起初不任用韩非，现在看到情势危急，不得不派遣韩非出使秦国。

　　韩非是公元前233年抵达秦国的。秦王非常高兴，但一时还没有对韩非加以信任和重用。韩非的同窗学友李斯出于嫉妒，又惧怕韩非得势会影响到自己的地位，就在秦王面前故意诋毁韩非。正好韩非曾上书劝秦王先伐赵、缓伐韩，给李斯找到了口实。李斯便鼓动上卿姚贾一起去面见秦王，诋毁说："韩非是韩国国君的儿子，最终肯定是为保存韩国着想，而不是为秦国吞并诸侯着想，这毕竟是人之常情嘛。现在大王如果长期不重用韩非却将他留在秦国，以后还是要放他回国，这恐怕会给自己留下无穷后患！还不如趁早加以罪名，依法处死他，以绝后患。"秦王听了，认为说得很有道理，就把韩非投入监狱，交给法官审讯治罪。李斯又派人送毒药给韩非，逼他自杀。韩非想要面见秦王，为自己辩解，向秦王表明自己的忠心，但李斯不让他晋见。韩非无可奈何，在李斯的威逼之下，只能服毒自尽了。不久秦王就后悔了，派人去赦免韩非，但为时已晚，韩非已经死在狱中。

在简单地记完韩非的一生之后，司马迁不禁发出这样的感叹："韩非知道向君主进说之难，写了《说难》，文章谈得很详细很清楚，但他最终还是因为游说人君而死在秦国，不能自我解脱。我真是为他感到悲哀啊！"

关于韩非之死，另外还有不同的说法，由于史料有限，还不能得到证实。

Han Feizi

was a famous philosopher and prose writer in the Warring States Period (475–221 BC); most important of all, he was the leading figure of the philosophical school of Legalism. Few records can be found about his life, and what we know about Han Feizi today is mainly based on "Biographies of Laozi, Zhuangzi, Shen Buhai and Han Feizi" in *Records of the Grand Historian* written by Sima Qian (145–87 BC) of the Western Han Dynasty.

Han Feizi was born in the State of Han in the late Warring States Period. Little is known about his living years, so many researchers infer that he was born around 280 BC and died in 233 BC (the 14th year of the reign of Emperor Shi Huangdi of the Qin Dynasty). He was born in the royal family of the King of Han; more specifically, he was "one of the many princes of the State of Han," namely, a son born to a concubine of the King of Han. Knowledge of Han Feizi's birth is of much help for us to understand his doctrines. We can well imagine that the eminent position and the living environment which allowed him to get up close to the center of power must have played an important role in the development of his thoughts and doctrines. Since he was brought up in the royal palace, it was not possible for him to share interests and tastes with the populace or even the middle- and lower-ranking officials. Such being the case, his doctrines were bound to be different from those of his contemporaries, such as the Confucian school, the Mohist school and the Agriculturalist school. Han Feizi's ideas actually had little in common with the lives of ordinary people, and the only purpose was nothing but the defense for the throne and the upholding of the monarch's power as the supreme authority. Since he was the son of a concubine of the King of Han, he took the name of the state "Han" as his surname and "Fei" was his given name. At that time, everyone had both a name and a style name, but the style name of Han Feizi was not passed down. As one of the great thinkers before the Qin Dynasty, he was also respectfully addressed as "Hanzi" and "Han Feizi".

Han Feizi had an impediment in speech, so he was not good at arguing or expressing himself, but he was especially apt in writing essays and books. In psychology, this phenomenon is called "compensation reaction", just like the fact that blind people usually have a keen hearing. At that time, scholars of different schools mostly depended on persuasion to convince the monarchs if they wanted to put their own doctrines into practice. As luck would have it, Han Feizi, who was endowed with intelligence, keen observation and a quick mind, suffered from the inability to express himself by speech. We can well imagine that such physiological inhibition might have exerted certain influence over the construction of his doctrines to some extent when he couldn't find an effective way to free himself from it.

Han Feizi was interested in the learning of "laws and governing methods", namely, regulating people by laws and controlling them by manipulative methods. According to Han Feizi, the state should be run by the rule of law, and laws should be made to define right and wrong, give reward to those who have rendered outstanding services, impose punishment on those who have committed crimes, and be applicable to everyone impartially without consideration of personal interests. The monarch is to take control over his subjects, so he should master a set of governing methods. Such views were the canons of the Legalist school and could be further traced back to the thoughts of "Huang and Lao", namely, Huangdi (the legendary Yellow Emperor) and Laozi (the famous Taoist philosopher in the 6th century BC to the 5th century BC). At the time when Han Feizi pursued his studies, the only prominent scholar who attached importance to the learning of "laws and governing methods" was Xunzi (circa 313 BC–230 BC), one successor of the Confucian school. Xunzi inherited the thoughts of the Confucian school, but he was open-minded enough to ignore the sectarian bias and absorbed the ideas of various schools, including elements of the Legalist school. Therefore, Han Feizi, interested in the learning of "laws and governing methods" since his childhood, had great admiration for Xunzi and went to ask for permission to study under his tutorship. Han Feizi then became a disciple of Xunzi and studied together with another famous man, Li Si. Han Feizi and Li Si both became representatives of the Legalist school later. Li Si was born of a common family in the State of Chu and could be considered as a practitioner, while Han Feizi was born in the royal family of the State of Han and could be regarded as a theorist. Han Feizi was much more talented than Li Si, which Li Si admitted himself. At an age when all states were constantly at war with each other, Han Feizi naturally went back to his hometown after finishing his study, both as a man of the State of Han and as a son of the King of Han, in the hopes of rendering service to his state. By contrast, Li Si was anxious to put his political talents to good use after learning the ways to run a state from Xunzi. In his opinion, the King of Qin was a promising ruler and had great ambition in conquering all the other states, so he could bring his talents to full play in the State of Qin. Therefore, he went to serve the King of Qin and was promoted to an important position.

The State of Han was the least powerful among the seven warring states. Seeing the perennial poverty and weakness in the State of Han, Han Feizi sent in many memorials to the King of Han out of patriotism, hoping that the king could carry out political reforms to make the state prosperous, but his propositions were never adopted. At that time, the ministers in power in the State of Han all ganged up for selfish purposes and momentary profit, so they spared no effort in driving away those "men of stratagem" who advocated political reforms and demanded for the rule of law. Under such political circumstances, Han Feizi had to step out of the vanity fair of political struggle and retreat to his study to preach his own political views by writing books and expounding his theory. Based on the historical experience of ruling a state and the present social conditions, Han Feizi wrote many essays such as "On Solitude and Indignation", "Five Kinds of Vermin", "Internal and External Collections of Stories", "On Various Matters" and "On the Difficulty of Persuasion", which were as lengthy as they were brilliant.

Han Feizi's views did not receive due attention in the State of Han, but his famous essays such as "On Solitude and Indignation" and "Five Kinds of Vermin" were introduced into the State of Qin. The King of Qin, who later became Emperor Shi Huangdi of the Qin Dynasty, had set his mind on building up a hegemony by unifying all the warring states. Therefore, after reading Han Feizi's essays, the king was very pleased, for the Legalist thoughts of Han Feizi and his view of establishing a centralized government coincided with the King of Qin's ambition of seeking hegemony. The king sighed with joy, "Wow! What a great person he is! Only if I could meet the author of these essays and have a heart-to-heart talk with him, I would have no regret upon my death!" Li Si, then a high minister in the State of Qin, told the king that these essays were written by Han Feizi, who was living in the State of Han at the moment. Hearing this, the king was overjoyed. He was anxious to achieve his ambition of building up a hegemony, so he thought Han Feizi was bound to be able to help him realize the great cause of unification as soon as possible. In order to meet this brilliant man, the king even dispatched troops to launch an attack against the State of Han to compel the King of Han to yield Han Feizi. The King of Han did not employ Han Feizi at first, but he had to send Han Feizi to the State of Qin as an envoy in face of the critical situation at the present moment.

Han Feizi arrived in the State of Qin in 233 BC. The King of Qin was very pleased to see him, but didn't assign him to any important post or show any trust in him at first. Yet, Han Feizi's former classmate Li Si became jealous. Afraid that Han Feizi would get the upper hand once gaining power, Li Si deliberately slandered Han Feizi in the presence of the King of Qin. It happened that Han Feizi once sent a memorial persuading the King of Qin to attack the State of Zhao and to delay the attack against the State of Han. Li Si used this opportunity to plant false accusations against Han Feizi. He went to meet the King of Qin with Senior Official Yao Gu and said, "Since Han Feizi is the son of the King of Han, he consequently must think about protecting the State of Han instead of helping the State of Qin to seize the other states. That might probably bring endless trouble in the future. Therefore, it would be better to charge him with a guilt and execute him by law, so as to remove the cause of future trouble." Hearing this, the king thought that Li Si's words were quite reasonable. He then threw Han Feizi into prison to await trial and possible sentences. Li Si sent poison to Han Feizi to force him to commit suicide. Han Feizi wanted to see the king to defend himself and to show his loyalty, but all his efforts were stopped by Li Si. Intimidated by Li Si, Han Feizi had no alternative but to commit suicide by taking the poison. The king soon regretted his earlier decision, so he sent someone to grant Han Feizi a pardon, only to find Han Feizi had died in the prison.

After briefly recording the life of Han Feizi, Sima Qian couldn't help commenting in a sorrowful tone, "Han Feizi knew well how hard it was to convince the monarch to accept his doctrines, so he wrote the essay 'On the Difficulty of Persuasion', which gave clear and detailed exposition on that matter. However, he died at last for lobbying the monarch in the State of Qin when he was unable to relieve himself from such a fate. How I grieve for him!"

There are other versions about Han Feizi's death, but they cannot be confirmed owing to the lack of historical records.

韩非子智慧故事
Wisdom of Han Feizi

1. 子罕以不贪为宝

　　春秋时期宋国有一位叫子罕的贤臣。当时宋国有个乡下人得到了一块玉璞，就把它进献给子罕。子罕不肯接受。献玉的乡下人说："这块玉璞我已经拿给雕琢玉器的工匠看过了，玉工认为它是宝物，所以我才敢进献给您呀！如此美玉只有您这样的君子才配得上，像我这样地位低下的小人可不配使用。"子罕说："你把美玉看成珍宝，我把不接受你的玉看成珍宝。如果你把玉给了我，那么我们两个人都失去了各自所宝贵的东西。你还是把这玉拿回去，让我们各人都保有自己的宝物吧。"

　　《韩非子》用这个故事来说明《老子》所说的"把没有欲望当作欲望，不要把难得的财物看得贵重"的道理。这个故事也见于《左传·襄公十五年》。《左传》记载的还多出了下面一段内容：献玉的人很恭敬地叩头，然后对子罕说："小人怀中藏着宝玉，难免被贼人惦记，到哪里都不安全啊。还是把它送给您吧，这样我就可以免于被人谋财害命了。"于是子罕就把美玉放在自己住的地方，让玉工雕琢它，然后又卖了出去，把钱给了献玉的人，然后送他回家去了。《韩非子》中子罕说"我以不受子玉为宝"，《左传》中则记载子罕说"我以不贪为宝"。"以不贪为宝"成为名言，更得到后人的传颂。

"以不贪为宝"，是两千多年前的子罕都已经明白了的道理，现代的某些官员却反而做不到，这实在是一种悲哀。一些贪官贪污受贿、以权谋私，以为钱多权重就是宝，全然不知这个"宝"也是个祸。直到为"宝"所累，丢官弃职，身陷牢笼，甚至送掉了卿卿性命，才知道哀叹"不贪真好"。早知今日，何必当初？

IT IS A VIRTUE TO BE FREE FROM GREED

There lived a virtuous minister called Zihan in the State of Song in the Spring and Autumn Period. At that time, a countryman of Song got an uncut jade and sent it to Zihan as a present, but Zihan would not accept it. The countryman who presented the jade said, "I have had it examined by a jade carver, who believed it to be a real treasure. Therefore, I dare to present it to you because only a gentleman like you deserve such a fine jade, while a lowly man like me is not worth it at all." Zihan said, "You consider this fine jade as a treasure, but I consider not accepting it as a treasure. If you give it to me, we will both lose our own treasures. Thus you'd better take it back, so that we can both keep our own treasures."

Han Feizi uses this story to show the idea that *Laozi* described as "regarding having no desire as a desire and not regarding rare wealth as valuable." This story can also be found in *The Chronicles of Zuo* with additional content that goes as follows. The man who presented the jade kowtowed with great respect and said to Zihan, "If I hide the precious jade in my bosom, thieves would inevitably be thinking about it, so it won't be safe wherever I go. I'd better give it to you, so that I would escape the fate of being murdered for it." Therefore, Zihan placed the fine jade in his own living place and had it polished by a jade carver. Then he sold it out, gave the money to the man, and sent him home. Zihan said "I consider not accepting the jade as a treasure" in *Han Feizi*, while he said "I consider being free from greed as a treasure" in *The Chronicles of Zuo*. Therefore, "being free from greed is considered as a treasure" became a well-known saying passed down from generation to generation.

"It is a virtue to be free from greed." Zihan, living over two thousand years ago, understood that, but some officials at present day, unfortunately, don't seem to pay heed to it at all. Some corrupt officials embezzle money, take bribes, and abuse their power for personal gains. They consider more money and power to be a "treasure", having not the least idea that this "treasure" is also a misfortune. They will not realize with regret that "it is good to be free from greed" until they are exposed, expelled from their official posts, put into prison, and even sentenced to death. If they had known what was going to happen, would they have been that greedy?

2. 宋人刻象牙楮叶

　　有个擅长雕刻的宋国人，他用象牙雕刻楮树的叶子，打算献给国君，花了三年时间终于完工了。这象牙楮叶尺寸宽窄合度，上面的筋脉、绒毛和色泽栩栩如生，即使将它混杂在真的楮叶中，也辨别不出来。宋国人的手艺得到了全国上下的一致好评，他也因为这一功劳而在宋国当了官。当时道家的著名代表人物列子听到此事却不以为然，批评说："假如自然界要经过三年才长成一片叶子，那么有叶子的东西可就太少了！"

　　韩非用这个故事来说明《老子》所说的"仰仗万物自然而然地发展而不敢勉强去做"的道理。他认为，"万物都有常态，应该因势利导。如果顺应了万物的常态，那么静止的时候就能够保持本性，活动的时候就能够顺应规律。"在讲了这个故事之后又议论道："所以不依靠自然条件而仅凭一个人的本事，不顺应自然法则而表现一个人的智巧，那就都是用三年时间雕刻一片叶子的行为了。所以冬天里种出的庄稼，即使是种植庄稼的始祖后稷也不能使它多产；丰年里旺盛的庄稼，就算是没什么本事的奴仆也不能使它枯败。仅凭一人的力量，就是后稷也不足以成事；而只要顺应自然规律，就是奴仆也会成事有余。"

　　当然，这个故事从老子、列子等道家人物所反复强调的顺应自然、不忤造化、不违天时的思想出发，完全否定了人为的仿自然的艺术，这一点也是不可取的。逼真地模仿自然的艺术，其价值并不在于与自然物比实际用处，而主要在于展示人对"美"的创造和欣赏能力，展示作为"万物之灵"的人类区别于动物的灵巧和智慧。

CARVING IVORY INTO A PAPER MULBERRY LEAF

There lived a man good at carving in the State of Song. He spent a good three years carving ivory into a paper mulberry leaf, which he intended to present to the king as a gift. The paper mulberry leaf made of ivory looked like a real leaf, with vivid veins, villi and lifelike colors. No one can tell it from real leaves when they were mixed together. The craftsmanship of this man of Song won unanimous praise from all over the state, and he was also given an official post for such an accomplishment. Liezi, a representative figure of the Taoist school, thought otherwise when he heard about it. He said in criticism, "If it took three years for a leaf to grow in nature, there would be few things with leaves."

Han Feizi uses this story to explain the idea that "we should let all things in nature grow as they do instead of imposing force on them", which first appeared in *Laozi*. He thought, "As all things generally stay in their normal state, we should guide them along their course of development. If they keep their normal state, they can keep their nature when being still and grow by their own laws when set in motion." After telling this story, he argues, "Therefore, relying on one's own ability instead of natural conditions or flaunting one's own smartness by working against the laws of nature is the same kind of folly as spending three years to carve a leaf out of ivory. Thus, even Houji, the first ancestor of all farmers, couldn't make the crops more productive if they are planted in winter; even an unskillful servant would not make the crops fail if they are harvested in a bumper year. Relying on a single person's power, even Houji cannot accomplish anything; on the other hand, even a lowly servant can get things done if he conforms to the laws of nature."

Still, this story follows the Taoist view, as emphasized repeatedly by Laozi and Liezi, that one should conform to the laws of nature without violating natural rules and seasonal changes. That leads to the downplaying of the human art of imitating nature. However, the value of the art of vividly imitating nature lies not in competing with natural objects in terms of practical use, but in displaying man's ability of creating and appreciating beauty and in showing the ingenuity and wisdom which distinguish man, "the culmination of all being", from an animal.

3. 墨子做木鸢

　　墨子用木头制作了一只飞鸢，经过三年才制成，只飞了一天就坏了。他的弟子说："先生的手艺真巧，竟能达到让木鸢高飞的境界。"墨子说："车插销是牛车上细小而关键的部件。我比不上制造插销的人手艺高超，他们用细小的木头，费不了一天的功夫，就能使牛拉的大车牵引三十石的重量，走很远的路，出很大的力，并且可以用很多年。现在我做了木鸢，三年做成，才飞了一天就坏了。"惠子听到后，评论说："墨子是'大巧'、真正的巧——他知道做车插销是真正巧的，而做木鸢是笨拙的。"

　　风筝起源于中国，一般认为，墨子制造的这只"木鸢"就是中国见于记载的最早的风筝。墨子名翟，战国初期鲁国人，是墨家的创始人。据一些古书记载，墨子是一位真正的"草根"哲学家，是出身于手工业工匠的"士"，熟悉木工和其他手工技术，所以他能做出这样精巧的"木鸢"。

这个故事与上一个"宋人刻象牙楮叶"的故事寓意有相近之处，都表现出某种程度上的"实用主义"，反对违反自然、没有多大实际用处的工巧。古人排斥各种精深繁复但实用性不大的手工业品和艺术品，一概斥之为"奇技淫巧"，这在一定程度上阻碍了中国古代科学技术的发展。

MOZI MAKES A WOODEN HAWK

Mozi (the founder of Mohism) made a flying hawk out of wood, which took him as long as three years, but it only flew for one day and then broke down. His disciples said, "You are so clever that you can make a wooden hawk fly into the sky." Mozi said, "A bolt is a tiny but crucial part in an oxcart. I cannot match those who make the bolt, for it just takes them less than a day to make such a tiny object with thin wood slices, which enables an oxcart to carry a heavy load of thirty *dan* over a great distance. And the bolt can be used for many years. Now I spent three years just on a wooden hawk, which broke down after flying for only one day." Hearing this, Huizi (a diplomat and philosopher) commented, "Mozi is a great man, a truly ingenious man — he knows that a cart bolt is a clever contraption while his wooden hawk is a clumsy one."

Kites originated in China. It is generally believed that the "wooden hawk" made by Mozi was the earliest kite to be recorded in history. Mozi, whose name was Di, was born in the State of Lu in the early Warring States Period. He was the founder of the Mohist school. According to the records in ancient books, Mozi was a "grass-root" philosopher, a craftsman-turned scholar. He was familiar with carpentry and other handiwork skills, so he could make such an exquisite "wooden hawk".

The moral of this story has something in common with that of the previous story "Carving ivory into a paper mulberry leaf", for they both show a certain degree of "utilitarianism" and objection to the craftsmanship that goes against the laws of nature and does not have much practical use. The ancient people rejected sophisticated handiworks and elaborate artworks which were not quite practically useful, and even dismissed them as "queer skills and vicious ingenuity". Such belief had in effect hampered the scientific and technological development in the ancient China to a certain extent.

4. 上有所好，下必甚焉

　　越王勾践筹划攻打吴国，想要老百姓不惧死亡为他卖命。有一次他外出时，看见一只发怒的青蛙，就手扶在车前的横木上向它致敬。随从说："干吗对一只发怒的青蛙致敬？"越王说："因为这只青蛙气势汹汹的啊。"武士们听到后，都说："一只气势汹汹的青蛙，越王都向它致敬，何况勇敢的武士呢？"于是这一年之中，就有十多位勇士请求为越王抛头颅，洒热血，战死沙场。越王准备向吴国复仇，就试行这样的教育：放火焚烧高台后，击鼓令人前进；大家纷纷向烈火中冲去，为什么呢？因为进火有赏。靠近江边后，击鼓令人前进；大家纷纷向江水中冲去，为什么呢？因为进水有赏。临作战时，人们断头剖腹而义无反顾，为什么呢？因为作战有赏。

　　齐桓公非常喜欢穿紫色的衣服，齐国上下从大臣到百姓都模仿桓公穿紫色衣服，于是紫色布料的价格猛涨，当时五匹素布还抵不上一匹紫色的布。齐桓公为此深感忧虑，他对大臣管仲说："因为我喜欢穿紫衣服，弄得全国上下都喜欢穿紫衣服，紫色布料现在贵得离谱，还一天比一天往上涨价，停都停不下来，对此我该怎么办呢？"管仲说："君王想要制止这种状况，自己先带头不穿紫衣服不就得了？您就对近侍说：'我现在特别厌恶紫衣服的气味。'如果在这个时候近侍中恰巧有穿紫衣服进见的人，您一定要说：'稍微退后一点，我厌恶紫衣服的气味。'"桓公说："好吧。"就照着去做了。结果，在这一天之内，君主的侍从官就没有一个穿紫衣服的了；到第二天，国都中就没有一个人穿紫衣服了；到第三天，整个齐国境内就没有一个人穿紫衣服了。

同类的例子《韩非子》还举出了很多，例如，齐桓公爱好女色而心性妒忌，所以一个叫竖刁的人便自行阉割以便掌管内宫；齐桓公爱好美味，吃尽了各种山珍海味后觉得没什么新鲜的了，只有人肉没有吃过，易牙就蒸了自己的儿子去进献给桓公，以求得宠爱。领导者若表现出自己的意向，属下为了博得领导者的欢心，就会揣摩领导者的心意，以便假意迎合。韩非对此的态度是，一方面强调君上要保持神秘，不要轻易表现出自己的意图，以免被臣下窥测利用；另一方面，君上也可以有意表现出正面的、自己想要的态度来对民风加以引导。勾践向怒蛙致敬，表现出自己崇尚勇武精神，由此鼓舞士气，使民众争相赴汤蹈火，便可以用来作战。据史籍记载，吴、越交战，越国敢死队百人，冲至吴军阵前，全部剖腹自杀，十分壮烈，致使吴军阵脚大乱，全线溃败。

由齐桓公好服紫和邹君好服长缨的故事，我们还可以看出普通民众盲目追赶"流行"的可笑。服紫和服长缨从流行到不流行，都出于对君主的盲目模仿，或是出于君主的提倡和禁止。对于那些穿紫衣带长缨、后来又不再穿带的一般人来说，并不是出于自己的真心喜爱或厌恶，他们的行为实在是没有什么道理。现代社会中流行大潮此起彼伏，多半也属于此类。我们应该保持自己的独立，不要被所谓"流行"的大潮所淹没。

THE UPPER CLASS SHOWS A PREFERENCE, AND THE LOWER CLASS FOLLOWS SUIT WITH GREAT FERVOR

King Goujian of Yue was planning to attack the State of Wu, so he wanted the people to risk their lives to fight for him without fear. Once he went out and saw an angry frog. Then he placed a hand on the beam in the front of his cart to show respect to it. His attendant said, "Why did you show respect to an angry frog?" The King of Yue said, "Because this frog has a threatening manner." Hearing this, the warriors all said, "The King of Yue shows respect to a fierce frog, not to mention brave warriors." As a result, over a dozen warriors volunteered to shed their blood and lay down their lives on the battlefield for the King of Yue. When the King of Yue prepared to take revenge on the State of Wu, he tried out the following methods to educate his people. When a tower was set on fire, drums were beaten for warriors to march forward. Then, everyone rushed into the fire. Why? Because they would be rewarded if they rushed into the fire. When the warriors came near a river, drums were beaten for them to march forward. Then, everyone jumped into the river. Why? Because they would be rewarded if they jumped into the river. When marching into a battle, the warriors were willing to lay down their lives with no thought of turning back. Why? Because they would be rewarded if they fought bravely in a battle.

Duke Huan of Qi was especially fond of purple clothes, so people all over the state, from ministers to common people, all copied him in wearing purple clothes. As a result, the price of purple cloth skyrocketed so that five bolts of plain cloth were not as expensive as one bolt of purple cloth. Duke Huan of Qi felt so anxious about it that he said to a minister called Guan Zhong, "Just because I like purple clothes, people all over the state like to wear purple clothes. As a result, the price of purple cloth has gone unreasonable. What's more, the price is going higher each day, with no prospect of getting down. What should I do?" Guan Zhong said, "If you want to remedy this situation, you might as well take the lead in refusing to wear purple clothes. You could tell your attendants, 'It makes me sick to smell purple clothes.' If an attendant happens to meet you in purple clothes, you must say, 'Take a small step backward as I dislike the smell of purple clothes.'" Duke Huan said, "All right." Then he did what he was told. Consequently, no attendant wore purple clothes within a day; on the second day, no one wore purple clothes in the capital; on the third day, no one wore purple clothes in the whole state.

Han Feizi also gives many other examples of this sort. For example, Duke Huan of Qi indulged himself in women and was jealous by nature, so a man called Shu Diao castrated himself so as to be put in charge of the concubines of the duke. Duke Huan of Qi loved delicious food, but as he had tasted all kinds of delicacies, he felt nothing was new except human flesh. Then, a minister Yi Ya presented his own son, steamed on a platter, to Duke Huan in order to curry favor. If a leader shows his own preferences, his subordinate will try to figure out his mind and behave pretentiously in order to win his favor. According to Han Feizi, on the one hand, the monarch should remain mystic, never showing his own intention rashly, in case it should be spied out and made use of by his subjects; on the other hand, the monarch can also exhibit positive attitudes to be followed by the people. Goujian saluted to an angry frog to show his respect for bravery, which consequently boosted the morale of the people and made them eager to be the first to conquer all difficulties and dangers. Such bravery could be used when fighting battles. According to historical records, when Wu and Yue were at war, a "death squad" of 100 men of Yue rushed to the frontline of the Wu troops and committed suicide by cutting open their own bellies. Such heroic death completely demoralized the Wu troops and led to the State of Wu's defeat.

From the story about Duke Huan of Qi's love of purple clothes and that about the King of Zou's love for long-tasseled hats, we can find ridicule in the public behavior of blindly pursuing "fashion". Wearing purple clothes or long-tasseled hats grew from fashionable to unfashionable either out of blind copying of the monarch's dress or out of the monarch's advocation or prohibition. As for those people who wore purple clothes or long-tasseled hats and then quit it, they didn't do so out of their own likes or dislikes, and their behavior was indeed unreasonable. The trends of fashion in the modern society, rising and declining one after another, more or less fall into this category. We should keep our own independence so as not to be manipulated by the so-called "prevailing" trends.

5. 谷阳献酒

　　春秋时楚共王和晋厉公曾在鄢陵大战，结果楚军战败，楚共王的眼睛也被乱箭射中。战斗正激烈的时候，楚军将领司马子反感到口渴，就要水喝。他的侍仆谷阳拿了一杯酒来给他。子反大喝一声，说："嘿！一边去！这是酒啊。你小子想害我啊？"谷阳安慰他说："您放心，不是酒。"子反就接来喝了。子反这人一向嗜酒如命，口渴时喝酒更觉酒味甜美，一喝就停不下来，结果喝醉了。战斗结束后，楚共王不甘心失败，还想再战，派人去召司马子反。子反正喝得酩酊大醉，没有办法，只能以心脏不舒服为由推辞不去。楚共王心里犯疑，于是乘车亲自前往察看。一进子反的帐中，居然闻到一股浓烈的酒味。共王气哼哼地回去了，说："今天的战斗，我自个儿都受了伤。想依靠这位大将吧，这位朋友却又醉成这样。司马子反他是忘了楚国的神灵，不把将士民众的生死放在心上啊！这仗我没法儿再打了！"于是将军队撤离鄢陵，把司马子反处以死刑，陈尸示众。韩非对此总结说："所以侍仆谷阳献酒，并不是因为他仇恨子反，他的内心是忠爱子反的，其本意并不是要害他的主人，但是最终却导致了子反被杀。所以说，滥行小忠，便是对大忠的祸害。"谷阳是所谓"好心办坏事"，可谓"小忠害了大忠"。像这种"表面看来是对他好其实结果是害了他"的事情，我们今天生活中仍然屡见不鲜。典型的例子如父母无原则地溺爱、纵容子女，结果轻则使子女一无所长、难以成才，重则使子女走上邪路，这可以说是"小爱害了大爱"。所以韩非说，"只有点小聪明的人不能让他去谋划大事，只有小忠诚的人不能让他掌管法令。"

　　子反贪杯，也可以看出子反"掩耳盗铃"、"自欺欺人"的心理。他明知是酒，也清楚打仗的时候不能喝酒，但其实早就心痒难耐了。所以谷阳一说这不是酒，他马上就为自己找到了借口，接过来就喝了，结果误了大事。我们在生活当中，也常常碰到明知某事不能做，却又往往要给自己寻找种种牵强的借口去做的事，值得以此为戒。

GU YANG OFFERS A CUP OF LIQUOR

King Gong of Chu and Duke Li of Jin once fought a battle at Yanling in the Spring and Autumn Period. It turned out that the troops of Chu were defeated, and King Gong of Chu got one of his eyes shot by a flying arrow. When the battle got fierce, General Sima Zifan of Chu felt very thirsty, so he asked for water. His attendant Gu Yang gave him a cup of liquor. Zifan shouted, "Hey! Go away! This is liquor. Do you want to get me killed?" Gu Yang then soothed the general, "Please don't worry. It is not liquor." Zifan took the cup of liquor and drank it. Zifan was always a compulsory drinker, so when he was thirsty, he felt the liquor was even more palatable. As a result, he couldn't stop drinking after taking the first cup and got drunk at last. After the battle was over, King Gong of Chu wouldn't resign himself to failure. He thought about fighting another battle again, so he sent for Sima Zifan. Zifan was utterly drunk. He had no choice but to say that he had a sick heart as an excuse for not coming. King Gong of Chu became quite suspicious, so he went to see what was going on by himself on a chariot. As he entered the camp of Zifan, to his great surprise, he got the strong smell of liquor. King Gong went back in great anger, saying, "In today's battle, I got myself wounded. I had hoped to rely on this great general, but he should have gotten so much drunk. He must have forgotten about the gods of Chu and the lives of soldiers and people. How can I go on with this war?" Therefore, after ordering the troops to withdraw from Yanling, the king had Sima Zifan executed and his body exposed publicly. Han Feizi concludes, "The attendant Gu Yang presented liquor to Zifan not because he hated the general. Instead, he loved his master deeply. He didn't mean to hurt his master, but his action finally led to the death of Zifan. Therefore, petty loyal behaviors conducted unwisely would be harmful to great loyal deeds." Gu Yang simply "did something wrong though he had good intention". This is called "bringing harm to great loyal deeds by conducting petty loyal behaviors." In our life today we still can find a lot of cases like this, in which one seems to do something helpful for others but brings harm to them at last. A typical example is like this: parents pamper their children and allow them too much latitude without principle, and the indulgence might prevent their children from learning necessary skills and becoming successful. What's worse, they might get their children fall into malevolence. This is called "petty love bringing harm to great love." Therefore, Han Feizi says, "The one with petty tricks shouldn't be entrusted with matters of great importance, and the one with petty loyalty shouldn't be tasked with the rule of law."

Zifan was excessively fond of drinking, and from his story we can also see his "self-deceiving" psychology. He knew perfectly well that it was liquor in the cup, and he was aware that he shouldn't drink alcohol when engaged in a battle, but he had already itched to drink. Therefore, when Gu Yang said it was not liquor, he gladly found an excuse for himself and drank the liquor at once, thus sealing his own death warrant. In our daily life, we often find such cases in which we know quite well something should never be done, but would always find various weak excuses to do it. We should take the story of Sima Zifan as a lesson.

6. 唇亡齿寒

　　春秋时，晋献公想要去讨伐虢国。但晋国跟虢国之间还隔着一个虞国，晋国必须向虞国借道。晋国的大夫荀息对晋献公说："您最好用垂棘的宝玉和屈产的良马去贿赂虞国君主，再向他借道，他一定会答应我们的。"晋献公舍不得，说："垂棘的宝玉是我的传家宝，屈产的良马是我最心爱的骏马。万一虞君他接受了我的礼物又耍赖不肯借道，那可怎么办呢？"荀息说："他不给我们借道，就必定不敢接受我们的礼物。假如他接受了礼物，借道给我们，您放心，那块玉璧就好比是从我们自个儿的内府里取出来藏到外府，那匹骏马就好比是从我们自个儿的内厩里牵出来拴到外厩一样。您不用担心。"晋献公说："好吧，就这么着吧。"于是让荀息带着宝玉和良马，去贿赂虞公，向他借路。虞公是个贪财的家伙，一看这么好的宝玉良马，马上就打算一口答应了。这时虞国贤大夫宫之奇劝谏说："您可不能答应啊。俗话说得好：

'辅车相依，唇亡齿寒。'我们虞国和虢国的关系，就好比车轮和起辅助保护作用的木板，就好比牙齿和嘴唇。护木依附着车轮，但车轮本身也要依靠护木。嘴唇缺了，牙齿就会暴露出来受寒。虞虢两国的地理形势正是这样。我们和虢国一向互相救援，互为倚仗，并不是在互相施恩，而是为了更好地自保。假如借道给晋国，那么如果虢国早上被灭掉的话，虞国晚上就要跟着灭亡了。千万不能借，希望您不要答应。"虞公不听，最终还是借道给晋国了。荀息率军讨伐虢国，大获全胜。过了三年，又发兵伐虞，灭掉了虞国。荀息牵着三年前送出去的骏马，拿着三年前送出去的玉璧，回来报告晋献公。献公高兴地说："玉璧嘛，还是和以前一样啊。不过呢，马却长了几岁了。"

"辅车相依，唇亡齿寒"是当时流行的谚语，比喻关系密切，利害相关。韩非用晋借道于虞以伐虢的故事，来说明君主的十种过错之第二"贪图小利"，故事末尾总结说："那么，虞公兵败国灭的原因是什么呢？是贪恋小利而不考虑它的危害。所以说，贪图小利，便是对长远的大利益的危害。"现在一些常见的诈骗案例，比如捡钱分钱、大变钞票、低价抛售"家传金佛"等之所以屡屡得逞，就是因为骗子抓住了人们"贪小利"的弱点。贪小利者最后往往吃大亏，任何时候我们都不能忘记先哲们总结出来的这一教训。当然，韩非要说的还有一层意思，那就是灾祸常常在还没有征兆的时候就开始了，我们避免灾祸应该从这个时候就开始着手。作为臣子的宫之奇抢在祸害刚露苗头时就想出了办法，但君主却不采纳，其亡国也就不足为怪了。

IF THE LIPS ARE GONE, THE TEETH WILL BE EXPOSED TO THE COLD

In the Spring and Autumn Period, Duke Xian of Jin wanted to launch a punitive expedition against the State of Guo. But the State of Yu lied between Jin and Guo, so Jin had to request a passage from Yu. Xun Xi, a senior official of Jin, said to Duke Xian of Jin, "You may want to bribe the Duke of Yu with the precious jade from Chuiji and the fine horse from Quchan and then ask him to lend us a passage. In that case, he is sure to comply with our request." Duke Xian of Jin, reluctant, said, "The precious jade from Chuiji is my heirloom, and the fine horse from Quchan is my favorite. What if the Duke of Yu accepts my gifts but refuses shamelessly to lend us a passage?" Xun Xi said, "If he doesn't want to lend us a passage, he surely dare not accept our gifts. If he takes our gifts and lends us a passage, please rest assured that it is just as if the precious jade is taken out of the inner part of our house to the outer part and as if the horse is led out of our inner stable to our outer stable. You don't have to worry at all." Duke Xian of Jin said, "All right. Do as you say." Then, the duke let Xun Xi take away the precious jade and the fine horse to bribe the Duke of Yu for a passage to Guo. The Duke of Yu was a greedy man, so he agreed at once when he saw the precious jade and the fine horse. At this moment, a senior official of Yu called Gong Zhiqi objected, "You must decline that proposal. As the saying goes, 'Wheels and wheel guards are dependent on each other, and the teeth will suffer the cold if the lips are gone.' The relationship between Guo and Yu is just like that between wheels and wheel guards and that between teeth and lips. Wheel guards which protect the wheels are attached to wheels, but wheels can't turn without wheel guards. If the lips are gone, the teeth will be exposed to the cold. The geographical situations of Guo and Yu are just like this. Guo and Yu always help each other and rely on each other. We are not bestowing favors upon each other; we do this to protect ourselves better. If we lent a passage to Jin, Guo would be defeated in the morning while we would be destroyed in the evening. You can't lend a passage to Jin. I wish you would never agree." The Duke of Yu would not listen, and he lent a passage to Jin at last. Xun Xi led troops to attack Guo and won a great victory. Three years later, he led troops to attack Yu and finally destroyed it. Then, Xun Xi retrieved the jade and the horse which were sent away three years before as a bribe and reported to Duke Xian of Jin. The duke was so pleased that he said, "The jade is as fine as before, but the horse was a few years older."

"Wheels and wheel guards are dependent on each other, and the teeth will suffer the cold if the lips are gone", a popular saying at that time, serves as a metaphor for close relationship and mutually beneficial interests between two parties. Han Feizi uses the story of Jin requesting a passage from Yu to attack Guo to show the second of the ten mistakes usually made by monarchs, "hankering after petty profits." At the end of the story, Han Feizi concludes, "Then, what is the reason for Yu's destruction? It's because the duke coveted small benefits without considering the possible great harm. Therefore, hankering after petty profits means a loss of greater interests in the long run." Nowadays some cheap scams, such as dividing a bundle of money after picking it up on the road, turning blank paper into money with magic, and selling "heirloom gold statues of Buddha" at a lower price, are pulled off again and again because the swindlers take advantage of people's weakness of "hankering after petty profits". Those who hanker after petty profits usually suffer great losses, so we should never forget this lesson summed up by the sages of the past. Han Feizi also puts forward an idea that a disaster usually starts before there are any noticeable signs, so we should take precautions to prevent a disaster from jutting out its head in the first place. Gong Ziqi thought out a solution before the disaster started to show up, but the monarch would not take it. No wonder the State of Yu was destroyed at last.

7. 智子疑邻

在《说难》中，韩非连续讲了两个故事：

从前宋国有个富人，有一天下大雨，他家的围墙被淋塌了。他儿子说："赶紧把围墙修好吧，要不然会招贼的。"一位邻居老人出于好心，也这样提醒他。到了晚上，家里果然遭了贼，很多值钱的家什都被偷走了。富人一家都称赞儿子很聪明，却对邻居老人起了疑心。

春秋初年的郑武公，想要讨伐胡国。他先把自己的女儿嫁给胡国君主，来讨他的欢心，麻痹他的戒心，然后问大臣们："我想用兵，哪一个国家可以攻打呢？"大夫关其思回答说："胡国可以攻打。"武公勃然大怒，把关其思推出去斩了，说："胡国是我们的联姻之邦，关系就像亲兄弟一样，你却建议去攻打它，是什么道理啊？"胡国君主听说了这件事，认为郑国是友好之邦，于是不再防备郑国。结果郑国趁机偷袭胡国，占领了胡国大片国土。

《韩非子》总结这两个故事说："关其思和那位邻居老人的话都是很恰当的，但重则被杀掉，轻则被怀疑；可见，并不是认识事物有困难，而是如何合适地处理这种认识很困难。"同样的事情和道理，不同的人去说，或者同一个人向不同的人去说，都会有不同的效果。那个儿子和邻居老头儿的话都说对了，关其思的话也正是郑武公心中所想，可是儿子被称赞，邻居老头儿却被怀疑，关其思还招来杀身之祸。可见游说、进言是否被采纳接受，并不完全在于是不是有道理、是否是实话，还在于以下两点：首先，游说、进言是不是正能迎合别人的需要，所以当时游说之士，往往想方设法揣摩君主的意图，努力投其所好；其次，在于你与对方关系的深浅密切程度，所以当时游说之士要晋见国君，一般都要先找君王的宠臣来引荐，以得到对方的信任。如果引荐者没有找对人，国君先就把你当"外人"看，那么即使你才高八斗，也常常不能得到重用。现在人们还常说"什么人说什么话"，意思是我们应该说符合自己身份的该说的话，否则就会多惹祸端。还有句话叫"交浅言深"，指的是跟人交情浅，谈话却很深入，言谈有失分寸，说的就是反面的情况。

CONSIDERING THE SON A GENIUS AND THE NEIGHBOUR A SUSPECT

Han Feizi tells two stories in succession in the essay "On the Difficulty of Persuasion."

Once upon a time, there lived a rich man in the State of Song. One day, it rained heavily and the enclosing walls of his house collapsed because of the rain. His son said, "Repair the wall at once, or our house will be visited by thieves." An old neighbour also warned him so out of good intention. When the night fell, his house was really visited by thieves and many valuable things were stolen. The rich man's family all praised the son as clever but became suspicious of the old neighbour.

Duke Wu of Zheng in the early Spring and Autumn Period wanted to attack the State of Hu. He married his own daughter to the Duke of Hu to please and lull the latter. Then he asked his ministers, "If I want to move troops, which state can I attack?" Senior Official Guan Qisi answered, "The State of Hu is a good choice." Duke Wu flew into a rage and had the senior official executed. He said, "Hu is the state with which we have formed an alliance by marriage, so we are like brothers. But now you suggest I should attack it. What's the point in it?" Later the Duke of Hu heard about this and thought Zheng was a friendly state, so he lowered his guard against Zheng. Consequently, Zheng seized this opportunity to launch a surprise attack on Hu and captured most of its territory.

Han Feizi says in conclusion about these two stories, "The words of Guan Qisi and the old neighbour are both appropriate, but one got beheaded in the serious case and the other was suspected in the less serious one. Therefore, there is difficulty not in understanding things but in how to deal with the understanding in an appropriate way." When the same thing and the same truth are suggested by different people or to different people by the same one, there might be different results. The son of the rich family and the old neighbour both told the truth, and Guan Qisi's words actually revealed a piece of Duke Wu's mind, but the son was praised, the old neighbour was suspected, and Guan Qisi was killed. Therefore, whether one's persuasion or advice will be adopted or not depends not entirely on whether it is reasonable or whether it is true. It also depends on whether the persuasion or advice caters for the audience's need, so those scholars who tried to persuade the monarchs to adopt their views at that time all used every means to figure out the monarchs' intention and tried to cater to their tastes. Secondly, it depends on the relationship between the advisor and the audience. Thus, at that time, if those scholars wanted to talk with a monarch, they all tried to ask a favorite associate of the monarch to introduce them, so that they already enjoyed the monarch's trust when seeking an audience. On the contrary, if they didn't find the right person to introduce them, the monarch would treat them as "outsiders". In that case, even though they were endowed with great talent, they usually couldn't be given important positions. Nowadays people still talk about "what kind of person says what kind of words", which means we should say the right words appropriate for our status; otherwise, we would invite a lot of trouble. There is also a saying "remote relationship but intimate talk", which means having a deep conversation when the relationship is not close enough. That is clearly an undesirable situation.

8. 和氏璧

　　春秋时期，楚国有位叫卞和的人，在荆山中发现了一块未经雕琢的璞玉。他拿去奉献给楚厉王，厉王让玉匠鉴定。玉匠说："这只是块普通的石头！"厉王认为卞和是骗子，就砍掉了他的左脚。厉王死后，武王继位。卞和不死心，又捧着那块玉璞去献给武王。武王让玉匠鉴定，玉匠又说："这只是块普通的石头！"武王也认为卞和是骗子，就砍掉了他的右脚。武王死后，文王登基。卞和就抱着那块玉璞在荆山下面嚎啕大哭，一连哭了三天三夜，眼泪全流干了，最后眼里都哭出了血。文王听说后，就派人去了解他哭的原因。派去的人问道："天底下受刑被砍断脚的人多了去了，也没见他们像你这样啊。为什么偏偏你哭得这么惨呢？"卞和说："我不是因为脚被砍掉而哭的。我是因为明明是宝玉，却被说成普通的石头才哭的；明明是忠贞之士，却被说成是骗子。这才是我最悲伤的地方。"文王于是让玉匠加工这块玉璞，果然得到了宝玉，再进一步将宝玉雕琢成玉璧，用卞和的名字命名为"和氏之璧"。在这个故事里，韩非用卞和喻指像自己一样的法术之士，用和氏璧喻指其所怀有的法术，用卞和两次受到刖刑、和氏璧两次不被人所识喻指法术之士和法术的不幸遭遇。我们则可以从中领悟到与人才有关的一些道理。有时候，发现人才就像经历了三代楚王才最终认识到和氏璧一样困难。有才能但没有得到好的条件而不得施展的人，就好比美玉藏在玉璞中不为人所知。而那些已有名气的人物，就好比已经雕琢完美的宝玉。

和氏璧在中国历史上可是大大有名。传说此璧冬暖夏凉，百步之内蚊虫不敢飞近，为稀世之宝。成语"完璧归赵"的"璧"就是这块"楚和氏璧"。战国时和氏璧辗转落入赵惠文王之手，被秦国的昭王知道了，昭王便派了位使臣到赵国，要以十五座城池来跟赵国换取和氏璧。蔺相如带着此璧到秦国，几经周折，将和氏璧完好地自秦送回赵国，这就是"完璧归赵"的典故。成语"完璧归赵"比喻把原物完好无损地归还原主。秦统一中国后，和氏璧又转入秦始皇之手，秦始皇命令玉工将其雕琢为玉玺。这玉玺长、宽、高均为四寸，四周还雕饰着五龙图案，玲珑剔透，巧夺天工。秦始皇爱不释手，将它奉为神物。汉灭秦后，和氏璧几经沧桑又到了汉高祖刘邦手中。刘邦把和氏璧作为传国玉玺代代相传，一直传了12代皇帝。后来王莽篡政，派人胁迫孝元皇太后交出玉玺。皇太后见国破家亡，一怒之下将玉玺取出摔在地上，这个传世国宝当场被崩掉一角，后来又命能工巧匠进行整修，用黄金镶上缺角，于是得名"金镶玉玺"。这稀世国宝，自三国以后即不知去向了。

俗谚说"有眼不识金镶玉"，多用来比喻见识浅陋，缺乏识别事物的能力，其中的"金镶玉"一般认为就是上面所说的"金镶玉玺"。

THE HE'S JADE

In the Spring and Autumn Period, there lived a man called Bian He in the State of Chu. Bian He found an uncut jade in Jingshan Mountain. He took the jade to King Li of Chu, who then asked a jade carver to appraise it. The jade carver said, "It's just a common stone." King Li thought Bian He was a cheat and had his left foot cut off. After King Li died, King Wu succeeded to the throne. Bian He didn't give up hope, so he took the jade to King Wu. King Wu asked a jade carver to appraise it again, and the jade carver also said, "It's only a common stone." King Wu also thought Bian He was a cheat and had his right foot cut off. When King Wu died, King Wen came to the throne. Then Bian He held the jade in his arms and cried at the foot of Jingshan Mountain for three days and three nights without end, until his tears ran out and blood came out of his eyes. Hearing about this, King Wen sent a man to ask about it. The man said to Bian He, "There are many people in the world whose feet were cut off. Why did you cry in such grief?" Bian He said, "I didn't cry because my feet were cut off. I cried because a precious jade was said to be a stone and a loyal man a deceiver. This is what actually makes me feel sad." Then King Wen asked a jade carver to chisel the jade and really got an invaluable treasure. He then had it carved into a round jade ornament and named it after Bian He: the He's Jade. In this story, Han Feizi means to say that he himself, as well as all the scholars of the Legalist school, is like Bian He. The He's Jade is used as a metaphor for all the doctrines he had developed, and Bian He's tragedy of suffering the inhuman punishment twice and the jade's fate of not being recognized twice are analogies for the misfortune of the Legalist scholars and their doctrines. We may also gain an insight from this story about talented people. Sometimes, finding talented people is just as difficult as recognizing the He's Jade by the three of kings of Chu. Talented people who can't give their talents full play due to a lack of favorable conditions are like fine jade hidden in its raw material which is not easily recognized by everyone, while those who have enjoyed favorable conditions to make achievements are like perfect carved jade.

The He's Jade is very famous in the Chinese history. It is said this jade was a rare treasure: it felt warm in winter and cool in summer, and kept mosquitoes away within a distance of a hundred steps from it. The word "jade" in the idiom "returning the jade intact to the State of Zhao" refers to the He's Jade. In the Warring State Period, the He's Jade passed through many owners and finally rested in the care of King Huiwen of Zhao. Hearing about the news, King Zhao of Qin sent an envoy to Zhao, demanding to exchange fifteen cities for the He's Jade with Zhao. Lin Xiangru, a wise minister of Zhao, took the jade to Qin and at last returned to Zhao with the jade intact after undergoing a lot of hardships. This is the allusion called "returning the jade intact to the State of Zhao". This idiom is often used as a metaphor for returning something to its owner in perfect condition. After Qin's unification of China in 221 BC, the He's Jade was passed on to the hands of Emperor Shi Huangdi of the Qin Dynasty, who asked jade carvers to carve it into an imperial seal. This seal was four *cun* in length, width and height, with carved patterns of five dragons on all its sides. It was so ingeniously and exquisitely carved that its superb craftsmanship excelled nature. Emperor Shi Huangdi of the Qin Dynasty was so fond of it that he would not let go of it; he honored it as sacred. After the Han Dynasty replaced the Qin Dynasty in the 3rd century BC, the He's Jade was passed on to Liu Bang, Emperor Gaozu of Han, after a lot of twists and turns. Liu Bang passed on the He's Jade as the imperial seal for his dynasty for twelve generations. Later, Wang Mang usurped the power of the throne in the 1st century and ordered his troops to force Empress Dowager Xiaoyuan to surrender the imperial jade seal. Seeing the country conquered and her home lost, the empress dowager took out the jade seal and threw it on the ground in a fit of pique. Consequently, a corner of the imperial jade seal was broken off. Later, skillful craftsmen made repairs on the seal by trimming the broken corner with gold, and thus came the name "the jade seal trimmed with gold". This rare treasure was nowhere to be found after the Three Kingdoms Period in the 3rd century.

Later, there appeared a proverb saying that "although one has eyes he cannot see the jade trimmed with gold", usually used as a metaphor for shallow-minded people who lack knowledge, experience or the ability to identify valuable things or talents. The "jade trimmed with gold" in this proverb is generally believed to be the imperial seal made from the He's Jade.

9. 孙叔敖善建善抱

　　春秋时，楚庄王援救郑国获得了胜利，又在河雍地带打猎，然后回国。回国后论功行赏，要奖赏令尹孙叔敖。出人意料的是，孙叔敖只要了一块汉水附近的贫瘠土地。楚国的法律是，享受俸禄的大臣，到第二代就要收回封地，只有孙叔敖的封地保留了下来。原因是这块土地太贫瘠了，没人想要，也就没人跟他家争，因而他的后世子孙得以代代享有这块封地。

　　《韩非子》在这个故事末尾总结说："所以《老子》说：'善于树立的就不会被拔出，善于抱持的就不会脱开。子子孙孙因为善于树立、善于抱持而世守封地，代代香火不绝。'说的就是孙叔敖这种情况。"孙叔敖是历史上著名的贤人，他此举可谓深通"以退为进"、"示人以弱"的道理。人人都爱宝贝，然而人与人心中的宝贝不同。孙叔敖心目中的宝贝，在平常人眼中不是宝贝，实际却是真宝贝。试问他就算要到丰饶秀美的封地，但两代之后就要被收回，土地都没有了，丰饶秀美又有什么用呢？子孙仍然难免受穷。一般人越是为子孙后代打算，越是想要丰饶的封地。而孙叔敖是"善建者"，他反其道而行之，最后达到了大家都没有达到的心愿。

SUN SHU'AO IS GOOD AT ESTABLISHING AND PRESERVING HIS MANOR

In the Spring and Autumn Period, King Zhuang of Chu won a victory in the battle to rescue the State of Zheng. Then he went hunting around the region of Heyong before returning to his own state. Back home, the victorious king wanted to award Sun Shu'ao, a meritorious minister, according to his contribution in the battle, but Sun Shu'ao just asked for a patch of barren land near the Hanshui River. According to the laws of Chu, the manors of those officials who enjoyed salaries from the government were to be taken back in their second generation. Only Sun Shu'ao's manor was passed on to his descendants because the land was so poor that no one would like to take it. Therefore, his descendants were able to enjoy this manor from generation to generation as no one wanted to fight for it with them.

Han Feizi concludes at the end of this story, "*Laozi* says, 'Those who are good at establishing things will not be pulled out; those who are good at preserving things will not be shaken off. Their descendants could keep their manors and continue their family lines from generation to generation because they are good at establishing and preserving manors.' That is the case of Sun Shu'ao." Sun Shu'ao was an outstanding minister well-known for his wisdom. His action of choosing a barren land as his manor can well illustrate his deep understanding of the idea that "one should make concessions in order to gain advantages and leave the impression of being weak to others". Everyone loves treasure, but they take different things as treasure in their minds. The treasure in Sun Shu'ao's mind is not a treasure in common people's eyes, but it is a real treasure. If he had received a fertile manor from the king, it would have been taken back in his second generation. When the land was gone, what could his descendants benefit from it even though it was fertile? In that case, his descendants could hardly avoid the fate of living a poor life. Generally, the more a person wants to plan for his descendants, the more anxious he is to get a fertile manor from the king. Nevertheless, as Sun Shu'ao was "a person good at establishment and preservation", he did exactly the opposite and fulfilled the wish that others failed to accomplish.

10. 讳疾忌医

　　春秋时期有个名医叫扁鹊。他去拜见蔡桓公，站了一会儿后，对桓公说："您有病，现在在表皮上，不治疗的话恐怕会加深。"桓公听了感到颇为不快，说："你们这些做医生的，总喜欢医治些没病的人，把这个当作自己的功劳。"过了十天，扁鹊又去拜见桓公，说："您的病已经发展到肌肉了，不治疗的话就更严重了。"桓公听了更为不快，理都不理睬他，扁鹊只好走了。过了十天，扁鹊又拜见桓公说："您的病已经发展到了肠胃，不治疗就不好收拾了。"桓公越发不快。又过了十天，扁鹊看见桓公，转身就跑。桓公很奇怪，特意派人去问他。扁鹊回答说："病在表皮，是药物熏敷就可以治好；深入到了肌肉，针灸还可以治好；再深入到了肠胃，清热的汤药也还可以治好；要是深入到了骨髓，那就是老天爷的管辖范围了，谁都没有办法了。现在君主已经病入骨髓，因此我就不再求见了。"过了五天，桓公果然身体疼痛，派人去找扁鹊，扁鹊已经逃往秦国。于是桓公病重死掉了。讲完这个故事后，韩非作了总结："所以良医治病，趁它还在表皮就加以治疗，这都是为了抢在事情细小的时候及早处理。事情的祸福都有刚露苗头的时候，所以圣明的人总是能够及早地加以处理。"祸福的由来都是起于小事，所以要及早采取措施，防止事情发展到不可收拾的地步。

这个故事最直接的意义是可以教给我们对待疾病的态度：不能像蔡桓公那样"讳疾忌医"，有病要及时医治。要不然，小病成大病，大病成顽疾，顽疾成不治之症，再后悔就晚了，成语"病入膏肓"讲的就是这个意思。《韩非子》在这个故事的上文说道："有形状的东西，大的必定从小的发展而来；历时经久的事物、聚集起来的东西，必定从细微的开端积累而来。所以《老子》说：'天下的难事必定开始于简易，天下的大事必定起步于微细。'因此要想控制事物，就要从微细处着手。千丈长的大堤，因为蝼蚁营造小小的窟穴而导致溃决；百尺高的房屋，因为烟囱漏出一点点的火星而导致被焚毁。……要谨慎地对待容易处理的事来避免大灾大难的发生，郑重地对待细小的漏洞以避免大祸临头。"我们日常生活中要重视培养敏锐的观察力，注意发现各种事情的细微征兆，以便及早"未雨绸缪"，对将要发生的事情作好防范准备和应对措施。

从这个故事，我们还可以在进言与纳言方面得到一些经验教训。扁鹊治病能从皮肤上的小毛病着手，不让它恶化到不可医治的地步，其医术无疑是极高明的。他对桓公所说的话也完全是出自一名医生的天职，然而桓公根本听不进去。看来，比起那些心怀鬼胎、屡进谗言，而被君主宠信的佞臣，扁鹊的进言艺术恐怕还有待提高。另一方面，作为纳言之人，我们要注意把说话人的身份跟其言语是否正确区分开来。固然，桓公所说的"医生总是喜欢医治些没病的人当作自己的功劳"，有它一定的道理，不同职业的人说话确实都容易带有职业的局限。但问题是桓公的这个判断跟他是否确实有病的事实，两者之间并没有必然关系。我们今天常常需要跟不同的专业人士打交道，听取他们的意见以作出各种决定，也要注意这一点。

HIDING THE SICKNESS FOR FEAR OF TREATMENT

There was a famous doctor called Bian Que in the Spring and Autumn Period. He went to visit Duke Huan of Cai. After standing for a while, he said to the duke, "You have an illness in epidermis, which will become more serious if it is not taken care of." Duke Huan was displeased and said, "You doctors always like to claim credit for yourselves by treating those who are not sick." Ten days later, Bian Que visited Duke Huan again. He said, "Your illness has developed to your muscles. It will get worse if you don't have it treated." Duke Huan was annoyed again. He ignored Bian Que completely, and the doctor had to take leave. After another ten days, Bian Que went to see Duke Huan again. He said, "Your illness has developed to your intestines and stomach. If you don't get it treated, it will be very difficult to cure." Duke Huan became even more unhappy. When Bian Que saw Duke Huan after another ten days, he turned around and ran away at once. Duke Huan was confused, so he sent an associate to ask the doctor about it. Bian Que answered, "When the illness is in epidermis, it can be cured by fumigation and external application of medicine; when it gets into the muscles, it can also be cured by acupuncture; when it comes to the intestines and stomach, it can still be cured by taking a heat-dispelling decoction of medicinal herbs; but when it goes deep into the marrow, it is at the mercy of Heaven as nobody could cure it. Now the duke's illness has been spread to his marrow, so I will no longer ask to see him." Five days later, Duke Huan really felt pains in his body. He then sent for Bian Que, but the doctor had already escaped to the State of Qin. Consequently, Duke Huan died of serious illness. After telling this story, Han Feizi says in conclusion, "A good doctor always chooses to cure a disease when it is still in epidermis, for he wants to solve the problem before it becomes serious. Both fortune and misfortune develop from a barely noticeable beginning, so capable and virtuous men always take care of them as early as possible." Great events develop from trivial matters, so measures should be taken early to prevent them from getting out of control.

The story can teach us the right attitude toward illness: we shouldn't behave like Duke Huan of Cai who avoided seeking medical advice though obviously sick. An illness should be treated in time; otherwise, minor ones would become serious, serious ones would become persistent, and persistent ones would become incurable. Then it will be too late to regret. The Chinese idiom that "the disease has spread to the vital organs" just means something to this effect. *Han Feizi* says in the context ahead of this story, "Anything that has a certain shape must undergo a process of development from the small to the big. What grows through a long time or what has been accumulated must start from something very small and tiny. *Laozi* says, 'Every difficult thing in the world must start from something easy; every great thing in the world must start from something trivial.' Therefore, if one wants to have control over something, he should start to deal with subtle details. A dyke one thousand *zhang* long could collapse because of the tiny holes dug by ants; a house one hundred *chi* tall could be burnt down because of little sparks leaked from the chimney. ... One should be cautious when dealing with easy problems so as to prevent great disasters from happening, and should be serious when dealing with small flaws so as to prevent great misfortunes from befalling him." Therefore, we should use our keen observation to watch out for subtle signs of various things so as to "repair the house before it rains" (also a Chinese idiom) and make precautions against, and find solutions to, anything which is going to happen.

From this story we can also draw some lessons about offering advice and listening to others' advice. When giving treatment, Bian Que could start with a small ailment in the skin and prevent it from getting worse and becoming incurable; therefore, he was obviously a superb doctor. What he said to Duke Huan was completely out of his good intention towards a patient, but Duke

Huan couldn't listen to him at all. Compared with those who harbored malicious schemes and made false accusations again and again but whose words were all accepted by the monarch, Bian Que might want to improve his skills of offering advice significantly. On the other hand, as the one who listens to others' advice, we should always distinguish the status of the speaker from the correctness of his words. There may be some truth in Duke Huan's words that "doctors always like to claim credit for themselves by treating those who are not sick." The advice offered by professionals is often inherent with certain professional limitations. However, the problem is that Duke Huan's judgement based on Bian Que's status as a doctor has nothing to do with the fact that he was indeed ill. Nowadays we often need to consult professionals and listen to their advice in order to make various decisions, so we should be careful in making judgements.

11. 箕子见微知著

　　从前商纣王制作了一副象牙筷子，太师箕子就感到非常担忧。他知道，有了象牙筷子，就一定不会在普通的陶器里使用，而一定会配合使用犀牛角杯或玉杯；象筷玉杯就一定不会用来吃豆子熬成的素汤，而一定要用来吃牦牛、大象、豹子的胎儿这样的奇珍异味；吃牦牛、大象、豹子的胎儿就一定不会穿粗布短衣，不会在茅屋下面食用，而一定要穿多层的织锦衣服，住上宽敞的房屋和高台。按照这个方式追求下去，那么普天下的东西也不够他享受，都不能满足他的贪欲了。箕子害怕后果严重，所以深为这样的开端而担忧。过了五年，商纣王摆设肉林，建炮烙之刑，登上酒糟堆成的山，俯临装满酒液的池子，残暴地杀戮臣下和人民，最终灭国亡命。因此箕子看见象牙筷子，就预感到了天下的祸害。

　　《韩非子》用这个故事来说明《老子》所说的"能够看到事物的萌

芽状态，就叫做明"的道理。箕子见微知著，见到微小的迹象就知道事物的苗头，见到事情的开端就知道它的实质、发展趋势和最终结果，所以见到象牙筷后箕子就恐惧了，就能预见到肉林、酒池这样的奢侈，可谓明察。这个故事的积极意义在于提醒人们要防微杜渐，"勿以恶小而为之"，不能"大错不犯、小错不断"。

　　人们常把这个故事与西方的"狄德罗效应"相提并论。18世纪法国有个哲学家叫丹尼斯·狄德罗，他是当时赫赫有名的思想巨人。一次朋友送给他一件质地精良、做工考究的酒红色睡袍，他非常喜欢。可是当他穿着华贵的睡袍时却觉得家里哪儿都破旧不堪，为了与睡袍配套，他更换了地毯、家具等等物品，终于家中的物品都跟上了睡袍的档次。可是这位大哲学家仍觉得很不舒服，因为"自己居然被一件睡袍胁迫了"，更换了那么多他原本无意更换的东西。他把这种感觉写成了一篇文章，题目就叫《与旧睡袍别离之后的烦恼》。整整过了两百年之后，在1988年，美国人格兰特·麦克莱肯读了这篇文章，感慨颇多。他认为这一个案具有典型意义，集中揭示了消费品之间协调统一的文化现象，并借用狄德罗的名字，将这一类现象概括为"狄德罗效应"。后来，"狄德罗效应"引起了越来越多人的关注，而且被运用了到社会生活的各个方面。

　　"狄德罗效应"也称为"配套效应"，简单来说就是"越得到越不足"，也就是说人在没有得到某种东西时，心里很平衡，生活很稳定，而一旦得到某种东西了，反而开始不满足，认为自己应该得到更多。

JIZI SEES HOW THINGS WILL DEVELOP FROM THE SLIGHTEST SIGNS

Once upon a time, King Zhou of Shang had a pair of chopsticks made of ivory, and Jizi, a wise minister, felt very worried. Jizi knew that the ivory chopsticks couldn't be used in ordinary pottery, but must be matched with precious cups made of rhinoceros horns or jade, that ivory chopsticks and jade cups wouldn't be used for vegetarian soup made of beans, but must be used for rare delicacies such as yaks, elephants or leopard feti, and that when one ate yaks, elephants or leopard feti, he wouldn't be wearing short clothes made out of coarse cloth and wouldn't be living in a thatched hut; instead, he would be wearing multi-layered clothes made out of brocade and living in spacious houses and towers. If he continued to pursue things like these, all the wealth in the world wouldn't be enough for him to enjoy or squander. Jizi was quite afraid that this would bring about unwanted consequence, so he felt great fear for such a beginning. After five years, King Zhou of Shang entertained himself with the "trees of meat", started the "hot bronze pillar" torture, and mounted the hill piled up with distillers' grains to look down at ponds filled up with wine. He also started to kill his officials and subjects cruelly. Finally, the people rebelled and put an end to the Shang Dynasty and King Zhou's life. Therefore, when Jizi saw ivory chopsticks, he foresaw the disasters that all the people were to suffer.

Han Feizi uses this story to show what *Laozi* describes as "being able to see things in the burgeoning state is called being wise." Jizi saw how things would develop from the slightest signs. That is, he knew what was coming when seeing minute phenomena; he also knew how things would come into being, develop and end when seeing the beginning. Therefore, he felt deep fear when seeing the ivory chopsticks and could foresee the "trees of meat", the "hot bronze pillar" torture and such luxury as the ponds of wine. He was indeed a man of keen observation. The value of this story lies in warning people of checking erroneous ideas from the outset, so as "not to engage in evil even if it's small" (a Chinese idiom) and not to "make no major mistakes but many minor ones."

People often compare this story with "the Diderot Effect" in the West. In the

18th century, there was a French philosopher by the name Denis Diderot, a "giant of thought" at that time. Once a friend sent him a scarlet robe of fine quality and excellent workmanship, which he liked very much. But when he wore the elegant robe, he felt that his home was so old and shabby as compared with the new robe. In order to match the robe, he replaced the old carpet, furniture and so on, until everything in his home was on par with the elegance of the robe. However, this great philosopher still felt uneasy because he hadn't expected that he himself "got coerced by a robe" so that he replaced so many things he hadn't intended to replace. Therefore, he wrote an essay entitled "Regrets on Parting with My Old Dressing Gown". Two hundred years later, when an American called Grant McCracken read this essay in 1988, he was struck by a feeling of familiarity. He thought this individual case was quite typical in revealing the cultural phenomenon of consumer goods matching each other, so he borrowed the name of Diderot to summarize this kind of phenomena as "the Diderot Effect", which later aroused widespread attention and was thus applied to various aspects of social life.

The Diderot Effect is also called "the Matching Effect", which, to be put simply, means "the more one gets the more he needs." Namely, one usually feels balanced when he hasn't got a certain thing, so he could live a stable life. However, once he gets a certain thing, he starts to feel dissatisfied instead and thinks that he should get more.

12. 箕子不知日期

　　商纣王不分昼夜地饮酒，因狂欢而忘记了日期。问他身边的人，都不知道。就派人去问太师箕子。箕子对自己的随从说："纣王他做了天下的主子，可自己和左右的人都忘记了日期，国家恐怕是很危险了。这情况大家都不知道而我一个人知道，我恐怕也危险了。"就推说自己也喝醉了酒，不知道日期。

　　屈原的《楚辞·渔父》中说自己被放逐的原因是"举世皆浊我独清，众人皆醉我独醒"。所谓"木秀于林，风必摧之"，又所谓"出头的椽子先烂"，在众人皆醉的情况下自己不能独醒，应该"与世浮沉"，不要表现出自己的明察，否则就危险了，很容易招来杀身之祸。在乱世里，装傻的功夫很重要，是有效的明哲保身之道。孔子曾经评价春秋时卫国的大夫宁武子说："宁武子这人，在国家太平时节，便聪明；在国家昏暗时节，便装傻。他那聪明，别人赶得上；那装傻，别人就赶不上了。”成语“愚不可及”就出自这里。随着历史的演变，“愚不可及”语义也有了很大变化，最初是指大智若愚，非常人所能及，现在则是指愚蠢无比。

JIZI DOESN'T KNOW THE DATE

King Zhou of Shang indulged himself in drinking day and night until he forgot about the date as he was carried away by wild pleasure. He asked people around him, who all had no idea. Then he sent someone to ask his minister Jizi about it. Jizi said to his own attendants, "King Zhou has been the master of the whole country, but he and the people around him all forget about the date. That means the country will probably be in danger. When people all have no idea except me, I will probably be in danger." Therefore, he replied that he didn't know the date either because he was drunken.

Qu Yuan (famous poet, circa 340 BC–278 BC) wrote in "The Fisherman" in *The Songs of Chu* that the reason for his exile was that "I am clean when the world is muddled, and I am sober when everyone else is drunken." As it is said, "if a tree stands out in the forest, the wind must blow it down." As another saying goes, "Rafters that jut out rot first." Therefore, when everyone else is drunken, one shouldn't remain sober, but should "drift with the current of the times." One shouldn't show his keen observation in that case; otherwise, he risks encountering dangers and possibly a fatal disaster. In an age of social unrest, the skill of pretending not to know is very important, for it is an effective means of playing safe. Confucius once commented on Ning Wuzi, the Senior Official of the State of Wei in the Spring and Autumn Period. He said, "Ning Wuzi was clever when the country was in peace and tranquility; he played the fool when the country was in disorder. Others can match him in wisdom, but no one can match him in playing the fool." The idiom "being a hopeless fool" comes from these comments. With the development of history, the meaning of this idiom underwent great changes. It initially referred to a person of great wisdom assuming a look of folly that no ordinary people could feign. Now it simply refers to an extremely stupid person.

13. 一鸣惊人

　　春秋时期的楚庄王，继承王位后已经执政三年了，可一直就没有发布过命令，没有处理过政事。左右臣下对此很是担心，但又不好或不敢直言劝谏。有一次，右司马侍座（王坐着，臣下陪侍站立在旁边），就抓住机会想了个办法委婉地劝谏楚庄王。他用隐语对庄王说："有一只鸟，栖息在南边的土丘上。三年了，从没张开过翅膀，不飞也不叫，默默无声。大王您说这是什么鸟呢？"庄王一听就明白了其言外之意，胸有成竹地回答说："三年不展翅，是用来长羽翼的；不飞也不叫，是用来观察民众的风俗习惯的。虽然没有起飞，一飞必定冲天；虽然没有鸣叫，一鸣必定惊人。您别管了吧，我已经知道了。"过了半年，庄王就亲自处理政事了。他废除的事情有十件，兴办的事情有九件；诛杀了五个大臣，进用了六个有才德的隐士。结果很快就把国家治理得井井有条。他起兵伐齐，在徐州打败齐国，在河雍战胜晋军，在宋地会合诸侯，从此称霸天下。

成语"一鸣惊人"、"一飞冲天"就出自这个故事。一叫就使人震惊，一飞起来就直冲到了天上，都用来比喻平时没有突出的表现，一下子做出惊人的成绩。西汉司马迁的《史记》也记载有楚庄王之后的齐国大臣淳于髡劝谏齐威王的事迹，与上面故事内容大同小异。楚庄王是春秋时代楚国著名的贤君，公元前 613 年～前 590 年在位。他少年即位，面临朝政混乱的局面，为了稳住事态，不过早暴露自己的意图，所以表面上三年不理朝政。他这么做实有深意，一方面是以静制动，暗地里等待合适的时机，同时静心观察，虚心学习治国之道；另一方面借此考察群臣，同时也麻痹邻国。后来楚国在楚庄王的统治下日渐强盛，楚庄王也成为春秋五霸之一。《韩非子》在这个故事结尾评价说："庄王不让小事妨碍自己的长处，因而能有大名；不过早把自己的意图表露出来，因而能有大功。"用来说明《老子》所说"贵重的器物制作费时，因此完成晚；宏大的声音需要聚集才能发出，故而稀少"的道理。

从另一个角度来说，楚庄王的"一鸣惊人"不是偶然的，和他三年来的认真观察、虚心学习是分不开的。现在有些人平时不愿努力，不愿付出，总幻想一鸣惊人、一夜成名，这是注定行不通的。

AMAZING THE WORLD WITH A SINGLE BRILLIANT FEAT AFTER A LONG DORMANCY

King Zhuang of Chu in the Spring and Autumn Period didn't issue one order or administer any state affairs for three years after succeeding to the throne. All the officials were worried about this but were afraid to make admonishments directly. Once, the Right Minister of War was waiting on the king (with the king seated and the ministers standing aside). He found a way to persuade the king tactfully. He said to the king in enigmatic language, "There is a bird perching on the hillock in the south. It hasn't extended its wings to fly or made any sound for three years. Does Your Majesty know what kind of bird it is?" At these words, King Zhuang immediately knew the implied meaning and answered with calm assurance, "It hasn't extended its wings for three years because it takes the time growing its wings; it has remained still and silent because it is observing the people's customs and habits. Though it has never flown, it must be able to shoot up into the sky once it takes off; though it has never made a sound, it must be able to amaze all once it cries. I've got it, so it's not your business now." After half a year, King Zhuang started to deal with the state affairs. He abolished ten laws and established nine new ones; he executed five corrupt ministers and employed six capable and virtuous hermits. As a result, the state was run in perfect order. He then dispatched troops to attack the State of Qi and conquered it in Xuzhou. He also defeated the troops of Jin in Heyong and convoked the other kings in the place of Song. From then on he became one of the most powerful kings at the time.

The idioms "amazing all with one cry" and "soaring up into the sky with one start" both come from this story. They are good metaphors for a person who makes no outstanding achievement in usual days but suddenly achieves an amazing feat. In *Records of the Grand Historian* written by Sima Qian in the Western Han Dynasty, there is a similar story: A minister of the State of Qi called Chunyu Kun made admonishments to King Wei of Qi in the time later than that of King Zhuang of Chu. King Zhuang was a virtuous monarch of Chu, who reigned from 613 BC to 590 BC. He ascended the throne in his youth, at a time when the state was in total chaos. In order to keep the situation from getting worse and not to disclose his intention too early, he pretended to stay away from state affairs for three years. There was indeed profound meaning in his behavior: on the one hand, he remained passive, so that he could bide his time and concentrate his mind on observing the situation and learning the ways of running a state with an open mind; on the other hand, he could examine the ministers and slacken the neighbouring states' vigilance. Later, the State of Chu was growing more powerful and prosperous under the leadership of King Zhuang of Chu, and the king himself became one of the Five Overlords of the Spring and Autumn Period. *Han Feizi* comments at the end of this story: "King Zhuang wouldn't let trivial matters get in the way of his strength, so he could achieve such a feat; he wouldn't disclose his intention earlier, so he could make great achievements." It explains the argument put forward in *Laozi*: "It takes a long time to make precious things, so they are finished late; it takes tremendous effort to produce resonating sounds, so they are rarely heard."

Speaking from another angle, King Zhuang of Chu's "amazing the world with a single brilliant feat after a long dormancy" is not a rare case. It has a lot to do with his careful observation and modest learning attitude during those three years. Nowadays some people don't want to work hard or exert any effort. They just have all sorts of ideals in their mind, always dreaming that they would amaze the world with a single brilliant feat or become famous overnight. They are doomed to be disappointed.

14. 目不见睫

　　春秋时期的楚庄王，有一次想发兵攻打邻近的越国。他的臣下杜子进谏说："大王您为什么想要去攻打越国呢？"楚庄王说："越国政治混乱，兵力弱小，我们正可以趁机灭掉它啊。"杜子说："愚臣很是为此事担忧。人的智慧，往往就好比眼睛。眼睛能看见百步之外的东西，却不能看见自己的眼睫毛。大王您的军队曾被秦国和晋国打败，丧失了数百里的土地，这就是兵力弱小啊；有个大盗叫庄蹻的在境内公然率众造反，官府却不能加以禁止，这就是政治混乱啊。大王您的兵力弱和政治乱，并不在越国之下。您反而想去攻打越国，这就是我前面所说的智慧如同眼睛，见远不见近啊。"庄王于是采纳了他的意见，停止了攻打越国的行动。

　　《韩非子》把这个故事归结为"所以了解事物的困难，不在于看清别人，而在于看清自己"，用来说明《老子》所说的"能自己认识自己，就叫做明"的道理。杜子劝谏的原话是："智如目也，能见百步之外而不能自见其睫。"后来缩短为成语"目不见睫"，原意是说眼睛看不见自己的睫毛，比喻没有自知之明。

西方有句谚语："看到他人眼中的刺，却看不到自己眼中的梁木。"这话出自《圣经》。《圣经·马太福音》第七章记载耶稣说："为什么看见你弟兄眼中有刺，却不想自己眼中有梁木呢？你自己眼中有梁木，怎能对你弟兄说'容我去掉你眼中的刺'呢？你这假冒伪善的人，先去掉自己眼中的梁木，然后才能看得清楚，以去掉你弟兄眼中的刺。"这和"目不见睫"非常相似，有异曲同工之妙。中国谚语说"人贵有自知之明"，《孙子兵法》说"知己知彼，百战不殆"，讲的都是这个道理。

THE EYE CAN'T SEE ITS LASHES

Once King Zhuang of Chu of the Spring and Autumn Period intended to attack a neighbouring state Yue. A minister Duzi gave counsel by asking, "Why does Your Majesty want to attack the State of Yue?" King Zhuang of Chu said, "Since Yue is in a state of political chaos and possesses little military strength, we could just take this chance to defeat it." Duzi said, "I am worried about this. A man's wisdom is just like the eye, which can see things a hundred steps away but can't see its own lashes. Your Majesty's troops were once defeated by Qin and Jin, which resulted in a great loss of land. This shows the weakness of our military forces. A robber called Zhuang Qiao openly gathered a crowd to rebel, but the government failed to suppress the rebellion. This shows the chaotic state of our political situation. Your Majesty, our state doesn't possess great military forces and is in a state of political chaos, so our situation is no better than that of Yue. But Your Majesty wants to attack Yue now, and your wisdom is like the eye – seeing things clearly in the distance but ignoring things close by." King Zhuang then gave up the idea of attacking Yue.

Han Feizi sums this story up as follows: "The difficulty in understanding the world lies not in seeing others clearly, but in seeing oneself clearly." That illustrates the idea discussed in *Laozi*: "It is wise to know oneself." The original counsel offered by Duzi goes like this: "Wise as the eye is, it can't see its own lashes though it can see things a hundred steps away." Later, it was put into the idiom "The eye can't see its lashes", which is used to describe a person with no knowledge of himself.

There is a biblical saying, "One sees the mote in other's eye but can't see the beam in his own eye." In Chapter Seven of the Gospel of Matthew in the Bible, Jesus Christ said, "And why beholdest thou the mote that is in thy brother's eye, but considerest not the beam that is in thine own eye? Or how wilt thou say to thy brother, 'Let me pull out the mote out of thine eye'; and, behold, a beam is in thine own eye? Thou hypocrite, first cast out the beam out of thine own eye; and then shalt thou see clearly to cast out the mote out of thy brother's eye." That is similar to the story mentioned above about the eye unable to see its own lash. The two stories are indeed like different versions of the same idea. The Chinese sayings "knowledge about oneself is wisdom" and "knowing the adversary and knowing yourself" both clarify this idea.

15. 商汤让国

商汤伐灭了当时的天子夏桀，接下来本该接任夏桀的诸侯国共主地位，但他又怕天下人说自己是因为贪图权位而伐桀的，会因此落下坏名声，就表示想要把天下让给当时一位很有威望的贤人隐士——务光，以表现自己坦荡无私的胸怀。同时呢，他又怕务光会真的接受了天子之位，便暗中派人跟务光说："汤杀了君主，却想把弑君的坏名声转嫁到您的头上，所以才说要把天下让给您的。"务光左右为难，最后跳黄河自尽了。

务光为什么只能无奈自尽？他接受吧，会落下弑君夺权的罪名，这与他避世修身的人生宗旨相去太远，他深深为此感到羞耻；他推辞吧，当时商汤已是实际的天下共主，强权之下恐怕也由不得他。这种形势下务光实际上已经进退两难，走投无路。而商汤通过此举，不仅洗刷了自己弑君夺位的恶名，而且又顺理成章地当上了天子。商汤搞的这一套把戏，后人或以褒奖的态度说成策略，或以贬低的态度说成奸谋。这跟后代的王莽、魏文帝曹丕、晋武帝司马炎等人实为篡位却要装扮成"禅让"一样，都是要给自己受人非议的行为找一块光明正大的"遮羞布"。

KING TANG OF SHANG CONCEDES THE THRONE TO OTHERS

King Tang of Shang attacked and killed King Jie of Xia. Naturally King Tang should have replaced King Jie of Xia to be the head of all the states, but he was afraid that people would say that he attacked King Jie to usurp power so that he would receive a bad reputation. Thus he declared that he wanted to concede the throne to a virtuous hermit Wuguang, who enjoyed high prestige at the moment, to show he was an open-minded and selfless man. At the same time, he was also worried that Wuguang would be so naive as to really accept the offer to be the king, so he secretly sent a message to Wuguang, "King Tang killed the old king but wanted to impute the bad reputation to you. That's why he said he wanted to give away the throne to you." Wuguang was caught up in a dilemma and consequently drowned himself in the Yellow River.

Why did Wuguang have no alternative but to commit suicide? If he accepted the offer, he would subject himself to the blame of killing the old king, which went too far away from his life goal of living a sequestered life to seek self-cultivation, and he would be ashamed of that. If he turned down the offer, it was really not up to him to do so under the great power of King Tang who was already the actual head of the states then. Under such circumstances, Wuguang indeed had no way out but to kill himself. However, through this little trick, King

Tang of Shang not only wiped off his bad reputation of murdering the old king to seize the power, but also could ascend the throne with good reason. This trick of King Tang of Shang was either praised positively as a strategy or criticized negatively as a conspiracy. In the later dynasties, there were similar cases of "conceding the throne": Wang Mang (45 BC–AD 23), Cao Pi (Emperor Wen of Wei, 187–226) and Sima Yan (Emperor Wu of the Jin Dynasty, 236–290) pretended to abdicate the crown to other people yet their real intention was to usurp the power for themselves. The trick of "conceding the throne" was used repeatedly as a convenient cover for the despicable actions of the Chinese usurping regents.

16. 蚤虱之流

　　宋国大臣子围将孔子引见给本国的太宰。孔子离开之后，子围进来，询问太宰对孔子的看法。太宰说："孔子真是伟大呀！我见过孔子之后，再看你，就如同渺小的跳蚤、虱子一样了。我现在就要将他引荐给君主。"子围怕孔子被君主看重，就告诉太宰说："恐怕君主见过孔子之后，再来看你，也就会跟你现在看我一样，把你看作如同跳蚤、虱子一般了呀！"于是，太宰就没有将孔子引见给宋君。

　　伟大的贤人出现，既会使一般人很自然地仰望折服，同时也容易使一些心胸狭窄的人产生妒嫉之心。有些下属往往因为怕自己被比下去而失宠，失去已有的地位，因此不推荐比自己优秀的贤人。"武大郎开店——高的不要"是常见的社会现象，如何开辟合理选拔人才、不蔽贤人的有效途径，这个古代君主常常面临的问题，也需要当代社会的各级管理者们认真思考。

MEN LIKE FLEAS AND LICE

Ziyu, a minister of Song, introduced Confucius to the Great Steward of the state. When Confucius left, Ziyu came in to ask the Great Steward about his views on Confucius. The Great Steward said, "What a great man Confucius is! After meeting him, I feel that compared with him, you are just as insignificant as a tiny flea or louse. So I would like to introduce him to the king at once." Ziyu was afraid that Confucius would won the king's good graces, so he told the Great Steward, "I'm afraid that the king will see you the same way you see me after meeting Confucius: he will see you as insignificant as a flea or louse." Therefore, the Great Steward didn't introduce Confucius to the King of Song.

When a great man of virtue appears, he will not only make common people naturally look up to him and feel awed, but also will easily cause some people to be jealous at the same time. Some subordinates usually won't recommend to their superiors capable people better than themselves for fear of being dwarfed and thus losing the favors and positions they have already earned. It is a common phenomenon that "The dwarf Wu Dalang would not employ anyone taller than himself in his business." It was always a headache for ancient Chinese monarchs to appoint the right people the right positions through an efficient and unbiased system of talent selection, and the problem has still been a major concern in the modern society.

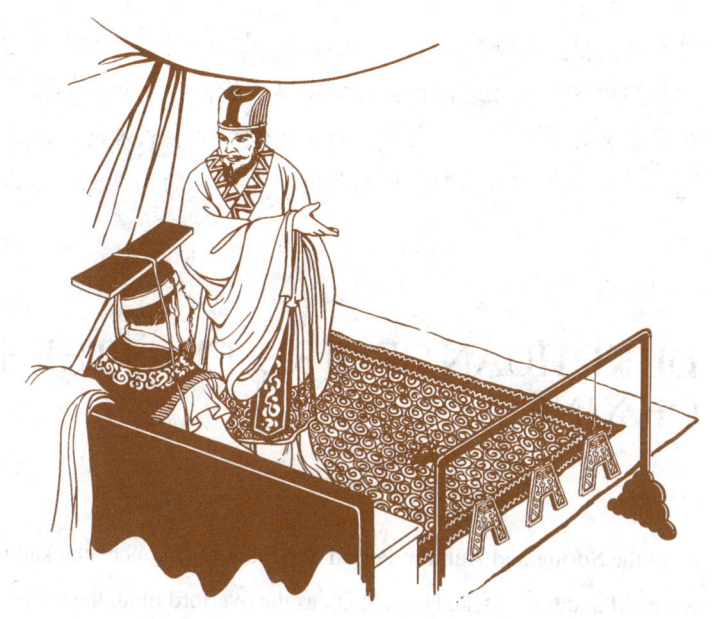

17. 齐桓公救邢

　　春秋时，有一次晋国讨伐邢国，当时齐桓公作为诸侯霸主，打算发兵前去解救。齐国大夫鲍叔牙说："现在就去为时太早了。如果不让晋国一直打下去把邢国灭亡，晋国就不会疲惫，国力就不会变弱；晋国不疲惫，国力不变弱，那么我们齐国的地位就不会相对地重要起来。况且扶持处于危险中的国家的功德，比不上恢复已经灭亡的国家的功德大。您不如晚一点等齐灭了邢国之后再去救它，一来这样可以使晋国疲惫，齐国才能真正得到好处；二来等邢国灭亡后再帮助他们复国，那样的名声才真正美好。"齐桓公于是听从其说，按兵不动，没有立即去救援邢国了。

　　鲍叔牙的计谋，就是所谓"坐山观虎斗"、"坐收渔人之利"。在我们今天看来，此计使得本来可以快速平息的战乱无端拖延，邢国百姓无辜多遭兵荒马乱、家破人亡之苦，未免显得有些残忍。但从为本国谋求最大利益来说，又难以彻底否定。中国几千年来政治哲学发达，这一类的政术经验和理论积累极为丰富，我们今天应该加以开发，应用在军事、外交和经济等方面。对于我们日常生活来说，这个故事起码也可以启发我们做事要把握恰当的时机，从而实现利益最大化。

DUKE HUAN OF QI RESCUES THE STATE OF XING

In the Spring and Autumn Period, the State of Jin once attacked the State of Xing. At that time, Duke Huan of Qi, as the overlord of all the states, planned to send troops to rescue Xing. Bao Shuya, an eminent minister in the State of Qi, said, "It's too early to go now. If we don't allow Jin to keep attacking Xing until Xing is conquered, Jin won't be worn out, and its power won't be weakened; if Jin isn't worn out and its power isn't weakened, our position won't become relatively more important. Furthermore, the merits of rescuing a state in danger are not as great as those of restoring a conquered one. You might as well wait a little longer to rescue Xing until it is conquered by Jin. In that case, for one thing, Jin will become worn out, and Qi will reap the benefits. For another thing, when we help Xing to recover its state after it is conquered, we will get good reputation." Duke Huan of Qi followed Bao Shuya's advice to hold the Qi troops and didn't go to the rescue of Xing at once.

Bao Shuya's strategy is called "sitting on top of the mountain to watch two tigers fight" or "reaping the spoils of victory without lifting a finger". In our point of view today, this strategy prolonged a war that could have been brought to an end and made the innocent people of Xing suffer more from the ravages of war, with their houses in ruins and family members dead or scattered. That is rather cruel. On the other hand, this strategy helped to bring maximum profit for the State of Qi, and in this sense it is viable. There is a rich legacy of sophisticated political philosophies, experiences and theories in the Chinese history, which can still be applied to today's military decision-making, diplomacy and economy. On a lesser scale, this story also instructs us to do things at the opportune time in order to maximize the profit.

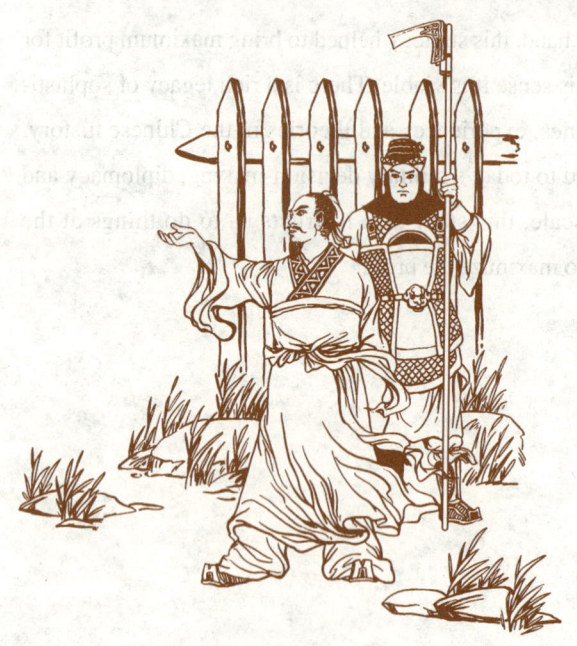

18. 伍子胥出逃

　　楚国人伍子胥一家被奸臣所害，满门抄斩。他一人逃出虎口，准备越境逃往吴国（伍子胥的故事参见第259页"费无极用计杀郤宛"）。这一天来到昭关，被守卫边境的官吏抓住了。伍子胥说："你知道国君为什么要抓我吗？"官吏说："不知道。"伍子胥说："国君搜捕我，是要索取我家的一颗宝珠。这颗宝珠实际上已经丢掉了——我拿不出来，所以要逃跑。现在如果你抓我去见大王，我就会说是你把宝珠抢走，吞到你肚子去了！"官吏听了伍子胥的话，觉得有道理：如果他抓捕伍子胥，最后君主要取回宝珠，必定会剖开他的肚子，他就没命了，于是就悄悄地放走了伍子胥。

　　伍子胥可谓颇有急智。在危急关头，他用一番话巧妙地把自己的利害与这位守关官吏捆到了一起，使自己原来的敌人变成了自己的盟友。古人说："利同则合，利分则争。""利"不单指利益，也包括预期可能的危害。俗话说的"拉上贼船"，现在的腐败官员用"一起分过赃"来结成攻守同盟，都是这个道理。当然这些都是反面的例子，在我们的生活和工作中，如果遇到矛盾冲突或不好解决的疑难问题，也不妨通过一定的办法或者说"谋略"，来使跟自己有冲突的人变得跟自己利害与共，合理地利用"利同则合"来解决问题。

WU ZIXU'S ESCAPE

Persecuted by a treacherous court official, Wu Zixu and his whole family in the State of Chu were to be executed. Only Wu Zixu managed to escape a narrow death. He planned to slip through the borders to seek shelter in the State of Wu (Please refer to the story entitled "Killing a Rival with a Borrowed Knife" on page 260 for more information about Wu Zixu). One day, he came to the Pass of Zhaoguan and was captured by an official stationed at the frontier. Wu Zixu said, "Do you have any idea why the king wants to catch me?" The official said, "No, I don't." Wu Zixu said, "The king searches for me in order to retrieve a precious pearl that my family owns. Actually, the pearl has been lost, so I have to run away as I don't have it with me. Now if you take me to the king, I'll say that you have taken the pearl and swallowed it." The official thought it over and was alarmed: if he turned Wu Zixu in, the king would want to get the pearl by cutting open his stomach, which would kill him for sure. Therefore, he secretly released Wu Zixu.

One may well say that Wu Zixu was quick-witted. At the critical moment, he used his clever words to attach his own interests to those of the official at the frontier, turning the adversary into his ally. As an ancient saying goes, "With same interests people become allies, while with different interests people fight each other." "Interests" here do not merely refer to profit but also include potential harm. As another popular saying goes, "One can't get off the pirate ship once onboard." Today, corrupt officials conspire to cover each other's back by "sharing the spoils together". Both of the above sayings mean the same thing. Of course, those are both negative examples. In our daily life and work, if we encounter conflicts or knotty problems, we might just as well tie our own interests to those of the opposing party by certain means or "tactics". In this way, we are consciously making use of the strategy of "forming an alliance with people sharing the same interests" to solve the problem.

19. 卫人之妻求神

　　卫国一对夫妻在祈祷时，妻子向神灵祈求说："让我没有灾难，得到一百捆布币。"丈夫很奇怪，问道："为什么要得这么少？"妻子回答说："超过这个数目，你就会用它去买小老婆了。"

　　人和人的利益不同。小到家庭之中，亲密如夫妻之间，尚且有各自不同的利益。妻子祈求财富，对于她自己来说，当然是越多越好。但财富是家庭共有的，如果过多了，丈夫用来买了小老婆，就会威胁到自己的地位，所以她很"聪明"地选择了一个不大不小的数目。看起来，任何事物，哪怕是财富和权势，都不是越多就越好。有时候太多了，反而会给自己带来麻烦或伤害。所以人必须把握一个合适的度，合适的才是最好的。

A CLEVER WIFE ASKS FOR BLESSINGS FROM GOD

When a couple in the State of Wei were asking for blessings from god, the wife said, "Bless me to be free from disasters and to get a hundred bundles of cloth." Her husband was very surprised, so he asked, "Why do you ask for so little?" The wife answered, "If we got more than this, you would use it to buy a concubine."

Different individuals have different interests. Even between husband and wife in a small family, there might arise different interests. When the wife asked for wealth, of course, she wanted more for herself. But the wealth was shared by the family. If there was excessive wealth, her husband would use it to buy a concubine, who would pose a threat to her own position. Therefore, she "cleverly" chose a moderate amount of money. It seems that it is not always better to possess more, be it wealth or power. Sometimes, going to the excesses will bring about burden and harm to oneself. Therefore, one must maintain an appropriate amount, for only the appropriate is the best.

20. 兔死狗烹

　　越王勾践攻打吴国，吴王谢罪并宣布臣服，越王准备接受他的投降。越国上大夫范蠡和大夫文种说："不行啊。过去吴国曾打败越国，但没有灭亡我们，大王您亲自入吴侍奉吴王，卧薪尝胆，最终复了国。这是上天把越国给了吴国，而吴国不接受。谚语说'上天给予的你不接受，就会反过来成为灾祸。'现在上天反过来不帮助吴王夫差了，这正是他们受到的天灾啊。上天把吴国给了越国，我们应当拜两拜接受下来，把它灭掉。大王您不能答应吴王的投降要求。"吴国的太宰嚭听说后，送给大夫文种一封信，信上说："狡猾的兔子捕完了，好猎狗就会被煮来吃；敌国灭亡了，谋臣就会遭到杀害。大夫您为什么不放过吴国，让它成为越国的忧患呢？这样您也才能保全在越国的地位啊。"文种接信读罢，长叹一声说："要是越国杀掉谋臣，也将会遭到和吴国同样的下场。"

成语"兔死狗烹"就出自这个故事，比喻事情成功以后，把出过大力的人除掉，尤其是多用于比喻统治者杀害功臣，后来西汉的司马迁在《史记》中也说过这件事。《韩非子》从"利异"的观点出发，认为："群臣跟君主的利益不同，群臣自己之间的利益也不同，所以臣下没有一个是忠诚的。臣下的利益确定了，君主的利益就失去了。因此那些奸臣贼子，招致敌国军队来除掉国内私敌，用涉外事件来迷惑君主，假如能取得自己的私利，就会不顾国家的忧患。"臣下要保住自己受重视的地位，往往同时要设法保住使自己能起作用的对象。所以太宰嚭会劝文种说，对于谋臣来讲，保住敌国不被灭亡，自己在本国才会得到重用。后世官兵剿匪时往往有意不彻底剿绝，免得自己无事可干以致失去上头重视，有时甚至"养匪自重"，都是这个道理。

THE HOUNDS ARE KILLED FOR FOOD ONCE THE HARES ARE BAGGED

King Goujian of Yue defeated the King of Wu, who made an apology and declared to submit himself to the rule of Yue. King Goujian of Yue decided to accept Wu's surrender, but Fan Li and Wen Zhong, senior ministers of Yue, both said, "Please don't do that. The State of Wu had defeated us before, but they didn't destroy us. Then Your Majesty went to serve the King of Wu yourself and finally restored our state after undergoing self-imposed hardships. At that time, Heaven bestowed Yue upon Wu, but Wu didn't take it. As the proverb goes, 'If you don't accept what Heaven confers on you, it will conversely turn into a disaster.' Now Heaven doesn't help the King of Wu, which is just the disaster he is supposed to suffer. Now that Heaven bestows Wu upon Yue instead, we should kowtow to Heaven twice and take it by destroying it.

Therefore, Your Majesty shouldn't agree to the request of the King of Wu for surrender." Hearing this, Pi, the Great Steward of Wu, wrote a letter to Wen Zhong, saying, "When wily hares are all captured, good hounds will be cooked for food; when the enemy state is destroyed, the councilors will be killed. Why don't you let Wu off and make it become a worry for Yue? Only in that case can you keep your position in Yue." After reading this letter, Wen Zhong uttered a deep sigh and said, "If Yue kills its councilors, it is to suffer the same fate as Wu did."

The idiom "The hounds are killed for food once the hares are bagged" comes from this story and explains the case where devoted contributors are gotten rid of after victory is achieved. It is specially used to explain the cases of monarchs killing officials of merit. The story was later recorded by Sima Qian of the Western Han Dynasty. *Han Feizi* introduces the view of "different interests" and makes the following conclusion: "The interests of officials are different from those of the monarch, and the interests of the officials themselves are also different; therefore, no official is loyal. If the interests of the officials are secured, those of the monarch will be lost. Therefore, those treacherous officials would invite enemy troops to get rid of their private enemies in their own country and confuse the monarch with foreign affairs; they would disregard the suffering of their own country if they could gain profit for themselves." If officials want to keep their own important positions, they will often try every means to protect whatever could make them useful. Therefore, the Great Steward Pi would persuade Wen Zhong by saying that for a councilor, Wen Zhong should keep the enemy state from being destroyed so that he could be given an important position in his own state. Military officers of later generations often intentionally kept from wiping out the enemy completely in case they would lose favor when they had nothing to do. Sometimes they even "supported robbers and rebels to maintain their own importance" out of similar considerations.

21. 语言暗示也能杀人

　　齐国有个叫"夷射"的做"中大夫"的官员，有一次在齐王那里陪侍齐王喝酒。他喝得酩酊大醉后出来，倚靠在走廊门上。走廊门的守门人是个受过刖刑的名"跪"的人，所以被人称为"刖跪"。刖跪向夷射请求说："大人，您看您都已经喝成这样了，还有没有一点剩下的酒啊？您肯不肯赏给小人一点喝呀？"夷射斥骂道："滚！像你这样低贱的受过刑的人，怎么竟敢向我这样的尊长要酒喝！"刖跪二话不说慌忙退下了。等到夷射离开后，刖跪就把水泼在走廊门的檐沟下，弄得像尿湿的样子。第二天，齐王出来看见，很生气地责骂："谁这么大的胆子，敢在寡人这儿撒尿啊？"刖跪回答说："我没看见啊。不过呢……嗯……呃……好像昨天中大夫夷射在这儿站过来着……"齐王因而追究夷射的罪责，最后杀掉了夷射。

　　魏王臣子中有两个人与济阳君不和，济阳君就想了一个办法来除掉他们。他让人伪造王命谋划进攻自己，魏王很快就知道了有人伪造王命谋划进攻济阳君的事，当然他并不清楚这是济阳君自己一手策划的。魏王就派人问济阳君说："你与谁有仇？"意思是此事背后的主谋应该就是济阳君的仇人。济阳君回答说："我不敢和谁有仇。不过呢……也曾和两个人关系不好。但我想恐怕也还不至于到这种地步吧？"魏王问左右近侍，都说："确实如此。那两个人就是某某和某某。"于是魏王就杀掉了那两个人。

刖跪和济阳君最后对国君的回答，都不把自己的意图直接用语言表示出来，而是留有余地，或"暗示"对方，或"以退为进"，使听话的人根据语境自然地得出自己想要传达给对方的信息，而事后如果追究起来，又因为自己没有明说而留不下把柄。我们常听到一句话："宁得罪君子，莫得罪小人。"刖跪和济阳君就都是典型的小人。君子难斗小人，自古以来一直如此。君子不会因为芝麻大的一点小事忌恨一个人，即使对某人有看法，也不会采取下三滥的手段去对付他。小人则正好相反。小人记仇，报复心极强，而且深深埋藏在心底，甚至深入骨髓，片刻不忘，等到机会一到，立刻跳出来，睚眦必报，就像上面故事里的刖跪。小人不会计较什么脸面，也不计较什么影响，他们为达到目的可以不择手段。因此无论做什么，小人的"出牌"决不会按游戏规则，更不会讲道德原则，正如俗语所说的"明枪易躲，暗箭难防"。

INSINUATIONS CAN BE LETHAL

There was a man called Yi She who acted as a junior official in the State of Qi. Once he served the King of Qi in drinking. After getting utterly drunk, he came out and leaned against the gate in the corridor. The gatekeeper in the corridor was a man named "Gui", who had his feet cut off as a punishment (called "yue") and thus was also named "Yue Gui". Yue Gui asked Yi She, "My lord, you see you have gotten yourself so much drunken. Have you got a little wine left? Would you please give me a little to drink?" Yi She yelled at him, "Go away! How dare you, a humble man whose feet have been cut off as a punishment, ask such a honorable man as me for drink?" Without saying a word, Yue Gui left in a hurry. When Yi She left, Yue Gui splashed some water under the eaves as if someone had pissed there. On the next day, the King of Qi came out and saw it. He burst up in anger, "Who has the guts to piss in my place?" Yue Gui answered, "I didn't see it, but … er … er … it seemed that Junior Official Yi She stood there yesterday …" Consequently, the King of Qi held Yi She responsible and eventually killed him.

Two officials of the King of Wei were not on good terms with Prince Jiyang, so the prince thought out a way to get rid of them. He asked someone to fake the king's order to launch an attack on himself. Soon the King of Wei knew someone had faked his order to attack Prince Jiyang. Of course, he had no idea that it was plotted by Prince Jiyang himself, so he sent someone to ask Prince Jiyang, "Who has harboured hatred against you?" The king believed that the chief plotter behind this conspiracy should be an enemy of Prince Jiyang. Prince Jiyang answered, "I dare not be the target of anyone's hatred. However, … I wasn't on good terms with two men. But I don't think it's that serious." Then the King of Wei asked his attendants about it, and all the attendants said, "It's true. The two men are Mr. A and Mr. B." As a result, the King of Wei killed those two officials.

Neither of the final answers of Yue Gui and Prince Jiyang were a complete expression of what the speakers had in mind. They both left room for imagination, whether to "give hint" or to "retreat in order to advance", in order to make the listeners naturally arrive at the conclusion through careful insinuation. If the conclusion was later proved false, they wouldn't be held responsible because they didn't make the conclusion directly. We often hear a saying: "One would rather choose to offend a gentleman than a villain". Yue Gui and Prince Jiyang are both typical villains. It has always been the case since ancient times that a gentleman can hardly contend with a villain. A gentleman won't hate anyone because of a trivial matter. Even if he is dissatisfied with someone, he won't use base means to deal with it. A villain will just do the opposite. A villain is extremely revengeful: he nurses grudges deeply at the bottom of his heart or even deep into his marrow; he never forgets his grudges for a moment and will jump out to seek revenge for petty grievances once the time is ripe. Just like Yue Gui in the above story, a villain does not care about "face" or "reputation". He will stop at nothing to get what he wants. No matter what he does, a villain won't play by any rules of the game, not to mention according to any moral principle. That is best explained in a saying: "It is easy to dodge a spear thrust in the open, but hard to guard oneself against an arrow shot from ambush."

22. 以人言善我，必以人言罪我

　　赵国人鲁丹多次游说中山国君，意见总不被接受，他就散发了五十金去贿赂国君身边的近臣，请他们在国君面前为自己说好话。下次又见到中山国君的时候，还没有开口说话，国君就盛情款待他吃饭。鲁丹出来后，连住所都没回去，急急忙忙就离开了中山国。他的车夫说："您呆了这么久，花了这么大功夫，好不容易这次见面国君对我们的态度转好了，为什么要着急离开呢？"鲁丹说："因为他人的话才对我友好，也一定会因为他人的话来怪罪我。"鲁丹还未走出中山国境，公子就中伤他说："鲁丹是个间谍，是为赵国来刺探中山国的。"果然中山国君就听进去了，因此布置搜捕鲁丹并要加罪于他。

　　鲁丹说的"以人言善我，必以人言罪我"这话，可谓对人性的深刻认识。糊涂的人，可分为两种，或者是自以为是，一点儿也听不进别人的劝；或者是毫无主见，轻信别人的话。后一种人，他的爱憎，就很容易随着别人的看法而改变。鲁丹正是看出了中山国君属于后一种人，所以他虽然受到了中山君的热情款待，却还是要仓皇出逃，全身远祸。没有自己主见的人是不可相信的，更是不可依赖的。

SOLICITED GOODWILL DOESN'T LAST LONG

Lu Dan of the State of Zhao had tried to offer counsel to the King of Zhongshan for many times, but his advice never got accepted. Then he bribed the king's close officials with fifty gold coins, asking them to speak in his favor in the presence of the king. The next time when he went to see the King of Zhongshan, the king warmly welcomed Lu Dan and entertained him with a lavish feast before he had a chance to speak. After getting out, Lu Dan left the State of Zhongshan in a hurry, without even going back to his residence. His driver asked him, "You have stayed here so long and made so much effort before the king finally changed his attitude toward us this time. Why would you leave in such a hurry?" Lu Dan said, "If he treats me friendly because of others' words, he might as well lay blame on me because of others' words." Before Lu Dan crossed the borders of Zhongshan, the prince of Zhongshan spread slanderous rumors against him, saying, "Lu Dan is a spy employed by Zhao to gather secret information about Zhongshan." As Lu Dan had expected, the King of Zhongshan believed in the rumors. The king thus arranged for a search of Lu Dan and wanted to impose a guilt on him.

Lu Dan's words that "if one treats me nicely because of others' words, he will also lay blame on me because of others' words" showed his deep understanding of human nature. A foolish person either considers himself in the right, unable to listen to others' advice, or has no definite views of his own, readily placing trust in others' words. The attitude of the latter can be easily swayed by the others' views. Upon recognizing that the King of Zhongshan might be easily influenced by others, Lu Dan ran away in a hurry in order to get away from disasters as soon as possible, despite the fact that he finally received the warm treatment from the king. A man with no definite views of his own can never be trusted, not to mention to be relied on.

23. 大蛇负小蛇

春秋时，鸱夷子皮侍奉齐国的大臣田成子。有一次，田成子犯了事儿，要逃离齐国投奔燕国，鸱夷子皮背着出关的通行证跟随他一起出逃。到了望邑，子皮说："您听说过这个故事吗？说有一群蛇住在湖沼边上，有一年大旱，湖里的水都干了，蛇群准备搬家。有条小蛇对大蛇说：'要是咱们还跟平常一样，您走在前头，我跟在后面，人们看到了会认为这只不过是两条普通的过路的蛇，必然有人会想杀死我们。不如这样：我们互相衔着，您背着我往前走。人们看见了，就会把我看作神君，他们害怕我的话就不敢杀我们了。'于是它们就互相衔着，大蛇背着小蛇穿过大路。人们见了都纷纷躲避，说：'这小蛇，连大蛇都要侍奉他，一定是神君啊！'现在的情况是，您美而我丑，您气度非凡而我气质平庸，我作您的随从，在大家看来没什么可奇怪的。但如果反过来，以我为主，要是您扮作我的上宾，人们就会认为我是拥有千辆战车的国君；如果您扮作我的使者，人家就会认为我是拥有万辆战车的国君的卿相。我看不如您干脆扮作我的侍从吧，这样人们就会把我看作拥有万辆战车的大国的国君。"田成子接受了这个主意，就背着通行证跟随在邸夷子皮的后面装作侍从人员。到了客店，店主人非常恭敬而殷勤地招待他们，并献上了美酒佳肴。

邸夷子皮对一般人的心理把握极为准确，他装神弄鬼的手段大获成功。用现代社会的术语来说，他很会"包装"。所谓"包装"，对象或资源本身并没有什么实质性的变化，变化的是整合利用资源的方法。特异的包装、组合、造势，造成了独特、奇异的效果，令人刮目相看。普通的蛇就这样包装成了蛇神，普通的侍从臣子就这样包装成了万乘之君，今天的很一般的一个人也就这样被包装成了明星。所以，现在那些盲目崇拜"偶像"的追星族们和古时候把小蛇当作蛇神的糊涂路人没什么两样。

A BIG SNAKE CARRIES A SMALL ONE

In the Spring and Autumn Period, Chiyi Zipi served Tian Chengzi, a minister of the State of Qi. Once as Tian Chengzi violated the law and escaped from Qi to Yan, Chiyi Zipi followed his master on the journey, carrying a border pass on his back. When they arrived at a place called Wangyi, Zipi said to his master, "Have you ever heard about this story? It is said that there lived a group of snakes by the lakes and marshes. One year there was a severe drought. All the lakes dried up, and all the snakes had to move. A small snake said to a big snake, 'If we go as usual, with you walking ahead and me following you behind, people will think we are just ordinary snakes, so someone may want to kill us. We might as well try this: we go in tandem, with you carrying me on your back. When people see us, they will regard me as a god. Since they are afraid of me, they dare not kill us.' Then they went onto the road in tandem, and the big snake carried the small one on its back. When people saw the two snakes, they were panic-stricken and said, 'The small snake must be a god, as a big snake serves it.' Now the situation is like this: you are handsome while I'm ugly; you are impressive in bearing while I am plain in appearance. If I act as your attendant, people will feel nothing is wrong. But if we do the opposite, with me pretending to be the master and you acting as my distinguished guest, people will think I am a king with thousands of war chariots. If you pretend to be my envoy, they will think I am the prime minister of a king with tens of thousands of war chariots. In my opinion, you might as well pretend to be my attendant. In that case, people will regard me as the king of a big state who owns tens of thousands of war chariots." Tian Chengzi took the advice and then pretended to be an attendant walking behind Chiyi Zipi, carrying the border pass on his back. When they came to an inn, the owner served them with great respect and hospitality and entertained them with good wine and delicious food.

Chiyi Zipi accurately read people's mind, so his deliberate trick of mystification proved very successful. Put in modern terms, he was a public relations expert. The PR campaign does not make any essential change to an object or a resource, but it does change the way the target is presented to the public. By redressing, rearranging and promoting the target in a creative way, the PR expert helps to produce a unique and unusual effect and allows the public to see the target in a new light. In this way, an ordinary snake becomes a snake god and a plain attendant becomes a king with tens of thousands of war chariots in the same way as today's celebrities are presented to the public. Therefore, those fans who blindly worship their "idols" at present day are no different from the foolish passers-by who regarded the small snake as a god in the old times.

24. 老马识途

　　春秋时期，齐桓公带兵攻打山戎国，获得了胜利。山戎国王逃到了孤竹国。齐桓公紧追不放，又带着管仲、隰朋等向孤竹国进军。他们出征时正是春暖花开的季节，等到打败孤竹国回师时，已经秋去冬来了。出征时还有茂密的树林，现在尽是枯枝败叶；出征时只见遍地的鲜花，现在全是茫茫的白雪。来时道路的痕迹，现在一点都找不到了。结果齐国军队迷失了方向，被困在山里。这时，管仲说："我们可以利用老马的才智呀。"就放开军中的老马，任它们自己往前走，大军紧紧地跟随在后面，终于找到了来时的路。这个问题解决了，别的麻烦又来了。将士们长时间在山里行军，找不到水喝，口渴难耐。隰朋说："蚂蚁冬天住在山的南面，夏天住在山的北面。如果地上蚂蚁洞穴口上的浮土有一寸高的话，地下八尺深的地方就会有水。"于是按这个办法找到合适的地方挖掘，果然找到了水。最终齐桓公率领大军顺利地返回了齐国。

　　成语"老马识途"就是从这个故事来的，"途"就是路途、道路。现在一般用它来比喻有经验的人熟悉情况，了解规律，能为先导。又说"识途老马"，比喻对某种事物十分熟悉的人。

　　《韩非子》在这个故事末尾总结说："凭管仲的智慧和隰朋的聪明，他们碰到不知道的事儿，尚且不惜向老马和蚂蚁学习；现在的人，不知道用他们的愚蠢之心去向圣人的智慧学习，难道不是错误的做法吗？"人的认识能力有限，而事理是无穷尽的。要想越过眼前的障碍，既要向前人学习吸收人类已有的知识，也要随时向客观事物学习，探求未知真理，这才能成为真正的智者。"他山之石，可以攻玉。"讲的正是借助外在力量来为自己服务的道理。

AN OLD HORSE KNOWS THE WAY

In the Spring and Autumn Period, Duke Huan of Qi led troops to attack the State of Shanrong and won a victory. The King of Shanrong fled to the State of Guzhu, under hot pursuit by Duke Huan of Qi who marched his troops into the State of Guzhu with his ministers Guan Zhong and Xi Peng. When the Qi troops started the expedition, it was warm spring with flowers in blossom, but when they returned after defeating the State of Guzhu, it was already past autumn and approaching winter. When they set out, there were thick forests, but at the moment only dead twigs and withered leaves were seen; when they set out, there were flowers blooming everywhere, but at the moment only white snow blanketed the land. They couldn't find any trace of the way on which they had travelled. As a result, the Qi troops got lost in the mountains. At this moment, Guan Zhong said, "We could make use of the wisdom of old horses." Then he had all the old horses in the troops released and allowed them to go freely themselves. Closely following the old horses, the troops found their way back at last. But after this problem was solved, another arose. The generals and soldiers marched in the mountains for a long time without getting any water to drink, and now they were distressed by thirst. Xi Peng said, "Ants live on the southern slopes of the mountains in winter and on the northern slopes in summer. If there is one *cun* of soil on the surface of an ant hill, there must be water eight *chi* deep beneath it." Then they dug an ant hill according to this method and found water at last. Finally, Duke Huan of Qi returned to his home state with his troops successfully.

The idiom "An old horse knows the way" comes from this story. It is now used to describe the fact that an experienced person familiar with a certain situation can be relied on as the guide. It can also be put as "the old horse that knows the way", referring to the person who is familiar with a certain situation.

Han Feizi concludes at the end of the story, "Though Guan Zhong and Xi Peng were very wise, they could still learn from old horses and ants when they met problems they couldn't cope with. Then isn't it wrong for the people now in all their foolishness not to learn from the wisdom of the sages?" Human beings have a limited ability to understand things, but the laws of things are infinite. If one wants to overcome the present obstacle, he should not only learn the knowledge from his ancestors, but also learn from the physical world at any time to pursue the unknown truth. Only in this way can he become a real wise person. Another idiom "There are other hills whose stones are good for working jade" also explains the idea of employing external resources to serve one's own need.

25. 想迁到越国去的鲁人

　　从前鲁国有个人，很擅长编草鞋，他的妻子擅长织生绢。他想迁到南边的越国去。有人知道他的打算后告诉他说："你要这么做的话，一定行不通的。"那个鲁人问："为什么？"这个人解释说："南边的越国乃是水乡，风俗跟我们这里不同。草鞋是穿在脚上的，但越国人的风俗是打赤脚走路；生绢用来做帽子，是戴在头上的，但越国人的风俗是披头散发，不用戴帽。你带着你的长处，却前往根本没有用武之地的国家，怎么可能不碰壁呢？"

　　鲁国的这对夫妇，完全不了解越国的生活习惯，只凭自己的手艺来想当然，就要搬到陌生的越国去谋生，真是危险，幸好有他人及时相劝。这个鲁人不懂得一切事物都是以时间、地点和条件为转移的，做事要切合实际，实事求是，从实际出发分析客观条件，要在正确的时间和正确的地方做正确的事情，才能收到良好的效果。单凭老经验和主观愿望，做事选错了时间和地点，是注定要碰壁的。

A MAN OF LU WANTS TO MOVE TO YUE

Once upon a time, a man in the State of Lu was very good at weaving straw sandals, and his wife was good at spinning raw silk. He wanted to move to the State of Yue in the south. Someone knew his plan and told him, "If you do so, it won't work." The man of Lu asked, "Why?" The advising man explained, "The State of Yue in the south is a region of rivers and lakes, where there are different customs. We wear straw sandals, but the people of Yue all walk with bare feet according to their customs; silk is used to make hats, which we wear on our heads, but the people of Yue have their hair hung loose and don't wear hats according to their customs. Now if you go to a state where your strength can't be given full play, how will you not suffer a setback?"

This couple of Lu were completely ignorant of the living habits in the State of Yue. Boasting their own craftsmanship, they took everything for granted and wanted to move to Yue, a strange place for them, to make a living. That could be quite risky. Fortunately, someone came to give them a piece of timely advice. This man of Lu didn't understand that everything changes according to time, place and condition. One should make decisions based on the actual situation and seek truth from facts by analyzing objective conditions realistically and doing the right thing in the right place and at the right time. Only in this way can one expect to achieve good results. Merely relying on one's old experience and subjective wish, one will certainly choose the wrong place and time to do something inappropriate and thus is bound to suffer a setback.

26. 卫人嫁女

　　从前有个卫国人，在女儿出嫁时告诫她说："出嫁后，你一定要私下积聚财物。做人家的妻子而被休回娘家，是常有的事；夫妻俩能够在一起白头偕老，是很侥幸的。要自己留点钱以防万一呀。"女儿果然很听话，出嫁后一直偷偷地积攒私房钱。她婆婆发现后，认为媳妇私心太多，就把她休掉了。这个女儿带回家的财物，比带去的嫁妆多出一倍。她的父亲不归罪于自己没有教育好女儿，反而自以为聪明，为家里赚了钱，对此还沾沾自喜呢。

　　在当时那个社会，一个女子被夫家休了，遣送回娘家，无异于葬送了一生的幸福。这个卫国人和他的女儿不去反省自己的错误行为，反倒为自己的"先见之明"沾沾自喜。《韩非子》讲完这个故事之后总结说："现在那些当官的，往往贪赃枉法、聚敛钱财、唯利是图，就都是像这个卫国人和他的女儿一类的人。"看来，如果人过度地为自己的利益考虑，并自以为聪明，就会忘了自己应做的事情，把最根本的东西抛弃了。

A MAN OF WEI OFFERS HIS DAUGHTER IN MARRIAGE

Once upon a time, a man in the State of Wei warned his daughter when she was to get married, "You must collect money secretly after you get married. It is common for a wife to be abandoned by her husband, and it is fortunate for a woman to live with her husband till old age. Therefore, you should keep some money for yourself lest the former case should happen." His daughter followed his advice. She was secretly saving money for herself all the time after marriage. However, her mother-in-law found it out and believed the woman to be too selfish, so her husband's family kicked her out. The woman went home with all her collected money and possessions, which were twice the sum of her dowry. The man of Wei didn't attribute the failure of his daughter's marriage to himself for not being able to educate his daughter well; instead, he thought he was very clever for he earned money for the family, and he was quite proud of it.

In the feudal society at that time, a woman's lifelong happiness would be forfeit if she was divorced and sent back to her parents' home. The man of Wei and his daughter didn't reflect that it was their own fault that brought about such a sad consequence, but congratulated themselves for their "foresight". After telling this story, *Han Feizi* says in summary, "Today those officials often take bribes, bend the laws, accumulate wealth and seek profit for themselves, just like the man of Wei and his daughter." It seems that if one takes too much of their own interests into consideration and still thinks himself in the right, he will forget about his own role and abandon the most essential principles.

27. 不死之药

有一个人拿着号称吃了可以长生不死的药来到楚国，要将它进献给楚王。宫廷里主管传达的官员捧着药进宫去，遇上一位宫中的侍卫武官。那侍卫武官问道："你拿的是什么好东西？"传达官回答说："是不死之药。"侍卫武官问："这药可以吃吗？"传达官回答说："当然是可以吃的呀。"于是侍卫武官从传达官手里抢过药就吞了下去。楚王知道后，非常生气，就要杀掉那个侍卫武官。侍卫武官劝谏楚王说："我问过传达官这药可不可以吃，他说'可以吃'，所以我才吃了药。这证明我没罪，如果说那药是献给大王的，别人吃了就是犯罪，那么这罪责应该由传达官来承担。再说，如果那人献给大王您的真是'不死之药'，您就更不该杀我了。因为我吃了药却导致大王要杀我，那所谓'不死之药'反倒成了'死药'了，这就是献药者欺骗了大王。大王您如果杀了我一个无罪的小臣，等于是向世人宣布您被人欺骗的丑闻；您倒不如饶恕我，把我放了，这样一来，世人将会称颂您的英明和大度。"楚王听了侍卫武官的一番话，觉得很有道理，于是下令把他放了。

那位侍卫武官以巧辩脱罪，实际上是以一种巧妙的方式进谏。他利用了两点，一是"可以"一词的多义性给句子"这药可以吃吗？"造成的歧义。"可以"既可以表示客观上的条件可能，又可以表示主观上的意愿允许。于是"这药可以吃吗？"就既可以表示："这药是人可以吃的吗？"意思是吃了对人的身体会不会有什么坏处，又可以表示"这药我可以吃吗？"意思是我吃它是不是合法的。传达官理解的是第一层意思，侍卫武官辩解时说他理解的是第二层意思。二是他利用"不死之药"的本来含义，为楚王制造了一个二难推理：如果不死之药是真的，那么，既然他已经吃下了不死之药，楚王就应该杀死不了他；如果他被楚王杀死了，就证明不死之药是假的，而如果不死之药是假的，那么他就又罪不该杀。楚王如果杀死了他，就会陷入一个"悖论"困境。总之，他无论如何也死不了。古代帝王多醉心于追求长生不老之术，梦想能够将这至高无上的地位、权势和财富永远保有下去。侍卫武官有胆有识，"安全"地戳穿了"不死之药"的谎言，巧妙地达到了劝谏楚王的目的。

ELIXIR OF LIFE

A man came to the State of Chu with the so-called elixir of life and offered it to the king, claiming that the elixir could make one immortal. The court official in charge of reception was walking into the palace with the elixir in his hands when he ran into a guard officer. The guard officer asked, "What are you holding in your hands?" The official of reception said, "Elixir of life." The guard officer then asked, "Can it be eaten?" The official of reception said, "Of course, it can be eaten." Then the guard officer snatched the elixir from the official's hands and gulped it down. Hearing this, the King of Chu was angry and demanded the guard officer to be executed. The guard officer defended himself and admonished the king, "I have asked the official of reception if the medicine can be eaten, and he answered, 'It can be eaten,' so I ate it. That proves I'm innocent. If the elixir was presented to Your Majesty only and others were not allowed to eat it, the official of reception should take the responsibility. What's more, if what that man presented to Your Majesty is the real 'elixir of life', you shouldn't kill me. If Your Majesty wants to kill me because I ate the medicine, then the so-called 'elixir of life' turns into 'drug of death', which means that the man with the elixir deceives Your Majesty. If Your Majesty kills me, an innocent officer, it gives the message to the world that Your Majesty is deceived. Your Majesty might as well spare me and let me go. In that case, everyone will praise you for your wisdom and generosity." The king saw the sense in the guard officer's words and had him released.

That guard officer's smart defense for his action was in fact a clever way of persuasion. He made use of two points. Firstly, the polysemy of the word "can" caused ambiguity for the sentence "Can it be eaten?" The word "can" means both an objective possibility and a subjective permission. In that case, the sentence "Can it be eaten?" can be understood either as "Can it be eaten by man?", which means whether it will bring any harm to human body if one eats it, or as "Can it be eaten by me?", which means whether I am allowed to eat it. The official of reception understood the sentence in the former meaning, but the guard officer explained it in the latter meaning when defending himself. Secondly, he made use of the original meaning of the "elixir of life" to create a dilemma. If the elixir was real, the king shouldn't be able to kill him since he was supposed to be immortal after eating the elixir. If he was killed by the king, it showed that the elixir didn't work, which meant he was not guilty and thus shouldn't be killed. Therefore, if he was killed, the king would be caught up in a paradox. All in all, he couldn't die in either case. The ancient emperors and kings were all obsessed with the pursuit of the art of becoming immortal and the medicines that could bring eternal youth and immortality, in the wish that they could keep their supreme position, power and wealth forever. The guard officer had both courage and insight to expose the lies of "elixir of life" and persuade the King of Chu in a safe way.

28. 远水救不了近火

　　战国初年的鲁穆公，为了结交晋、楚这两个强国，把自己的儿子们派到这两个国家去做官，希望万一鲁国有难也好有个照应。他的大臣犁钮却认为这种做法并不能解决问题，就对鲁穆公说："越国是水乡之国，人们都善于游泳。可是，如果我们这里有个孩子掉进了水里，去请越国的人来相救，那么不等人家赶来，溺水的人早就淹死了，越国人再会游泳也没有用。又比如，如果失火了，到千里之外去取海水来救，海水虽然很多，但是大火也一定扑灭不了。这道理很简单：远水救不了近火。同样的道理，现在晋国和楚国虽然很强大，但是毕竟距离鲁国较远，而齐国距离鲁国较近。一旦鲁国受到齐国侵略，这种祸患靠晋楚两国恐怕也很难相救吧！"

　　《庄子·外物》记载了一个著名的"涸辙之鲋"的故事：庄子家里很穷，去向监河侯借粮食。监河侯说："好！我就要收租税了，等我收到以后，借给您三百金，好吗？"庄子气得脸色都变了，说："我昨天来这里时，在半路上听到有人喊救命，我回头一看，只见车辙里有一条小鲫鱼。我问它说：'鲫鱼啊！您这样喊我做什么呢？'它回答道：'我是东海神的臣子，今天不幸陷落在这干车辙里，您可有一斗半升的水救救我吗？'我说：'好。我正要到南方去游说吴越的国王，我请他们把西江的水引上来营救你，好吗？'鲫鱼气愤地变了脸色说：'我失掉了平常赖以生活的水，已经没法生存，我只求你给我一斗半升的水就能活命，你却说这么多废话。等你把西江水引来，我早就没命了，你还不如早一点把我挂到那卖干鱼的铺子里去呢！'"

这两个故事说明的道理显然很相近，都是比喻缓慢的救助办法不能解决眼前的急难。《韩非子》这里的原文"远水不救近火"后来成为成语，又演变为更通俗的"远水救不了近火"、"远水不解近渴"。民间还有歇后语"太行山上看运河——远水不解近渴"。

A FIRE CLOSE AT HAND CANNOT BE PUT OUT WITH DISTANT WATER

In the early Warring States Period, Duke Mu of Lu wanted to befriend the stronger states of Jin and Chu, so he sent his sons to be officials in these two countries, in the hope that they might help if Lu was involved in trouble. However, his minister Li Zu questioned the effectiveness of this plan and said to Duke Mu of Lu, "The State of Yue is a region of lakes and marshes, where people are all good at swimming. Nevertheless, if we go to ask the people of Yue for help when one of our children here is drowning in water, the child will already be lifeless before they get here. Let's take another example. If we go to get sea water thousands of *li* away to put out a fire here, the fire rages on though there's plenty of water in the sea. The reason is very simple: a fire close at hand cannot be put out with distant water. Similarly, though the states of Jin and Chu are both powerful now, they are far away from us after all, while the State of Qi is quite close. Once we are attacked by Qi, I'm afraid it will be hard for Jin and Chu to come to our help."

Zhuangzi records a famous story entitled "Fish Trapped in a Dry Rut". Zhuangzi had a poor family, so he went to borrow some grains from the superintendent of river courses. The superintendent said, "All right. When I get the revenue of my fief, I will lend you three hundred gold coins. Will that do?" Zhuangzi flushed with anger and said, "I heard someone calling me for help when I was on the way here yesterday. I turned around and saw a small carp in a cart rut. I asked it, 'Carp, why do you call me?' It answered, 'I'm a subject of the God of the East Sea. Unfortunately, I was trapped in this dry rut today. Will you save me with a bucket of water?' I said, 'All right. As I'm going to the south to offer counsel to the kings of Wu and Yue, I will ask them to divert the water from the West River here to save you. Will that do?' The carp flushed with anger and said, 'Now that I have lost the water I rely for existence every day, it has been impossible for me to survive. I only ask you for a bucket of water to maintain my life, but you speak so much nonsense. I would have already been dead when you diverted the water from the West River here. You might as well hang me in a dry-fish shop right now!'"

These two stories explain the idea that an urgent problem at hand can't be solved with slow ways of relief. The story of "A fire close at hand cannot be put out with distant water" in *Han Feizi* later became an idiom and evolved into popular sayings like "A present thirst cannot be quenched with distant water." There also appeared a two-part allegorical saying among the people: "Look down at the canal from the top of Taihang Mountains — A present thirst cannot be quenched with distant water."

29. 巧诈不如拙诚

　　乐羊担任魏国将领时，率军去攻打中山国。这时他的儿子正在中山，中山国君就把他的儿子杀掉煮了，做成肉羹送给乐羊。乐羊坐在帐幕下把肉羹吃了，整整吃了一杯。魏文侯对身边的一位大臣堵师赞说："乐羊因为我的缘故而吃了他儿子的肉，他真是忠心啊。"堵师赞回答说："他连儿子都吃了，还有谁不能吃呢？"乐羊从中山得胜归来，文侯奖赏他，却怀疑他的用心。鲁国贵族孟孙猎到一只小鹿，让秦西巴拿着送回家去。小鹿的母亲跟在后面哀啼，秦西巴不忍心，就把小鹿放掉，让它跟母鹿一起跑了。孟孙回来后，问秦西巴要小鹿。秦西巴回答说："我不忍心，就把小鹿还给它母亲了。"孟孙非常气愤，赶走了秦西巴。过了三个月，又把秦西巴召回来，让他做自己儿子的老师。孟孙的车夫说："从前您要加罪于他，现在又将他召回来给您的儿子当老师，这是为什么呢？"孟孙说："他对小鹿都不忍下狠心，何况对我的儿子呢？”

　　乐羊作为魏国的将领，两军相争时不为敌方的计谋所动，是值得称赞的。其实他对儿子的惨死表现出满不在乎的样子也就可以了。但他亲自吃儿子的肉，还一吃就是一大杯，固然使敌方的计谋落空，但也不禁使人对他的残忍不寒而栗了。这种行为表现，在韩非看来就是应该反对的"巧诈"。而秦西巴的行为虽然显得很傻，但出自内心的真诚，就是"拙诚"。针对乐羊因有功却遭到怀疑，秦西巴因有罪却备受信任这一现象，韩非的看法是，做得很巧的伪诈比不上显得很笨拙的真诚。

INSINCERE CLEVERNESS IS NOT AS GOOD AS SINCERE CLUMSINESS

Yue Yang, the military commander of the State of Wei, led his troops to attack the State of Zhongshan. At that time, Yue Yang's son happened to be in Zhongshan, so the King of Zhongshan killed Yue Yang's son, cooked him into meat custard and presented it to Yue Yang. Yue Yang sat in the tent and ate up the whole cup of meat custard. Hearing this, Duke Wen of Wei said to a minister called Du Shizan, "Yue Yang ate his son's flesh for my sake, so he is really loyal to me." Du Shizan answered, "If he can eat his son, who else will he not eat?" When Yue Yang returned from Zhongshan in triumph, Duke Wen rewarded him for his merits but became suspicious of his intention. Meng Sun, a nobleman in the State of Lu, caught a young deer and asked Qin Xiba to take it back home. The mother of the young deer followed Qin Xiba, crying sadly. Qin Xiba couldn't help sympathizing with them, so he set the young deer free to let it run away with its mother. When Meng Sun came back, he asked Qin Xiba for the young deer. Qin Xiba answered, "I don't have the heart to separate the young deer from its mother, so I set it free." Meng Sun was so angry that he drove Qin Xiba away. After three months, he called Qin Xiba back and asked Qin Xiba to be the tutor of his son. The driver of Meng Sun asked, "You blamed him before, but now you called him back to be your son's tutor. Why is that?" Meng Sun said, "He is kind-hearted to a young deer, let alone my son."

As a general of Wei, Yue Yang was not disturbed at all by the enemy's trick of killing his son when the troops of two sides were at war, and that was worth a pat on the shoulder. Supposing that he tried very hard to hide his grief over his son's death at the bottom of his heart and pretended not to care in the least in the presence of the enemy, it would be enough for him. However, he ate a whole cup of his son's flesh. Undoubtedly, it made the enemy's trick fall flat, but other people couldn't help feeling horrified at his cruelty. This kind of behavior was considered by Han Feizi as "insincere cleverness" that should be frowned upon. On the other hand, Qin Xiba's behavior, though apparently very silly, was out of heartfelt sincerity, or "sincere clumsiness". As for Yue Yang's fate of being suspected in spite of his contributions and Qin Xiba's fate of being trusted in spite of his fault, Han Feizi concludes that insincere cleverness is not as good as sincere clumsiness.

30. 三虱争讼

　　有三只吸血的虱子在互相争吵着，另一只虱子从旁经过，问道："你们在吵什么？"三只虱子说："我们都争着想占据猪身上最肥的地方。"那只过路虱子说："你们还瞎争些什么？眼看腊月祭祀就要到了，人们要杀猪祭祀，用茅草烤猪，火烧火燎的，你们也不担心马上没命了，怎么还在这些小地方计较呢？"三只虱子一听恍然大悟，明白了利害轻重，于是便聚在一起拼命吸食猪身上的血肉，结果母猪很快消瘦了。由于祭祀时人们习惯杀最肥的，这头母猪就活下来了，这些虱子也因此得以保全。

　　这则寓言旨在批评那些目光短浅的人。那三只虱子，只看到自己眼前的利益，却看不到大家共同的长远的利益，因而争夺不休。而那只旁观的虱子从大处着眼，往长远着想，看清了真正根本的利害关系，这就是所谓的"当局者迷，旁观者清"。人与人之间的分歧和利害冲突总是难免的，当我们在生活中遇到一些"蜗角之争"时，就应该反省一下，我们现在的争斗是否只是为了蝇头小利斤斤计较，是否就如"三虱争讼"一样的可笑？我们是不是应该放下目前的互相争夺，一起来看看有没有更远大的值得共同去努力的目标？

THE QUARREL OF THREE LICE

Three blood-sucking lice were quarrelling with each other when another louse passed by. The passing-by louse asked, "What are you quarrelling about?" The three lice said, "We all wanted to occupy the most greasy part of the sow's body." The passing-by louse then said, "What are you fighting for? Soon the sacrifice of the twelfth lunar month will arrive. Then people will kill pigs as sacrifice and roast the pork with burning straw. At that time, you will be burnt and smoked by fire. Aren't you worried about your life? Why on earth are you still fussing about such small matters?" These words were like a thunderclap striking at the three lice, and they suddenly realized the most important matter at hand. Therefore, they worked together to suck the blood of the sow with all their effort, and the sow soon became very lean. Since people were used to killing the fattest pig, that sow managed to survive, so these lice also saved themselves.

This allegory aims to be a satire of short-sighted people. Those three lice only saw their own immediate interests but failed to see their overall, long-term interests, so they kept quarrelling with each other. But that passing-by louse had the overall and long-term interests in mind, so it could point out the most important matter for the three lice. This is called "The involved parties are blind while the onlookers see the best." It is inevitable for people to have disagreements and conflicts of interests among themselves. When we come across "fights over interests as small as the antenna of a snail", we should start to reflect whether we are fighting for petty profits, whether we are as silly as the three lice quarrelling with each other, and whether we should give up the present fight and work together to see if there is any more profound goals to be achieved with concerted efforts.

31. 恶贯满盈

　　从前有个人，和一个极其凶狠蛮横的恶棍做邻居，他想："咱惹不起还躲不起吗？"就打算卖掉住宅搬到别的地方去。有人劝他说："这人就快恶贯满盈了，到时他自然会得到他该有的下场。你不妨再等待一下吧。"想卖住宅的这个人回答说："我就是害怕他会拿祸害我来满盈他的罪恶啊。"于是很快就搬走了。

　　《韩非子》在这个故事后总结道："所以说：'事情到了危急关头，是再也不应该拖拉的。'"我们做事应该当机立断，当断不断，反受其乱。既然看出了祸患的苗头，就不能犹豫，应该有针对性地采取行动。如果不能及时将其除掉，就应尽早躲避，不能拖拉。"恶贯满盈"后来成为成语，意为作恶极多，已到末日。

DON'T WAIT UNTIL THE LAST HARM IS DONE

Once upon a time, there lived a man, who had an extremely cruel villain as his neighbour. The man thought, "Since I can't afford to offend him, can't I just avoid him completely?" Then he decided to sell his house and move to another place. Someone persuaded him, "This villain has committed countless crimes and deserves to be punished in Heaven's name, so he will naturally meet the end he asks for in due course. You might as well wait a little longer." The man who wanted to sell his house answered, "I'm afraid that he will do the last harm to me." Then he soon moved away.

Han Feizi concludes at the end of the story, "Therefore, when the critical moment comes, one should never delay in making the decision." We should make prompt decisions in whatever we do. If we hesitate when a decision is needed, our indecision will breed trouble for us. When we have seen the early signs of a disaster, we should take actions with a clear aim instead of hesitating. If we fail to prevent the disaster in its early stage, we should avoid it as soon as possible instead of delaying. "Having committed countless crimes and deserving to be punished in Heaven's name" later became an idiom, which means someone has committed so many crimes that he is coming to the end of his days.

32. 中行文子出逃

　　中行文子是晋国朝中六卿之一，出逃时路过某个县城。随从说："这里的县官是您的老朋友，您不如去他那里休息休息，同时也暂且等待一下我们后面的车子。"文子说："你说的县官这个人啊，以前我喜爱音乐，他就送给我好琴；我喜爱佩戴在身上的玉饰，他就送给我玉环；这些都是在助长我的过失啊。用这样的手段来得到我的好感以求自己安身的人，我怕他也会拿我去换取别人的好感啊。"于是不作耽搁，赶紧离开了那县城。这个县官果然没收了中行文子后面随从的两辆车子，并进献给他的主子。

　　中行文子对人性的认识可谓深刻。以助长他人之恶而表现出的对他人的爱，不是真的出于爱，而是另有目的。这样的人也是没有道德原则的人，一旦别人对他已无利用价值，就什么事都干得出来了。这就提醒人们，当你春风得意的时候，要防备围在你身边的小人；无原则地取悦你的人，也可能拿你去作为无原则地取悦他人的礼物。要知道，别人对你是否好并不是最根本的，而且也是随时可能转变的，关键是要知道，他为什么喜欢你，为什么讨厌你。有了正确的认识，才会作出正确的判断和选择。

THE ESCAPE OF ZHONGXING WENZI

Zhongxing Wenzi was one of the six ministers of the State of Jin. Once he passed by a certain county during his escape. His attendant said, "The county magistrate here is one of your old friends, so you might go to his place to have a rest for the time being while waiting for the rest of our carts to catch up." Wenzi said, "The county magistrate you just mentioned sent me fine stringed instruments since I liked music and sent me jade rings since I liked to wear jade ornaments, and his indulgence encouraged my fault. Since he used such means to win my favor and to climb to a high position, I'm afraid that he would betray me to win others' favor." Therefore, he left the county in a hurry. Later that county magistrate indeed confiscated two carts of Zhongxing Wenzi's attendants lagging behind and presented the carts to his boss.

Zhongxing Wenzi really had a deep understanding of human nature. The "love" to others showed in the way of encouraging their fault is not real love, but ill-meaning indulgence. Those people who show such "love" are without any moral principles and will readily resort to betrayal once they believe that their target is of no use to them. Dear reader, please be warned: keep a comfortable distance from the fawning crowd who abandon their principles and are solicitous to satisfy your every whim if you happen to be in an advantageous position, for they do so with ulterior motives and will turn on you once they want to curry the favor of someone more important. You must remember that how you are treated is an inconsequential thing as compared to why you are treated that way — are you liked or disliked because of who you are or what you are? Once you have a clear understanding of that, you will make the right judgements and decisions.

33. 管鲍之交

　　管仲和鲍叔牙两人都是春秋初期齐国有名的贤臣，他们幼年时就交情深厚，两小无猜。齐襄公时，政令无常，襄公多次欺侮大臣，奸淫妇女，滥杀无辜。管仲和鲍叔牙担心齐国将会大乱，两人议论说："现在的君主昏庸极了，必定会被取代。齐国诸位公子中值得辅佐的，不是公子纠，就是公子小白。我和你每人分头侍奉一位公子，谁先成功，就收留另一个人。"于是管仲就随从侍奉公子纠出奔鲁国，鲍叔牙则随从侍奉公子小白出奔莒国。后来齐襄公果然被杀。鲁国派兵保护公子纠赶回齐国争夺王位，先由管仲领兵扼守莒、齐要道，以防小白先行入齐争夺君位。两相遭遇，管仲开弓射中了小白的衣带钩。小白假装被射死，公子纠误以为对手已去，就不再急着赶路，结果延误了行程。于是小白率先入齐，立为齐桓公。齐桓公率军大败鲁军，鲁国在齐国逼迫下杀死了公子纠，管仲也被鲁国人囚禁起来献给桓公。在鲍叔牙的推荐下，桓公任用管仲为相，在齐国执政。桓公在管仲的辅佐下成就霸业，并以霸主的身份，多次会合诸侯，使天下归一。对此，韩非十分感叹，说管仲的成功，离不开鲍叔牙的帮助。正如古语所说，“奴隶自己出售贵重的皮裘是卖不掉的，因为奴隶身份低贱，人们不相信他；士人自称善于辩说是没人信的，别人的推荐和鼓吹才显得可信。”管仲和鲍叔牙就像是一种叫翢翢的鸟，头重尾轻，到河边饮水时，为避免栽到河里，总是需要另一只鸟衔着它的羽毛，两者之间谁也离不开谁。

管仲和鲍叔牙两人相知最深，历史上就有了被人称道的“管鲍之交”的说法，用来比喻交情深厚的朋友。管仲自己曾经感慨地总结说，“生我者父母，知我者鲍子也。”学贯古今、经天纬地的奇才管仲也需要鲍叔牙的帮助，何况其他人呢？其实个人的能力再强也不能脱离社会而存在，他总是在别人的直接或间接的帮助下才能确保生存、获得成功的。这就是俗话说的“一个篱笆三个桩，一个好汉三个帮”。多交几个好朋友，有时会成为事业成功的重要因素。

THE FRIENDSHIP OF GUAN ZHONG AND BAO SHUYA

Guan Zhong and Bao Shuya were both wise ministers in the State of Qi in the early Spring and Autumn Period. They had been playmates in their childhood and had established profound friendship since then. At that time, Duke Xiang of Qi issued changeful decrees at random, frequently bullied ministers, raped women and killed innocent people indiscriminately. Guan Zhong and Bao Shuya were worried that Qi would be tossed into turmoil soon, so they talked to each other, “Now that the present monarch has brought such chaos to the state, he is bound to fail. Among all the Qi princes, either Prince Jiu or Prince Xiaobai looks promising enough to be the next duke. You and I go to serve one respectively, and whoever succeeds first should help the other." Therefore, Guan Zhong followed Prince Jiu to head for the State of Lu, while Bao Shuya followed Prince Xiaobai to go to the State of Ju. Later Duke Xiang of Qi was murdered. The State of Lu then sent troops to escort Prince Jiu back to Qi to contend for the throne. Guan Zhong led troops to hold the strategic pass between Ju and Qi, in case that Prince Xiaobai should enter Qi earlier to get the throne. When the two princes' armies were engaged, Guan Zhong, fighting for Prince Jiu, shot an arrow, which hit exactly on the bronze hook on Prince Xiaobai's clothes. Prince Xiaobai pretended to be dead. Prince Jiu thought his opponent had gone, so he no longer hurried on his way and finally delayed his trip. Then Prince Xiaobai got back first and became Duke Huan of Qi. Duke Huan of Qi defeated Lu in battle, so Lu was forced to kill Prince Jiu and imprison Guan Zhong, who was then sent to Duke Huan as a gift. With Bao Shuya's recommendation, Duke Huan appointed Guan Zhong as the prime minister to deal with political affairs. Duke Huan became the overlord of all the states with the help of Guan Zhong and convoked the other dukes for many times in the name of the de facto leader of China. Han Feizi commented with great affection that Guan Zhong, with all his wisdom, couldn't go anywhere without Bao Shuya's help. That is described in the saying: "A slave cannot sell precious fur by himself because his humble origin betrays him. Likewise, people won't believe a scholar if he claims to be eloquent himself. Others' recommendation and promotion can significantly boost the credibility." Guan Zhong and Bao Shuya are like a kind of bird called "little cuckoo", which has a heavy head and a light tail. When one bird drinks water from the river, there is always the need for another bird to hold the drinking bird's feather so that it won't fall into the river. In that case, they can't do without each other.

Guan Zhong and Bao Shuya were such loyal friends that there came the expression "the friendship of Guan Zhong and Bao Shuya", generally referring to people with profound friendship and one helping his friend in need. Guan Zhong himself once said emotionally, "It's my parents who gave me life, but it's Bao Shuya who really understands me." Guan Zhong was well-known for his great talent and praised as "well versed in the learning of both ancient times and his own age, and capable of administering the universe". Yet Guan Zhong needed the help from Bao Shuya, not to mention others. In fact, no matter how capable a man is, he can't break away from the society where he lives. He always needs to make a living and achieve success with others' direct or indirect help. As the saying goes, "A fence needs the support of three stakes, and an able fellow needs the help of three friends." To make friends sometimes will be vital for the success of one's career.

34. "海大鱼"

　　春秋战国时期，各诸侯国执掌国政的卿相，同时又多是有自己封地的封君，他们在自己的封地内具有独立的最高权力。为了巩固自己的权力，齐国靖郭君田婴在他的封地薛地加筑城墙，这件事遭到很多门客的劝阻。但田婴根本听不进去，也很不耐烦，他对通报人员说："我不见那些劝说的门客，你不要再为他们通报了。"有个请求接见的齐国门客说："我只要求说三个字。超过三个字，就请把我煮死好了。"田婴就接见了他。门客快步上前，对田婴说："海大鱼。"果然只有三个字，说罢掉头就跑。田婴叫住他，说："请告诉我你说的到底是什么意思。"门客说："我说过超过三个字就请把我煮死，我可不敢拿死来开玩笑。"田婴说："好吧，我允许你多说，希望你给我讲清楚。"门客回答说："我说的'海大鱼'就是指海里的大鱼。您听说过海里的大鱼吗？渔网捕不住它，射鱼的丝绳拖不住它，但它要是任性乱游脱离了水，蝼蚁都可以在它身上为所欲为呢。现在齐国也就是您的大海。您要能长期掌握齐政，还要薛地干什么？您要是失去了在齐国的大权，即使把薛地的城墙修得和天一样高，也没有什么用处啊。"田婴说："是，你说得很好。"就把在薛地筑城的事停了下来。

这则故事的精彩之处，在于那个齐人的"海大鱼"三个字。他善于进谏，用使人似懂非懂的"海大鱼"勾起了对方的好奇心，使田婴不自觉地从本来不许人进言变成主动要求进言者多说，看来选择合适的切入点是保证进言有效的前提。

"THE BIG FISH IN THE SEA"

During the Spring and Autumn Period and the Warring States Period, a prime minister in a state who controlled the state affairs was also the head in his own manor, where he instituted independent supreme power. In order to bolster his power, Tian Ying, entitled Prince Jingguo of the State of Qi, began to build defensive walls in his own manor, Xue. Many of his dependant guests tried to dissuade him from doing so, but Tian Ying would not listen at all. He even became so restless that he said to the usher, "I won't see those guests trying to persuade me, so you don't have to report them to me." A guest from the State of Qi asked to see Tian Ying and said, "I only hope to be allowed to say three words. If I say more, please boil me in a cauldron." Tian Ying then received him. The guest took a few quick steps forward and said to Tian Ying, "*Hai Da Yu* (the big fish in the sea)." He really said three words and then turned around to run. Tian Ying stopped him and said, "Please tell me what on earth you mean by that." The guest said, "If I say more than three words, you can boil me in a cauldron, so I dare not trifle with my life." Tian Ying said, "All right. I allow you to say more and hope you can explain that clearly to me." The guest answered, "'*Hai Da Yu*', the three words I said, refers to the big fish in the sea. Have you heard about it? The fishing net cannot trap it, and the fishing string cannot drag it out. However, once it leaves the water due to its poor judgement, even mole crickets and ants could do whatever they like on its body. Now the State of Qi is your sea. If you can stay in control of the state affairs of Qi for a long time, what do you want the manor of Xue for? If you lose your power in Qi, it won't be of any help even if you build the walls of Xue as high as the sky." Tian Ying said, "Right. You've got a good point." Then he stopped building defensive walls in Xue.

The best part of this story is the three words said by the guest from Qi, namely, "*Hai Da Yu*". He was good at offering advice, for he used the enigmatic words "*Hai Da Yu*" to arouse the listener's curiosity. As a result, Tian Ying unwittingly changed his attitude from forbidding anyone to offer advice to actively asking the guest to say more. It seems that choosing the right angle is the prerequisite for effective persuasion.

35. 三人成虎

　　战国时代，各国互相攻伐，为了使大家真正能遵守信约，国与国之间通常都将太子交给对方作为人质。魏国大臣庞恭，将要陪魏国太子一起到赵国去做人质，定于某日启程赴赵都邯郸。临行时，庞恭向魏王提出一个问题，他说："如果现在有一个人来对您说，他看见闹市熙熙攘攘的人群中有一只老虎，大王相信吗？"魏王说："我当然不信。"庞恭又问："如果有第二个人来对您这样说呢？"魏王说："那我也不信。"庞恭紧接着追问了一句："如果有三个人都说亲眼看见了闹市中的老虎，大王是否还不相信？"魏王说道："既然这么多人都说看见了老虎，肯定确有其事，所以我不能不信。"庞恭听了这话以后，深有感触地说："果然不出我所料，问题就出在这里！事实上，人虎相怕，各占几分。具体地说，某一次究竟是人怕虎还是虎怕人，要根据力量对比来论。众所周知，一只老虎是决不敢闯入人口集中的闹市区的。但现在三个人的言论就造出了一只老虎。赵国国都邯郸离魏国国都大梁，比起宫中离街市要远得多，议论我的人又不止三个。您要是听见他们纷纷说我的坏话，岂不是要断言我是坏人吗？临别之前，我向您说出这点疑虑，希望大王一定不要轻信人言。"庞恭走后，一些平时对他心怀不满的人开始在魏王面前说他的坏话。时间一长，魏王果然听信了这些谗言。当庞恭从邯郸回魏国以后，魏王就再也不愿意召见他了。所以韩非说："言之为物也以多信。"意思是言论这东西，在很多人都同样那么说时，就很容易令人相信。

　　成语"三人成虎"就出自这个故事，也说"三人成市虎"，比喻谣言重复多次，就能使人信以为真。"曾子杀人"的故事常常被拿来跟"三人成虎"相提并论。孔子的弟子曾子离别了老母，离开家乡到费国去。不久，费国有个和曾子同姓同名的人杀了人。有人听到这个消息，也没有弄清情况，就去告诉曾子的母亲："听说你的儿子在费国杀人了。"这时，曾子的母亲正在织布，听了这个消息，头也不抬地回答说："我的儿子是决不会杀人的！"照样安心地坐着织布。过了一会儿，又有人来说："曾子杀人了！"曾子的母亲仍不理睬，还是织她的布。过了不久又跑来一个人，同样说："曾子杀人了！"听了第三个人的报告，曾子的母亲害怕了，立即丢下手中的梭子，急急忙忙地跳墙跑了。

　　看起来，流言蜚语一多，就有人会信以为真；随声附和的人一多，白的也会被说成黑的。但"谣言止于智者"，聪明人不会轻信别人的话，他以实践作为衡量认识是否正确的标准，实践决定认识。

THREE PEOPLE ARE ENOUGH TO FABRICATE A TIGER

In the Warring States Period, the states often attacked each other. In order to make every one truly abide by agreements of truce, the states usually sent their own crown princes to each other as hostages. Pang Gong, a minister of the State of Wei, was going to accompany the crown prince of Wei to the State of Zhao as the hostage, and the date had been settled for them to go to Handan, the capital of Zhao. Before their departure, Pang Gong asked the King of Wei a question, "If a man comes to tell Your Majesty now that he saw a tiger in the bustling crowd in the market, will Your Majesty believe it?" The king said, "I certainly won't believe it." Pang Gong asked again, "What if a second man comes to tell Your Majesty the same thing?" The king said, "I won't believe it, either." Pang Gong then pressed the question, "If three men claim to have seen a tiger in the bustling market in person, will Your Majesty still disbelieve it?" The king said, "Since so many people all say they have seen the tiger, it must be true. I have to believe it." At these words, Pang Gong mused and said, "As expected, this is where the problem lies. In fact, man and tiger both fear each other to some extent. Specifically speaking, whether man are afraid of tiger or vice versa depends on the balance of the strengths of the two parties in the specific situation. As we all know, a tiger dare not break into a bustling downtown area with a lot of people. However, now three men's words create a tiger. The distance between the capital of Zhao, Handan, and the capital of Wei, Daliang, is much longer than that between the palace and the market. Besides, there will be more than three people who will talk about me. If you hear them speak ill of me, won't you develop the idea that I'm an evil man? Therefore, I tell you about my doubts before my departure, in the hope that you won't easily place trust in others' words." When Pang Gong left, some people who had harbored grudge against him started to speak ill of him. As time went by, the King of Wei really believed their false accusations. When Pang Gong came back from Handan, the King of Wei was no longer willing to see him. Therefore, Han Feizi says, "The credibility of what is said also depends on how many times it is repeated." It means that the more people give the same account of an opinion, the more it appears "believable".

The idiom "If three people give testimony of a tiger, it will sound true" comes from this story. It can also be put in this way: "If three people give testimony of a tiger in the bustling market, it will sound true." This idiom is used to explain the idea that when a rumor is repeated many times, it can almost be regarded a fact; therefore, sometimes rumors can obscure the truth. The story "Zengzi has killed a man" is usually mentioned in the same breath with the story "Three people give testimony of a tiger". According to this story, Confucius's disciple Zengzi left his old mother and hometown for the State of Fei. Soon after that, a man in the State of Fei who shared the same name with Zengzi killed a man. Someone got the news and told Zengzi's mother without confirmation, "I heard your son killed a man in the State of Fei." Zengzi's mother was weaving cloth. At this news, she answered without looking up, "My son will never kill a man." Then she went on weaving her cloth calmly. After a while, another man came and said, "Zengzi killed a man." Zengzi's mother still took no notice of it and continued to weave. A moment later, a third man came and also said, "Zengzi killed a man." Hearing the third man's report, Zengzi's mother became afraid, so she dropped the shuttle and jumped over the wall to run away in a hurry.

It seems that when rumors grow, people tend to believe them; when more people follow in the cry, a white object can be said to be a black one. However, "rumors will be exposed by the wise." A wise person will not repeat what others say. He tries to find out facts to determine whether a certain understanding is right or not. Only facts can be the basis of knowledge.

36. 滥竽充数

　　战国时的齐宣王爱听吹竽，又好讲排场，为他吹竽的就有三百人。他每次听吹竽，一定要叫这三百人一齐吹给他听。有个南郭先生，根本就不会吹竽，看到这个机会，就到齐宣王那里去，请求参加这个吹竽队。齐宣王很高兴，就把他编在吹竽队里，待遇跟别的乐师相同。这位根本不会吹竽的南郭先生，每逢吹竽，就混在乐队里，拿着竽装腔作势。这样一天天混过去，不曾被人发现。等到齐宣王死了，齐湣王接替王位。他和齐宣王不同，不喜欢听大家一起吹竽，而是喜欢叫吹竽的人一个一个地来吹给他听。南郭先生听到这个消息，只好逃之夭夭，不敢再冒充会吹竽的乐师了。

　　这就是成语"滥竽充数"的故事，比喻没有真才实学的人，冒充有本领，混在行家里充数；也可比喻以次充好。

　　美国总统林肯曾经说过一句很著名的话："有时候你可以欺骗所有

的人，你甚至可以一直欺骗某些人，但是你不能一直欺骗所有的人。"不学无术的人只能靠吃大锅饭混日子，当他独当一面的时候就会露出马脚。所以说做人一定要有真才实学，用人则应该重视逐一考察。

NANGUO PASSES HIMSELF OFF AS A MEMBER OF THE ORCHESTRA

In the Warring States Period, King Xuan of Qi loved listening to *yu*, a kind of wind instrument made of bamboo. As the king also loved extravaganza, he had an orchestra of three hundred people to play the instrument for him. Every time he listened to the music, he must have all these three hundred people play together. A man called Nanguo exploited this opportunity. He went to see King Xuan of Qi and asked for permission to join the orchestra though he wasn't able to play *yu* at all. King Xuan was very pleased, so he let Nanguo join the orchestra and receive the same pay as the other musicians. Every time the music was played, this Mr. Nanguo joined in the orchestra and made pompous gestures with the instrument in his hands, pretending to be playing. In this way, he muddled along from day to day without being discovered. When King Xuan died, King Min ascended to the throne. Unlike King Xuan, King Min did not like listening to all the musicians play together but loved to let them play one by one. At this news, Mr. Nanguo had no choice but to slip away as he would be exposed if playing alone.

This is the story of the idiom "passing oneself off as a member of the orchestra". It is used to describe the kind of person who has no genuine ability and learning but pretends to be capable and competent, passing himself off as a member among the experts. It can also be used for "selling seconds at best quality prices".

Abraham Lincoln, the 16th president of the United States, has a famous saying: "You can fool all the people some of the time, and some of the people all the time, but you cannot fool all the people all the time." Those who have neither learning nor skills can hope to muddle along by taking credit for the performance of capable people. When they are asked to do something alone, they will show their incompetence. Therefore, one should always have some skills and knowledge to rely upon, and employers should examine the performance of his employees one by one.

37. 美人掩鼻

　　战国时期，魏襄王送给楚怀王一位美女，楚怀王对她宠爱有加。怀王夫人郑袖很是嫉妒，但表面上并没有表露出来，反而对这位新美人大献殷勤。她作出非常疼爱这位美人的样子，对美人的照顾甚至比楚王更加细致入微。服饰玩物珍宝，凡是美人想要的，郑袖都挑选出来送给她。美人喜欢的宫室卧具，她也全部让出来。楚王见了后，感叹说："夫人知道我宠爱新来的美人，她也宠爱这位美人，甚至超过了我，这正是孝子奉养父母、忠臣侍奉君主的方式啊。"郑袖知道楚王已经不认为自己嫉妒，就对新来的美人说："大王非常喜欢你、宠爱你，但讨厌你的鼻子。你要想得到君王的长久宠爱，今后见君王时就最好把鼻子掩住。"于是美人听从了郑袖的话，每次见到楚王，常常捂住鼻子。楚王对郑袖说："新来的美人见我时常捂住鼻子，这是为什么？"郑袖作出一副欲说还休的样子回答："我也不知道啊。"在楚王的再三追问下，她才说道："不久前新人曾说过，她讨厌闻到大王的气味。"楚王发怒说："割了她的鼻子！"郑袖预先已经告诫过侍从："大王如果发了话，一定要听从命令立即去执行！"于是侍从就马上拔出刀来割掉了美人的鼻子。

郑袖陷害新美人计算周密，裁起赃来不露痕迹，有准备、有步骤地让楚王听信了她的谎言，并制造机会借楚王之手除掉了新美人，实在是可怕。生活中也不乏这种人，他们往往口蜜腹剑、两面三刀同时又演技高超，其真实面目往往颇难识破。韩非讲这个故事，重点在于阐明君主应"明察"以避免被近幸所欺骗的重要性。后来，人们以"美人掩鼻"为进谗离间之典，表示因嫉妒而设计陷害之意。

THE BEAUTY COVERS HER NOSE

In the Warring States Period, King Xiang of Wei gave a beauty to King Huai of Chu as a concubine, and King Huai of Chu loved his new concubine very much. Zheng Xiu, the wife of King Huai, was very jealous, but she didn't show her feelings in front of others. On the contrary, she did everything she could to please the new concubine. She pretended to be very fond of the new concubine and even gave more considerate and tender care to her than King Huai. Whatever the new concubine liked, be it clothes, playthings or jewels, Zheng Xiu would pick them out and send them to her. Even when the new concubine liked the bedding in Zheng Xiu's bedroom, Zheng Xiu would be willing to give it up to her. Knowing this, King Huai of Chu said in gratitude, "Since my wife knows I love the new beauty, she also loves her, and her love even exceeds mine. This is just the right way for a filial son to support his parents and for a loyal official to serve the monarch." When Zheng Xiu knew King Huai no longer thought she was jealous, she then said to the new concubine, "The king loves you very much, but he dislikes your nose. If you want to win enduring favor from the king, you'd better cover your nose from now on when you see him." Therefore, the new concubine followed Zheng Xiu's advice and often covered her nose when she met the king. The king said to Zheng Xiu, "The new beauty often covers her nose when seeing me. Why is that?" Zheng Xiu answered with pretended hesitance, "I don't know, either." When questioned repeatedly by the king, she said, "I heard her saying lately that she hated your smell." The king flew into a rage and said, "Chop her nose off." Zheng Xiu had warned the attendant in advance, "If the king gives an order, you must do as he orders at once." Therefore, the attendant took out his knife at once and chopped the new concubine's nose off.

Zheng Xiu's plot against the new concubine was so carefully designed that she showed no trace when making false accusations. She methodologically made King Huai of Chu believe in her lies and created a chance to get rid of the new concubine through the hands of the king. What a horrible woman she was! There is no lack of such people in our life. They are often honey-mouthed and dagger-hearted and like to play a double game. At the same time, they are highly skillful at pretending, so their true intentions are often very hard to be identified. When Han Feizi tells this story, he wants to emphasize that a wise monarch should be "perceptive" in order to avoid being deceived by his favorites. Later, people regard "the beauty covering her nose" as an allusion for a slandering behavior, namely, plotting against others out of jealousy.

38. 买椟还珠

　　墨家有个叫田鸠的人去见楚王，见面后没说上几句话，楚王就问田鸠："墨子是个声名显赫的学者。他亲自实践起来还是不错的，但他讲的话很多却不动听，为什么？"田鸠并没有直接回答，而是说了两个小故事。

　　第一个故事叫"秦君嫁女"。秦国君主把女儿嫁给晋国公子，出发时，没有装扮自己的女儿，而是叫晋国为他女儿准备衣服装饰。同时陪嫁的女子有七十人，秦君却在国内就给她们穿上了华丽的衣着。到了晋国后，晋国公子喜欢上了那些衣着华丽的陪嫁小妾，却看不上秦君的女儿。这可以叫做善于嫁妾，不能说是善于嫁女。

　　另一个故事叫"买椟还珠"。有个在郑国的楚国人，有一颗漂亮宝贵的珍珠，想要卖出去。他为了卖个好价钱，便动脑筋好好地将珍珠包装了一下。他用名贵的香木料"木兰"做了一个匣子（即"椟"），用桂椒香料把匣子熏得香气扑鼻。匣子外面镶嵌上珍珠、宝石和美玉作点缀装饰，再用翡翠镶边。这匣子看上去闪闪发亮，实在是一件精致美观的工艺品。这样，楚人将珍珠小心翼翼地放进盒子里，拿到市场上去卖。有个郑国人很喜欢这个匣子，买下来后，发现匣子里面还有一颗珍珠，于是把珍珠还给了这个楚人。这可以叫做善于卖匣子，不能说是善于卖宝珠。

最后韩非说："现在社会上的言论，都是一些漂亮动听的话，君主只看文采而不管它是否有用。墨子的学说，传扬先王道术，阐明圣人言论，希望广泛地告知人们。如果修饰文辞的话，他就担心人们会留意于文采而忘了其学说的内在价值，从而造成因为文辞而损害实用的恶果。这和楚人卖宝珠、秦君嫁女儿是同一类型的事，所以墨子的话很多，但不动听。"

成语"买椟还珠"就出自这里。今天这个成语多比喻人没有眼力，舍本逐末，常常用来讽刺像故事中的郑人那样不真正识货、不懂得某事物中真正有价值部分的人。做事情要有主次之分。楚人原本以为别人会欣赏他的珍珠，可是没想到给人的感觉却是精美的外包装超过了包装盒内东西的价值，以至于"喧宾夺主"，这可以说是一种很可悲的"异化"现象。当然，这也并不是说外部包装就不必讲究了，只不过任何事情都不能走到极端。古书说的"言之无文，行而不远"，就是说言语的文采也不可忽视。

KEEPING THE GLITTERING CASKET AND GIVING BACK THE PEARL

A man of the Mohist school called Tian Jiu went to see the King of Chu. Before they had much talk, the King of Chu asked Tian Jiu, "Mozi is an influential scholar. His practices are quite nice, but his talks are not entirely pleasant. Why?" Tian Jiu didn't answer it directly, but told the king two stories.

The first story was called "The King of Qin offering his daughter in marriage". The King of Qin married his daughter to the prince of Jin. At the departure of the entourage of the bride, the king didn't dress up his own daughter, but asked the State of Jin to prepare attires for her. However, the king dressed up the seventy maids who were sent as part of the dowry. When the entourage of the bride came to the State of Jin, the prince liked those magnificently dressed concubines but despised the plainly dressed bride, the daughter of the King of Qin. Therefore, the King of Qin was good at offering concubines instead of his daughter in marriage.

Another story was called "Keeping the glittering casket and giving back the pearl". A man of Chu, who lived in the State of Zheng, had a beautiful precious pearl and wanted to sell it. In order to get a good price, he racked his brains to dress up the pearl. He made a casket of a rare aromatic "magnolia wood" and perfumed it with cinnamon and spice. The outside of the casket was inlaid with pearls, jewels and jades as ornaments and edged with emeralds. The whole casket glittered with gems and was indeed a beautiful and delicate work of art. Then, the man of Chu carefully put the pearl inside the casket and took it to the market. A man of Zheng liked this casket very much, so he bought it. When he found the precious pearl inside the casket, he returned the pearl to the man of Chu. The man of Chu can be said to be good at selling the casket instead of the pearl.

In the end, Han Feizi concludes, "The speeches that prevail in the society now are full of beautiful and attractive words, and the monarchs only care about literary appeal instead of practical use. The doctrines of Mozi spread the ways and tactics of the ancient kings, clarify the sages' views and hope to educate the great majority of the people. If he uses smart diction, he is afraid that people will pay attention to the literary appeal instead of the intrinsic value, which would bring about the consequence that utility gives way to diction. It is the same as the man of Chu selling the pearl and the King of Qin offering his daughter in marriage, so Mozi talks a lot but doesn't talk in entirely pleasant ways."

The idiom "keeping the glittering casket and giving back the pearl" comes from this story. Today this idiom is usually used to describe the person who doesn't have good judgement or make sensible decisions. It is often used to satirize people who are not able to tell good from bad and don't understand the real valuable part of an item, just like the man of Zheng in the story. Whenever doing anything, one should have a clear sense of priority and know where the importance lies. The man of Chu had thought others would appreciate his pearl, but to his surprise, he gave them the impression that the exquisite casket outweighed the value of its content, leading to an "alienation" effect of "the wrangling guest taking the place of the host". Of course, it doesn't mean that there is no need for presentation — it just doesn't have to go that far as to overshadow its content. As an ancient saying goes, "If the language is not attractive, it won't stand the test of time." Therefore, literary appeal shouldn't be ignored as well.

39. 画鬼容易画狗马难

　　有个替齐王画画的门客，齐王问他："画什么东西最难？"门客回答说："画狗和马一类的动物最难。""那画什么容易呢？"门客回答说："画鬼怪最容易了。"狗和马是人们都熟悉的动物，天天在人们的面前出现，画得有一丝疏忽，人们就会提出疑问，所以很难画。而鬼怪是想像出来的东西，谁都没有真正见过，每个人都可以信手涂抹，没有像不像的问题，所以画起来再容易不过了。

　　检验真理的唯一标准就是实践，鉴定狗马画得好坏真伪，拿实物验证便一目了然。可是，正因为鬼的形象是没有实物可以加以对照验证的，所以画起来就容易随意捏造。韩非讲这个故事是要说明，人主听取言论，也要拿其实效来加以检验。当时的一些著名辩士，如魏牟、长卢子、詹何、陈骈、庄周之类，他们的言论虽然听起来深远广大、令人迷惑，但其实不切实际，虚幻无定，最容易随意捏造，就跟画鬼魅差不多。这个故事后世转为"画鬼容易画人难"、"画鬼容易画马难"、"画鬼容易画犬难"、"犬马难，鬼魅易"等成语。

IT IS EASIER TO DRAW A GHOST THAN TO DRAW A DOG OR A HORSE

The King of Qi asked a painter, "What is the most difficult thing to draw?" The painter answered, "Animals such as dogs and horses are the most difficult to draw." "Then what is the easiest thing to draw?" The painter answered, "Ghosts and monsters are the easiest to draw." Dogs and horses are common animals known to all. As they appear in front of people every day, everyone is familiar with them. Once the painter shows a slight negligence in the drawing, people will raise questions of likeness. Therefore, it's difficult to draw dogs and horses. But ghosts and monsters are imaginary because no one has ever seen them. Thus, everyone can draw whatever they like. There will not arise the question whether the drawing is true or not, so it couldn't be easier to draw ghosts and monsters.

Facts are the only yardstick to test truth. If you want to make judgements on a painting of a dog or a horse, just take a look at a real dog or a horse. However, things are not that straightforward with ghosts or monsters, as there are no such things in the real world. Han Feizi tells this story to explain that a monarch should put speeches and views to test by evaluating their actual uses. In Han Feizi's opinion, a lot of famous orators at that time, such as Wei Mou, Zhang Luzi, Zhan He, Chen Pian and Zhuang Zhou (or Zhuangzi), made up confusing and highly impractical speeches, which were actually easy to fabricate like the paintings of ghosts and monsters. This story is alluded to in many Chinese idioms, such as "It is easier to draw a ghost than to draw a man", "It is easier to draw a ghost than to draw a horse", "It is easier to draw a ghost than to draw a dog" and "Dogs or horses are difficult to draw, while ghosts and monsters are easy to draw. "

40. 郢书燕说

　　有个人从楚国的郢都写了一封信给燕国的相国。信是在晚上写的，写信的时候，烛光不太亮，这个人就对在一旁端火烛的仆人说："举烛。"意思是"把火烛举高一点。"可是，因为他在专心致志地写信，嘴里说着"举烛"，就随手把"举烛"两个字误写到信里去了。所谓"举烛"，并不是信的本意。但燕相收到信以后，看到信中的"举烛"二字，琢磨了半天，最后解释说："这'举烛'二字太好了。举烛，也就是崇尚光明；所谓崇尚光明，也就是要重视选拔贤人加以任用。"于是燕相把这封信和自己的理解告诉了燕王，燕王也非常高兴，就按燕相对"举烛"的理解，大力选拔贤能之才委以重任，燕国因此还真的治理得很好。郢人误书，燕相误解。国家治理是治理好了，但这根本不是郢人写信的本意。韩非的结论是："先王的言论，有涉及小事，当今社会上却理解为意义重大的；有涉及大事，当今社会上却理解为意义小的；

这是没有人能够真正弄清楚的。……先王的话有时像郢人写信那样，而后人理解起来，却大多属于'燕相看信，胡乱解释'一类。"韩非感叹说，"当代被提拔的学者大多都是像燕相这类的人。"

成语"郢书燕说"就出自这里，比喻自作聪明，穿凿附会，曲解原意。生活中常常有这样的情况：把简单的事情想复杂了，结果反而弄错了；反之，把复杂的事情简单化，也同样会犯错误。燕相就是自作聪明把简单的事情想复杂了。幸亏他歪打正着，得到了燕国大治的好结果，否则可就闹大笑话了。

THE PRIME MINISTER OF YAN MISINTERPRETS THE LETTER FROM YING

A man in Ying, the capital of the State of Chu, wrote a letter to the prime minister of the State of Yan. The letter was written at night, and the candle was not bright enough at that moment. The man said to his servant, who was holding the candle beside, "Lift the candle." What he meant was "hold the candle a little higher." However, as he was absorbed in writing, he wrote the words "lift the candle" in the letter conveniently while saying the words to his servant. Therefore, "lift the candle" was not what the letter intended to say. But when the prime minister of Yan received the letter and saw the words "lift the candle", he pondered for quite a while. At last he explained, "The words 'lift the candle' are wonderful. Lifting the candle means advocating light, and advocating light indicates paying attention to selecting talented people." So the prime minster told the King of Yan about this letter and his understanding. The king was also very pleased, and then he devoted great efforts to selecting talented people and appointing them to important positions according to the prime minister's understanding of the letter. As a result, the State of Yan was run much better than before. The man of Ying wrote the words by mistake, and the words were misunderstood by the prime minister of Yan. Though the state was run better than before, it was not the original intention of the man writing the letter. Han Feizi's conclusion goes like this: "Some of the views of the ancient kings only involved trivial matters, but the people of the present time understand them as significant; other views involved significant matters, but the people today regard them as trivial. No one can really find them out. ... Words of the ancient kings sometimes suffer the same fate as the letter written by the man of Ying, for they are usually misunderstood by later generations in the same way as the prime minister of Yan misinterprets the letter from Ying." Nevertheless, "scholars of the present day are mostly similar to the prime minister of Yan."

The idiom "The prime minister of Yan misinterprets the letter from Ying" comes from this story. It describes the kind of person who, considering themselves clever, stretches the original meaning and gives distorted interpretations. Such cases can often be seen in daily life: simple matters are thought as complicated, while complicated matters are deemed as simple — both may lead to mistakes. The prime minister thought himself clever, so he made a simple matter complicated. Fortunately, he was lucky to set things just right and helped the State of Yan run smoothly; otherwise, he would have made himself a complete fool.

41. 郑人买履

　　郑国有个打算买鞋的人，他先量好自己脚的尺码，然后随手把尺码放在一边，等到去赶集时却忘了带上。在集市上挑好鞋以后，这个人才想起来，说道："啊，我忘记拿尺码了。"于是赶紧返回家里去取。等到带上尺码再赶回集市时，集市早就散了，结果没有买到鞋。有人对他说："你为什么不用自己的脚去试鞋呢？"他说："我宁愿相信尺码，也不相信自己的脚。"对此，韩非发挥说："不能面对现实问题加以适当的处理，使之适合国家政事的需要，却一味地讲求先王之道，就如同郑人买履，相信尺码而不相信自己的脚。"

　　成语"郑人买履"就出自这里，用来讽刺只信教条、不顾实际的人。

　　故事中的郑人，大家听了觉得可笑，似乎愚不可及，现实生活中也许不会有这种人，但是它所比喻的人和事却古往今来到处都有。韩非实际上是用这个寓言把他所反对的做事方式推到了极致，用生活中浅显易明的事来打比方，其荒谬性立刻就显现出来了。值得思考的问题是，旧有的尺度和规范，在新的情况下会不会一成不变？真理的认识是来自生活，还是来自观念？

A MAN OF ZHENG WANTS TO BUY A PAIR OF SHOES

A man in the State of Zheng wanted to buy a pair of shoes. He first measured his feet and then conveniently put the measurement aside, so he forgot to take it when he went to the market. After he chose a pair of shoes, he suddenly remembered it and said, "Oh, I forget to take my measurement." So he went back home in a hurry to get it. When he got to the market again, the market had closed. As a result, he didn't get the shoes. Someone said to him, "Why don't you try the shoes with your own feet?" He said, "I would rather trust the measurement than my own feet." Han Feizi elaborates on this story, "If one doesn't make adjustments for existing problems in the state affairs, but blindly follows the ways of the ancient kings, he is no different from the man of Zheng who trusts the measurement instead of his feet when buying shoes."

The idiom "The man of Zheng wants to buy a pair of shoes" comes from this story. It satirizes the kind of people who would rather believe in dogmas than adjust to actual situations.

Everyone may have the feeling that the man of Zheng is too ridiculously foolish to exist in real life. Well, maybe no one is foolish enough to buy a pair of shoes according to a measurement instead of the size of his own feet, but throughout the history a lot of people do engage in follies in the same nature.

Han Feizi employs this allegory set in a familiar scenario to push the absurdity to the extreme and shows his disapproval of rigid dogmatism. Consider the following questions: Will the old rules and norms remain unchanged in new situations? Does the perception of truth come from practices or ideas?

42. 王登荐贤

　　王登任中牟县县令时，向当时晋国的封君赵襄子进言说："中牟有中章和胥己两位文士，他们的品行很好，学识很渊博，您何不举用他们呢？"赵襄子说："你让他们来见我，我将任命他们为中大夫。"赵襄子的家臣头目劝他说："中大夫是晋国的重要官位，现在中章和胥己他们没有什么功劳就得到这么高的职权，不符合晋国提拔大臣的原意。您恐怕也只是耳闻他们的名声，而没有亲眼看到他们的实效吧！"赵襄子说："我先前取用王登，就是已经既用耳朵听又用眼睛看过的了。现在王登选拔的人，如果又要我用耳朵去听和用眼睛去看，这样亲自考察，就永远没完没了了。"王登在一天内使中章和胥己两个人晋见赵襄子，两人被直接任命为中大夫，并被授予了土地和房屋。于是中牟县里有一半的人放弃耕田除草的农活，卖掉住宅和菜园，都去追随搞私学的文士去了。

韩非讲这个故事，是要说明"上有所好，下必风从"的道理，所谓"利益在什么地方，民众就归向什么地方；宣扬什么好名声，士人就拼死为它奋斗"。因此韩非反对君主重视提拔文学之士，因为那些搞私学的文士"国家没有战争时不耕田出力，国家有难时又不披甲打仗"，君主过分看重并提拔他们，必然导致民众群起效仿，最终极大地妨碍耕战。

当然韩非这个故事的意义还不止这些，它还提出了如何用人、培养人的问题。可以对诸葛亮与曹操作一个比较，诸葛亮事无巨细无不亲自过问，结果没有为蜀国培养出多少接班人才。曹操没他聪明，但曹操会用人，结果魏国人才辈出，发展壮大。看来，事必躬亲，即使鞠躬尽瘁，也不一定能够达到理想的结果。

WANG DENG RECOMMENDS TALENTED MEN

When Wang Deng acted as the county magistrate in Zhongmou, he offered advice to Zhao Xiangzi, one of the dukes in the State of Jin, "Two scholars in Zhongmou called Zhong Zhang and Xu Ji are men of integrity and great learning. Why do we not employ them?" Zhao Xiangzi said, "Ask them to see me, and I will appoint them as junior officials." The head retainer of Zhao Xiangzi persuaded the duke, "Junior officials are important positions in the State of Jin. Now that Zhong Zhang and Xu Ji haven't made any contributions yet, granting them such high positions seems to be in disagreement with the original intention of promoting officials in the State of Jin. You probably have heard about their names but haven't seen their real talent in person." Zhao Xiangzi replied, "When I employed Wang Deng, I used both my ears and my eyes. Now for the people Wang Deng has selected, if I still need both my ears and my eyes to examine them in person, then there won't be an end to it." Wang Deng arranged for Zhong Zhang and Xu Ji to see Zhao Xiangzi in one day. Then the two scholars were appointed junior officials immediately and granted lands and houses. As a result, half the people in the county of Zhongmou gave up their farm work and sold their houses and gardens to follow the two scholars who focused on private studies.

Han Feizi tells this story to explain the idea that "when the upper class shows a preference, the lower class follows suit with great fervor." As one may say, "The people always flock to the place where there are profits; scholars usually work desperately for whatever are promoted as good reputation." Therefore, Han Feizi disapproves of the monarch's promotion of scholars because those scholars who only focus on private studies "neither do farm work when the state is in peace nor put on armor to fight on the battlefield when the state is at war." If the monarch favors them and promotes them, the people will certainly follow suit in groups, which will bring great harm to farming and military service.

Of course, Han Feizi means more than that by telling this story, for it also puts forward the question of how to use and train personnel. Take Zhuge Liang (181–234) and Cao Cao (155–200) in the Three Kingdoms Period as an example. Zhuge Liang attended to each matter in person, be it important or trivial. As a result, he didn't train many talented people for the Kingdom of Shu. Cao Cao was not as clever as Zhuge Liang, but Cao Cao was good at making use of his personnel. As a result, the Kingdom of Wei prospered because it had a great number of talented people. It seems that one may not necessarily reach the ideal goal by attending to everything personally, even if he spares no effort in carrying out his duty.

43. 宋襄公式的仁义

　　公元前 638 年，宋、楚两国在泓水(今河南柘城西北)打了一仗，就是历史上著名的"宋楚泓之战"。当宋人已经摆好了阵势，而楚人还没有完全渡过河时，宋国司马子鱼快步上前向宋襄公进言道："敌众我寡，请在楚人渡了一半，尚未摆好阵势时出击，一定能把他们打垮。"宋襄公说："我听君子说过：'不要再伤害已经受伤的人，不要捉拿年事已高的人，不要在别人危险时再推一把，不要在别人窘迫时再逼一步，不要进攻没有摆好阵势的敌军。'现在楚军还没有完全过河，我们就去攻打，这是不合于仁义的。还是等到楚人全部过了河，摆好阵势，然后再击鼓让我们的战士们进攻吧。"子鱼说："君王不爱惜宋国的民众，不顾惜保全国家的根本，只不过为的是仁义的虚名罢了。"襄公说："你不要多说了，赶紧回到队伍里去！不然将按军法处置！"子鱼回到队伍时，楚人已经排好行列、摆好阵势了，襄公这才击鼓进攻。结果宋人大败，宋襄公也伤及大腿，三天后就死了。

韩非总结道："这就是追求亲自实行仁义带来的祸害。一定要依靠君主亲自去干，然后民众才听从，这就是要君主自己种田吃饭，自己排在队伍里打仗，然后民众才肯从事耕战。这样一来，君主不是太危险了吗？而臣子不是太安全了吗？"

韩非讲这个故事本来是想证明君主不宜事必躬亲的道理，而后人引用这个故事，主要是讥笑宋襄公的愚蠢。他被后人嘲笑了两千多年，到现代，毛泽东在《论持久战》中曾说："我们不是宋襄公，不要那种蠢猪式的仁义道德。"更是使得这个故事在当代中国普通人中流传甚广。不过，宋襄公身上所表现出来的讲究规则和人道的精神，其光明正大、堂堂正正的君子风范，从某种程度上来说，还是值得敬佩的。很多人在"成王败寇"心理的支配下，把一些堂堂正正的做法讥为"妇人之仁"，我国传统文化中各种阴谋诡诈之计非常发达，"脸皮厚、心地黑"的"厚黑学"大行其道，恐怕跟我们长期对宋襄公一类人物的彻底否定与嘲笑不无关系。

THE KIND OF BENEVOLENCE AND JUSTICE OF DUKE XIANG OF SONG

In 638 BC, the State of Song and the State of Chu fought a battle at Hongshui River (now the northwest of Zhecheng in Henan). When the troops of Song were arrayed for the battle, the troops of Chu hadn't crossed the river completely. Ziyu, the Minister of War of the State of Song, came up quickly to Duke Xiang of Song and said, "As the enemy outnumbers us, please launch the attack now when the Chu troops are in the process of crossing the river and haven't gotten themselves ready for the battle. In that case, we are sure to defeat them." Duke

Xiang of Song said, "I've heard gentlemen say, 'Don't hurt a wounded man; don't arrest an old man; don't push a man in danger; don't press a man while he is in difficulty; don't attack the enemy when they are not ready.' Now the Chu troops haven't crossed the river completely. If we launch the attack, it won't be an act of benevolence and justice. We'd better wait until all of them cross the river and get ready for the battle before we beat drums for our soldiers to attack." Ziyu said, "If you don't value the people's lives of Song and don't care about preserving the fundamental interests of our state, your reputation of benevolence and justice are nothing but hypocrisy." Duke Xiang said, "Stop talking and come back to your troops. Otherwise, I'll punish you according to the military law." When Ziyu came back, the Chu troops had been arrayed in battle formations before Duke Xiang of Song finally gave the order to attack. Consequently, the Song troops suffered a crushing defeat. Duke Xiang of Song was also wounded in his thigh and died three days later.

Han Feizi concludes, "This is the harm brought by pursuing benevolence and justice personally. If the monarch has to do everything in person before the people will follow, it means that the monarch has to do farming by himself and fight a battle by himself before the people will do farming and fight battles. In that case, is it too dangerous for the monarch? Is it too safe for the subjects?"

Han Feizi tells this story mainly to explain that the monarch shouldn't attend to everything in person, but when this story was cited in later generations, people usually sneered at the foolishness of Duke Xiang of Song, who was actually laughed at for over two thousand years. Mao Zedong wrote in his essay "On Protracted War", "We are not Duke Xiang of Song, so we don't want that kind of asinine benevolence and justice." That made the story even more popular among the people of China. Nevertheless, the positive quality that Duke Xiang of Song showed, such as abiding by rules and humanity, behaving like an upright gentleman and refusing to take advantage of the weak, should still be respected. Some people believe in the practical idea that "the winner is the king while the loser is the beggar", so they dismiss honest behaviors as "maudlin weakness". Throughout the Chinese history there is no lack of conspiracies and brazen evil-doers, which had even been glorified to a certain extent. Maybe that has something to do with the long-standing disdain for honest people like Duke Xiang of Song.

44. 韩昭侯与申不害

　　韩昭侯是战国时代韩国国君，在位期间申不害主持国政。有一次，韩昭侯对申不害感叹说："法度非常不容易推行。"申不害说："所谓法度，就是验明功劳而给予赏赐，依据才能而授予官职。现在君主设立了法度，却又听从近侍的请求，这是法度难以推行的原因。"昭侯说："您说得好！我从今以后知道该如何推行法度了，知道该听取什么意见了。"后来有一天，申不害向韩昭侯请求委任他的堂兄做官。昭侯说："你当初是怎么告诉我的？要是听从你的请求，不就破坏你的治国原则了吗？我没法采纳你的请求！"申不害诚惶诚恐地请求给自己以处罚。

　　申不害不愧为法家代表人物之一，短短的几句话就抓住了法治的精髓。然而事到临头，他也免不了私下求情，足见很多事情真是"易言而难行"、"说时容易做时难"。现实生活中有些人总是奉行"双重标准"，说的与做的，自己的与别人的，抽象的与现实的总是合不起来。申不害能有错即改，韩昭侯也没有做人情，这不是很容易的，两人都值得钦佩。

MARQUIS ZHAO OF HAN AND SHEN BUHAI

Marquis Zhao of Han was the monarch of the State of Han in the Warring States Period, during whose reign Shen Buhai presided over state affairs. Once Marquis Zhao of Han lamented to Shen Buhai, "Laws are so hard to enforce." Shen Buhai said, "Laws are used to give rewards according to evaluated contributions and to grant official positions according to individual talents. Now you have established laws but still sanction the requests of those close to you — that is the reason why laws become difficult to enforce." Marquis Zhao said, "You have a good point. I know how to enforce laws in the future and what kind of advice to heed." Later, Shen Buhai asked Marquis Zhao of Han to appoint his cousin as an official. Marquis Zhao said, "What did you tell me before? If I grant your request, am I violating your principles of running the state? I can't give my consent." Shen Buhai was ashamed of himself and humbly asked the marquis to give him punishment.

Shen Buhai was a good advocator of the Legalist school, for he explained the rule of law in just a few words. However, when it came to his personal matters, he resorted to asking for a personal favor from the marquis like the others. It serves to show that "speech is easy while action is hard," or "easier said than done." Today many people adopt a "double standard". They seem to draw a clear line between what they say and what they do, between what laws should be applied to them and what laws should be applied to others, and between goals and practices. Shen Buhai corrected his mistake the moment he realized it, and Marquis Zhao of Han stuck to his principles and didn't yield to inappropriate requests. Both were honest people and should be respected.

45. 韩昭侯处罚掌衣官和掌帽官

　　战国初期的韩昭侯，有一次喝醉酒睡着了。掌帽官怕他着凉，就给他身上盖了衣服。韩昭侯睡醒后很高兴，问近侍说："谁给我盖的衣服啊？"近侍回答说："是掌帽官。"昭侯便同时处罚了掌衣官和掌帽官。他处罚掌衣官，是认为掌衣官失职，该给自己盖衣服而没有盖；他处罚掌帽官，是认为掌帽官越权，盖衣服不属于其职权范围却擅自盖了。韩昭侯不是不担心寒冷，而是认为越权的危害超过了寒冷。对此，韩非总结说："所以明君驾驭臣下，臣下不准超越职守去立功，不准夸夸其谈，言行不一。超越职守就该处死，言行不一就该治罪。群臣应该专心于本职工作，言而有信，这样，他们就不可能结党营私了。"不准臣下越权，有时会造成本来可以处理好的政事，因有关官吏怕越权而不敢管，由此带来一些损害。但韩非认为，这也是值得付出的代价。

这一故事可能未必是历史事实。本书的不少富有戏剧性的历史故事，可能也是出于杜撰。这个故事的戏剧性在于有意突出近臣因爱君主而受罚的反差，故事的结局出乎普通人的预料。韩非正是通过这种强烈的对比，使自己的主张给读者留下十分深刻鲜明的印象。《韩非子》说："君主想要禁止不正之风，就要去审核臣下的言论和职事。做臣下的发表一定的言论，君主根据他的言论授予相应的职事，再根据他的职事要求他的政绩。政绩符合职事，职事符合言论的，就赏；政绩不符合职事，职事不符合言论的，就罚。所以群臣言大功小的要罚；这不是要罚小功，而是要罚政绩不符合言论的行为。群臣言小功大的也要罚；这不是不喜欢大功，而是认为政绩不符合言论的危害超过了所建的大功，所以要罚。"臣下功大也要受罚，这与常人的认知也是大不相同的。

PUNISHMENT FOR BOTH DUTIFUL AND UNDUTIFUL OFFICIALS

In the early Warring States Period, Marquis Zhao of Han once fell asleep after getting drunk. The official in charge of hats was afraid that the marquis would catch a cold, so he covered the marquis with clothes. After waking up, Marquis Zhao of Han felt pleased and asked his attendant, "Who covered me with clothes?" The attendant answered, "It's the official in charge of hats." Marquis Zhao then punished both the official in charge of hats and the official in charge of clothes. The official in charge of clothes was punished because he neglected his duty: he should have covered the marquis with clothes but he didn't; the official in charge of hats was punished because he overstepped his role: it's not his duty to cover the marquis with clothes, but he did. Marquis

Zhao of Han was not worried about catching a cold as much as incurring the harm of allowing his subjects to overstep their positions. As for this, Han Feizi concludes, "Therefore, when a wise monarch rules over his subjects, he would not allow them to overstep their authority to win honor or to indulge in big talk which doesn't match their actions. If one oversteps his position, he is to be put to death; if one fails to match his words with deeds, he is to be punished. The officials should keep their minds on their own jobs and remain true to their own words. In that case, they won't band together for selfish purposes." Forbidding the subjects to overstep their roles sometimes brings about harm to certain political affairs, which otherwise could be dealt with well but are consequently left unattended because officials are afraid of being accused of overstepping their authority. But in Han Feizi's opinion, it is a price worth paying.

This story might not be historically accurate, as is the case for many dramatic historical stories to be told in this book. What is dramatic about this story is the emphasis on the sharp contrast between the official's love for the marquis and the punishment he got for it. Thus, the ending of the story subverts the expectation of most people. Han Feizi just makes use of this sharp contrast to let his own views leave a strong and striking impression on his readers. *Han Feizi* says, "If the monarch wants to prohibit dishonest practice, he should examine his subjects' views and deeds. When a subject airs certain views, the monarch should assign him an appropriate post according to his views and then let him make political achievement according to his post. If one's political achievement agrees with his post which also conforms to his views, he is to be awarded; if one's political achievement doesn't agree with his post which doesn't conform to his views either, he is to be punished. Therefore, those subjects whose views outweigh their achievement should be punished. This is not to punish those with insignificant achievement but those whose achievement is in disagreement with their views. Those subjects whose achievement outweighs their views should also be punished. This doesn't mean that great achievement is not preferable but that the harm brought about by disagreement between one's views and achievement outweighs what has been achieved, and thus punishment is demanded." The idea of punishing the subjects who have made great achievement is quite different from people's usual beliefs.

46. 晋文公攻原得卫

　　春秋时期的晋文公攻打原城时，只携带了十天的粮食，于是和大夫约定在十天内收兵。十天到了，晋军却没能攻下原城，文公鸣金收兵，打算离开。这时有个从原城中出来的士人说："再有三天的时间，原城就会被攻下了。"群臣近侍向文公进谏说："原城内弹尽粮绝，力量已经耗光了，君主您暂且等一等吧。"文公说："我当初和将士们约好的期限是十天，现在到期还不离开的话，那就失掉了我的信用。得到原城却失掉信用，这种事我是不干的。"于是收兵离去。原城人知道后，都说："像他那样守信用的君主，我们怎么能不归顺呢？"就向晋文公投降了。卫国人听到后也说："像他那样守信用的君主，我们怎么能不跟从他呢？"随后也投降了晋文公。孔子听到后记下来说："攻打原国而得到卫国，靠的是信用。"

　　《韩非子》总结这个故事说："在小事上能够讲求信用，在大事上就能够建立起信用，所以明君要在遵守信用的基础上逐步积累声望。赏罚不讲信用，禁令就无法推行。"小信用有所成就之后，大信用才能确立起来。儒家也讲"民无信不立"，守信是古今中外共同的正面价值标准。凡是有人群交往之处，都应该以"信"待人处事。因为晋文公恪守信用，所以他赢得了各诸侯国的拥戴，成为继齐桓公之后的诸侯霸主。

AN ATTACK ON ONE CITY YIELDS TWO

In the Spring and Autumn Period, when Duke Wen of Jin attacked the city of Yuan, he took only enough provisions that could last ten days, so he arranged with his senior officials to return within ten days. However, Duke Wen didn't capture the city after ten days of attack. Then he beat the retreating drum and prepared to leave. At that time, a scholar from the city of Yuan said, "The city of Yuan will be captured if you press your attack for another three days." All the close officials then persuaded Duke Wen, "Since ammunitions and provisions have run out and people have been exhausted inside the city, it is in your best interest that you wait a little while." Duke Wen said, "I have agreed upon a time limit of ten days with my generals and soldiers. Now that the time is due, I will break my promise if I still don't return. I won't go back on my word just to get the city of Yuan." Then, Duke Wen withdrew his troops and left. When the people of Yuan heard about it, they all said, "How could we not come over and pledge allegiance to such a monarch who keeps his promise?" Therefore, they all surrendered to Duke Wen. Hearing about this, the people of Wei also said, "How could we not come over and pledge allegiance to such a monarch who keeps his promise?" Then they also surrendered to Duke Wen. Upon hearing this,

Confucius recorded the story and commented, "Duke Wen won the city of Wei when he attacked Yuan, because he is a man of credit."

Han Feizi concludes, "If one is able to keep his word in trivial matters, he can establish his credit in significant matters as well. Therefore, a wise monarch should gain credit by keeping promises. If he breaks his promises when giving rewards and punishments, no laws will be able to be enforced." Great credit can be established only when small credit is accumulated. The Confucian school also believes that "the government can't establish itself among its people if it doesn't win their trust." Honesty in keeping promises is always a commendable quality at all times and in all countries. Wherever people live together, they should treat each other with honesty. It is because of his honest behaviors that Duke Wen of Jin was able to win support from various states and became one of the Five Overlords of the Spring and Autumn Period.

47. 晋文公斩宠臣

　　晋文公重耳向大臣狐偃请教政事。一番对答之后，话题转到了如何才能让民众为我所用、为君主卖命上头来。文公问："要怎样做才足以让民众为我打仗呢？"狐偃说："让他们不得不去打仗。"文公说："不得不去打仗怎么讲呢？"狐偃回答说："有功必赏，有罪必罚，就足以让他们去打仗了。"文公说："怎样才能达到刑罚的最高境界呢？"狐偃回答说："刑罚不避开亲近和显贵的人，法治实施到你宠爱的人。"文公说："好。"第二天，文公下令在圃陆打猎，约定以中午为期限，迟到的按军法处置（先秦时期，会众田猎同时又是日常军事训练的一种形式，所以要按军法从事）。这时有个文公宠爱器重的名叫颠颉的人迟到了，执法官吏请君主定他的罪。文公掉着泪，很是为难。执法官吏说："请让我给他用刑。"于是腰斩了颠颉，并向百姓巡示，用来表明有法必依。此后百姓都非常害怕，说："颠颉那么受国君的宠爱和器重，尚且被按法治罪，对我们又有什么可手下留情的呢！"文公见百姓可以用来打仗了，于是就起兵攻打原国，战胜了对方。接下来又展开一系列军事行动，攻下很多地方，成就了霸业。晋文公能取得成功，没有别的原因，就是因为他听从了狐偃的主张，借用了颠颉的脊梁。

"令行禁止"是军队最重要和最基本的纪律。要做到这一点，有时不得不借助非常手段。有一个很有名的"孙子练兵"的故事，说的就是这个道理。吴王阖闾曾让孙子训练由宫中美女组成的队伍，来试验他的兵法。孙子将一百八十名宫中美女编为两队，任命吴王最宠爱的两位妃子作队长。训练中尽管孙子三令五申，反复向这些宫女宣布纪律，但她们依然只顾嬉戏，不听命令。于是孙子不顾阖闾的求情，把那两名作队长的吴王阖闾最心爱的妃子斩杀了。结果很快地这些宫女就依军令排兵布阵了。

让民众不得不战的办法，就是信赏必罚，特别是亲贵犯法也不能例外，对于君主的宠臣法令的执行也不能打折扣。韩非说晋文王的成功是因为借助了颠颉的脊梁，突出的就是信赏必罚。俗话说"杀一儆百"、"杀鸡给猴看"。"杀一"是否能"儆百"，还得看所杀的人是否合适。连君主最宠爱的大臣和妃子都不免因违法而被杀，就能起到足够的震慑作用，让民众看到执法公正无私，亲贵无赦，就会不得不服从号令，不得不去应征作战，作战时又不得不拼死尽力，争立战功。民众可用，是取信的结果。

DUKE WEN OF JIN EXECUTES HIS FAVORITE MINISTER

Duke Wen of Jin consulted a minister Hu Yan about state affairs. After several turns of questions and answers, the topic switched to how to make the people serve the monarch and work themselves to death for the monarch. Duke Wen asked, "What can I do to make the people fight for me?" Hu Yan said, "Leave them no choice but to fight for you." Duke Wen said, "What do you mean by leaving them no choice but to fight for me?" Hu Yan said, "Reward those who have rendered outstanding services and punish those who have committed crimes. That will be enough motivation for the people to go fighting." Duke Wen said, "What is the ultimate goal of giving punishment?" Hu Yan answered, "When giving punishment, you shouldn't avoid people close to you and in high positions, so that the laws will be applied to your favorites." Duke Wen said, "All right." In the following day, Duke Wen ordered a hunting party, and the time was fixed at noon. Anyone who arrived late would be punished according to the military law. At that time, hunting parties were a kind of military training, so the military law was applied. A man called Dian Jie, who was one of Duke Wen's favorite ministers, came late, and the law enforcer asked the monarch how to punish Dian Jie. Duke Wen wept in indecision. The law enforcer said, "Please let me punish him." Then he executed Dian Jie by cutting the man in two at the waist and paraded the body through the streets for the public to see, in order to show that the law was strictly observed. After that the people were all afraid, saying, "The Duke punished his most favorite minister according to law, not to mention us! How could he show mercy to us?" When Duke Wen saw the people could be motivated to fight, he launched an attack against the State of Yuan and defeated it. He then took a succession of military actions, seized a lot of lands and ascended to a dominant place among all the states. The reason for Duke Wen's achievement was simple: he followed Hu Yan's advice and made use of Dian Jie's broken spine.

"Strict enforcement of orders and bans" is the most important and fundamental military discipline. Sometimes desperate measures have to be taken to ensure that the principle will be followed. A well-known story called "Sun Tzu drills troops" is a good example. King Helü of Wu asked Sun Tzu to train an army made up of maids and concubines in the palace, in order to test Sun Tzu's military strategies and tactics. Sun Tzu divided the one hundred and eight maids and concubines into two teams and appointed two of the king's favourite concubines as captains. In the course of the drilling, though Sun Tzu announced disciplines to the maids and concubines again and again, they indulged themselves in having fun and paid no regard to Sun Tzu's orders. Then, despite the king's pleading, Sun Tzu executed the two incompetent captains who were the favorites of King Helü. As a result, the maids and concubines soon obeyed orders and marched in formations.

The way to "leave the people no choice but to fight" is to reward those who have rendered outstanding services and punish those who have committed crimes. The monarch's relatives and high officials shouldn't be exempt from the laws. The favorite ministers of the monarch, when committing a crime, should still be put to law. Han Feizi says that Duke Wen's success lies in the use of Dian Jie's broken spine, because this case highlights the principle of giving rewards to those who have rendered outstanding services and punishing those who have committed crimes. As the saying goes, "Execute one as a warning to others," or "Beat the dog before the lion." Whether "executing one" can "give a warning to others" depends on whether the person to be executed is worthy of being set as an example or not. Only when the monarch's favorite ministers and concubines cannot escape the fate of being killed for breaking the laws can the laws have enough deterrent effect. If the people see that the laws are enforced impartially and that none of the monarch's relatives or high officials can escape punishment, there will be overwhelming pressure on the people to abide by the laws, to enlist in the army, and to risk their lives for military glories during battles. The people can be motivated because the laws have credit.

48. 曾子杀猪

　　曾子是孔子弟子之一。曾子的妻子要上集市去，她的小儿子跟在后面哭闹着也要一起去。曾妻便哄儿子说："你回去，等我回来杀猪给你吃。"她从集市回来后，曾子真的就要去抓猪来杀。曾妻急忙阻拦道："我只不过是跟孩子说着玩哄他的。"曾子正色说道："小孩可不是开玩笑的对象。孩子年幼没有什么才智知识，要靠父母作出样子才会跟着学，完全听从父母的教诲，处处加以模仿。现在你欺骗了他，就是教他学你的样子骗人。做母亲的欺骗自己的孩子，那孩子就不会相信自己的母亲了。这不是教育孩子的好方法啊！"于是，曾子杀了那头猪，煮了肉给孩子吃。

　　这是一则很有名的家庭教育故事。这个故事告诉大家：在任何时候，都不能欺骗孩子。坦桑尼亚的著名诗人、小说家和语言学家夏巴尼·罗伯特在其散文名作《童年》中曾经这样说道："童年乃是人生的重要阶段。人的品性在童年开始形成。我们长大后成为什么样的人，取决于童年时的所学与所为。"不杀猪的失信看起来是小事，但也应该"勿以恶小而为之"。曾子不欺幼子，看起来简单，但却不是今天的家长都能做到的。

ZENGZI KILLS A PIG TO FULFILL A PROMISE

Zengzi was one of the disciples of Confucius. Zengzi's wife wanted to go to the market, but her youngest son, crying and screaming behind, also wanted to go there with her. Zengzi's wife then coaxed the boy, "Go back and wait at home, and I'll kill a pig for your dinner." When she came back from the market, Zengzi really went to catch a pig for the kill. Zengzi's wife hurried to stop him and said, "I just played a joke to coax our son." Zengzi said seriously, "You shouldn't play a joke with a child. As a child is young with little sense or knowledge, he can only learn by following the example of his parents. He totally follows the teachings of his parents and copies their behaviors all the time. Now that you cheat him, you are teaching him to follow your example and cheat others. If a mother cheats her own child, the child won't believe his own mother. That is not a good way to educate a child." Therefore, Zengzi killed the pig and cooked it for his son's dinner.

This is a famous story on family education. It tells us that a child should not be cheated in any case. Shaaban Robert, the famous Tanzanian poet, novelist and linguist, wrote in his famous prose "Childhood", "Childhood is an important stage in one's life. One's personality develops from his childhood. What kind of people we will grow to be depends on what we learn and do in our childhood." It seems to be a trivial matter to keep the pig and thus lose credit, but one "should not engage in evil even if it's small." Zengzi wouldn't cheat his son. It seems to be an easy thing, but not all the parents today could make it.

49. 楚厉王误击警鼓

　　春秋时的楚厉王曾立下制度：遇到军情警报，就敲起军鼓作为号召，通知民众一起防守。有一次他喝醉酒后，错误地敲响了军鼓，民众都非常惊慌，聚集起来准备防守。厉王派人安抚大家说："我是喝醉了酒和近侍开玩笑，才错误地击了鼓。"于是民众都松懈下来。过了几个月，又遇到军情警报，厉王再次击鼓，民众却都不去备战了。于是他马上更改命令，明确信号，这样民众才又信从了。

　　战国初期魏国的李悝，曾作军队将领。他警告左右营垒的军队说："小心警惕敌人，他们早晚就会来袭击你们。"像这样的警告说了好多次，但敌人却没有来。左右营垒的军队就都松懈下来，不再相信李悝了。过了几个月，秦人前来袭击他们，打起仗来，李悝号令不灵，几乎全军覆灭。关于这事的另一种说法是：李悝率魏军将要和秦人交战。他对左边营垒的军队说："快上！右边营垒的军队已经上阵了。"又骑马到右边营垒的军队说："快上！左边营垒的军队已经上阵了。"两翼军队都说："上阵吧。"于是都争先恐后地上了阵。过后第二年，再和秦人交战。秦人前来偷袭，一交手，差点儿将魏军全部消灭。

　　韩非讲的这两则故事同样是说明"信"的重要，只不过是从反面即以不讲信用的危害来说明的。如果不尊重法令，法令的信用屡次被破坏，法令就形同虚设了，会导致严重的恶果。历史常常表现为重复，从"楚厉王误击警鼓"中可以看到"周幽王烽火戏诸侯"的影子。周幽王因为要博得冷面美女褒姒的"千金一笑"，不惜屡次点燃烽火，让诸侯们误以为敌军来袭，率领军队来回空跑。结果犬戎真正入侵、幽王再燃起烽火时，就没有诸侯来救了，最终导致西周灭亡。不讲诚信，最终带来的将是更大的危害。

KING LI OF CHU BEATS THE ALARMING DRUM BY MISTAKE

In the Spring and Autumn Period, King Li of Chu set up a rule: if there was any urgent military situation or alarm, the alarming drum would be beaten as a call to inform the people to defend the state together. Once he beat the alarming drum by mistake after getting drunk, and the people were all in such a panic that they gathered to prepare for defense. King Li then sent his men to reassure the people, saying, "I got drunk and played a joke with my attendants, so I beat the drum by mistake." Then the people all let their guard down. After a few months, an urgent military situation arose, so King Li beat the drum again. But this time the people didn't prepare themselves for defense. Therefore, King Li changed the order at once to reconfirm the signal, and then the people began to trust him again.

Li Kui once acted as the general of the troops of the State of Wei in the early Warring States Period. He warned the troops in the left and right camps, "Guard against the enemy as they will attack us sooner or later." He gave such kind of warnings to them for several times, but the enemy didn't come. As a result, the left and right camps all let their guard down and wouldn't trust Li Kui any more. After a few months, the troops of Qin made an attack on them, and the armies of Wei and Qin were engaged. Since Li Kui's order was not obeyed, his Wei troops were almost wiped out. Another version of this story goes like this: Li Kui led his Wei troops and was about to engage the Qin troops. He said to the troops of the left camp, "Go to battle! The right camp has been in battle." He then rode to the troops of the right camp and said, "Go to battle! The left camp has been in battle." Both of the two wings of troops said, "Go to battle!" Then they all rushed to the frontline to fight in the battle. In the next year, the Wei troops fought with the Qin troops again. However, this time the Qin troops made a surprise attack and almost wiped out the Wei troops.

Both of the stories told by Han Feizi explain the importance of honesty, or more specifically, the grave consequences of being dishonest. If laws are disobeyed or discredited frequently, the laws will become useless, which will bring about tragic results. History often repeats itself: from the story "King Li of Chu beats the alarming drum by mistake", one can find similar elements of a more famous story "King You of Zhou makes fun of the dukes by burning beacon fires". Just to get a smile from his cold-faced concubine, which he considered "worth a thousand pieces of gold", King You of Zhou did not hesitate to burn the beacon fires again and again. The dukes thought that enemies were attacking and rushed to the capital with their troops to protect the king, only to find that they were fooled again and again. As a result, when the troops of Quanrong did invade the capital and King You burnt the beacon fires for real, no duke came to his rescue. Eventually, the Western Zhou Dynasty met its demise. Dishonesty only brings harm in the end.

50. 外举不避仇，内举不避亲

春秋时，晋国中牟地方的县令一职出现了空缺，晋平公问大夫赵武："中牟是我国的重要地区，是邯郸的重镇，就好比大腿、肩膀和胳膊之于人的身体一样重要。我想选用一个优秀的县令，派谁去好呢？"赵武说："邢伯柳可以。"平公很奇怪，问道："他不是你的仇人吗？"赵武回答说："私仇不关公事。"后来平公又问赵武："宫廷内库现在缺主管，派谁去担任好呢？"赵武说："我的儿子就行。"赵武举荐人才，在外不避开自己的仇人，在内不避开自己的儿子。他就是这样不考虑个人恩怨，前前后后一共举荐了四十六个人。

另一种说法说举荐邢伯柳的人是解狐。邢伯柳原是解狐的家臣，曾与解狐的宠妾私通。解狐发现后，将两人暴打一顿赶了出去。现在解狐又举荐邢伯柳去做官，邢伯柳以为解狐已经消除了对自己的仇怨，就前去拜谢，说："您开脱了我的罪过，我怎么敢不来拜谢呢？"解狐取过弓箭，拉开弓就迎头射去，说："我举荐你是为公，是因为你能胜任。而跟你有仇，这是我的私怨。我不能因为与你有私仇，就让君主不能了解、任用你。你赶紧走吧，我还是同原先一样怨恨你！"

据《左传》、《国语》等书记载，晋平公时的大夫祁奚（祁黄羊），退休时举荐自己的仇人解狐接替自己的职位担任中军尉。但解狐还未上任就去世了，于是祁奚又举荐自己的儿子祁午担任这个职位。祁奚的行为得到孔子的高度赞扬，也常被后世称引为"外举不避仇，内举不避亲"的著名例子。

我国古代选拔人才的科举制度，是隋唐时代才逐步起源、确立并一直发展沿用到清末的。在此之前，地位尊贵者的举荐，对于人才的脱颖而出是很重要很关键的。"外举不避仇"可能还有不少人能够做到，毕竟这既符合公正无私选拔人才的原则，又能得到他人的称赞。而"内举不避亲"就不一样了，它容易被人看成是为了一己的私利，中国人大多很在意他人的看法，不惧他人误解的勇气与内心的坦荡显得尤为重要。

WHEN RECOMMENDING TALENTS ONE SHOULD NOT AVOID ONE'S ENEMIES OR RELATIVES

In the Spring and Autumn Period, there was a vacancy of the county magis=
trate in Zhongmou of the State of Jin. Duke Ping of Jin asked a minister Zhao
Wu, "Zhongmou is an important region in our state and an important town in the
capital Handan. It is to us what legs, shoulders and arms to a human body, so I
want to appoint an excellent county magistrate. Who do you think can fill this
vacancy?" Zhao Wu answered, "I recommend Xing Boliu." Duke Ping was very

surprised and asked, "Isn't he your enemy?" Zhao Wu answered, "Personal grudge has nothing to do with public affairs." Later Duke Ping asked Zhao Wu again, "I need a person to take charge of the palace storehouse. Who should I appoint?" Zhao Wu answered, "I recommend my son." When Zhao Wu recommended talents, he didn't avoid his own enemy outside his family or his own son in his family. He was just such a man who didn't take into consideration his personal grudge or favor. He recommended forty six talents in all.

According to another version of this story, the man who recommended Xing Boliu was Xie Hu. Xing Boliu was originally a retainer in Xie Hu's home. Since he had an affair with Xie Hu's favorite concubine, the two of them were given a good beating and then driven out when Xie Hu found it out. Now that Xie Hu recommended Xing Boliu to fill the official vacancy, Xing Boliu thought Xie Hu no longer held any grudge against him, so he went to Xie Hu's home to express his gratitude. Xing Boliu said, "Now that you have forgiven my fault, how dare I not come to express my gratitude?" However, Xie Hu took out his bow and shot an arrow at Xing Boliu, saying, "I recommend you for the good of the public. That's because you are suitable for the position. But the hatred I hold for you is my personal concern. I won't prevent the monarch from knowing and employing you because of my hatred toward you. Go away at once because I hate you as much as before!"

According to historical records such as *The Chronicles of Zuo* and *Analects of States*, in the reign of Duke Ping of Jin, Senior Official Qi Xi recommended his personal enemy Xie Hu to take his own place as the general for training soldiers. However, Xie Hu died before taking office, so Qi Xi recommended his own son to fill this post. Qi Xi won high praise from Confucius for his impartial attitude and became a famous example for "recommending talents without avoiding one's enemies or relatives."

As a way to select talents for the government in the Chinese feudal dynasties, the Imperial Civil Examination System appeared in the 6th century and lasted until the beginning of the 20th century. Before that, the recommendation by a nobleman or a high-ranking official was an important means for a talented person to be recognized and given an important position in the officialdom. Probably the principle of "recommending talents without avoiding one's enemies" is relatively easy to follow, for after all this kind of practice not only conforms to the principle of impartially selecting talents but also can win others' respect. But "recommending talents without avoiding one's relatives" is different, for it may be regarded as earning personal profits for one's own sake. Chinese people usually care about others' view of themselves, so it is a valuable quality to be courageous enough to live with others' misunderstanding and maintain a peace of mind.

51. 狗猛酒酸

　　宋国有一个卖酒的人，他酿的酒非常醇美，待客非常殷勤，给客人量酒也非常公平，门外悬挂的用以招徕生意的酒幌子挂得又高又显眼，总之看起来各方面都做得很好，无可挑剔。但是，他的酒却始终卖不出去，由于存放的时间太长，酒都变质发酸了。这个卖酒的宋国人对此感到十分奇怪，想不通原因何在，就去向他熟识的地方长者杨倩请教。杨倩问道："你家养的狗凶吗？"他说："狗倒确实是凶。可是这跟酒卖不出去有什么关系呢？"杨倩说："你的酒卖不出去，就是因为人们怕你家的狗呀。你想，大家常支使小孩子去买酒，可是当小孩儿揣着钱拿着壶要进来买酒时，你家的猛狗却迎上来要咬他。这样一来，又有谁还敢到你家去买酒呢？所以你家的酒就只好放着变酸，卖不出去了。"

　　这事的另一种说法是：宋国卖酒的人中有个叫庄氏的，他的酒一直都很好。有人派仆人去买庄氏的酒，可庄家的狗乱咬人，仆人不敢进去，就到别家去买了酒。有人问道："为什么你不买庄氏的酒呢？"仆人大概不好意思承认自己怕庄家的狗，就找托词回答说："因为今天庄氏的酒酸。"由于庄氏的狗凶猛，他家好好的美酒就这样被人说成是酸的了。

一条恶狗看门，就能把一个好端端的酒店弄得门庭冷落，客不敢入；如果一个国家让坏人控制了某些要害部门，那后果必然是忠奸颠倒，社会腐败，百姓遭殃。韩非讲这个故事，正是要说明国家也有恶狗，而恶狗就是围在国君身边的奸臣。国君只有去除那些像恶狗一样的奸臣，国家才会兴旺强盛。由此想开去，对于我们个人来说，刚愎自用的坏脾气、人见人厌的恶习也是恶狗，它会把有益于自己修身进德的好意见、好建议吓走的。

THE FIERCE DOG AND THE SOUR WINE

There was a winemaker in the State of Song, who made excellent wine, served his customers warmly, and gave a fair deal for every customer. Besides, the shop placard was hung high and conspicuously outside the door to attract business. All in all, it seemed everything was done perfectly. Yet, he could not sell his wine, which went sour after being kept for too long. The winemaker was confused and couldn't figure out the reason. Then he went to consult a local elder Yang Qian, whom he was familiar with. Yang Qian asked, "Is your dog a fierce one?" The winemaker said, "The dog is indeed very fierce, but what does that have to do with the fact that I'm not able to sell my wine?" Yang Qian said, "You can't sell your wine because people are afraid of your dog. Just think about it: people usually ask their children to buy wine for them, but when a child comes to buy wine with money and a kettle, your fierce dog goes up to bite him. As a result, who dares to buy wine from your shop? Therefore, your wine has to be kept until it goes sour. It just won't sell."

Another version of this story goes as follows. There was a winemaker named Zhuang who sold wine in the State of Song. His wine was always good. A customer sent his servant to buy wine from Zhuang, but Zhuang's dog threatened to bite everyone that came near. The servant didn't dare to go in, so he bought wine from another wine shop. Someone asked, "Why didn't you buy wine from Mr. Zhuang's shop?" The servant perhaps felt embarrassed to admit that he was afraid of Mr. Zhuang's dog, so he made up an excuse, "Because the wine of Mr. Zhuang's shop is sour today." Just because Mr. Zhuang had a fierce dog, the good wine of his shop was said to be sour.

A fierce dog that keeps the door can make a good wine shop lose its business, as no one dares to go in. If the vital departments of a state was controlled by evil men, the state will suffer the consequences of social unrest, corruption, and suffering of the common people. Han Feizi tells this story to suggest that there are also fierce dogs in a country, who are none other than those treacherous courtiers around the monarch. Only when the monarch removes all these courtiers could the state become prosperous. Likewise, we may consider our self-centered attitudes and unwelcome bad habits as a fierce dog which drives away good advice beneficial for our self-cultivation.

52. 执法官和太子

　　楚庄王规定有关外朝的法规："群臣、大夫和诸位公子乘车入朝，马蹄不准践踏到屋檐下滴水处。有违犯的，宫廷执法官就砍断他的车辕，杀掉他的车夫。"有一天，太子入朝，马蹄踩到了屋檐下滴水的地方，宫廷执法官于是就砍断了他的车辕，杀了他的车夫。太子很愤怒，进去向庄王哭诉了事情的经过，说："您一定要替我报仇，杀了那执法官！"庄王说："不行。法是用来敬宗庙、尊社稷的。所以，像执法官那样能确定法制、遵从法令、尊敬社稷的人，是国家的臣子，我怎么可以诛杀？违犯法制、使法令失效、不尊敬社稷的行为，是臣下凌驾于君主之上、臣下侵犯君主的行为。臣下凌驾于君主之上，君主就会失去威势；臣下侵犯君主，君主的地位就会有危险。威势失去，地位危险，就不能保有国家，我还拿什么传给子孙呢？还拿什么传给你呢？"于是太子赶紧掉头跑开，躲避到外面露宿了三天，面朝北方一再叩拜，请求给予自己死罪。

关于这事的另一种说法是：楚国法令规定，车子不准行进到宫中的第二道门。楚王有一次紧急召见太子。当时天下着雨，宫中院子里有积水，人步行很难通过，太子就要把车子一直赶到第二道门。宫廷执法官说："车子不能到第二道门。到第二道门是不合法的。"太子说："君王召唤得很急，我总不能等没有积水了再下车走过去吧。"于是继续赶马向前。执法官就举起兵器刺向太子的马，摧毁了太子的马车。太子进去后，对楚王哭诉道："院子里积水很多，我赶车到了第二道门。执法官说不合法，举起兵器刺我的马，毁了我的车。父王您一定要杀了他！"楚王说："前有年老的君主我，执法官他不越规办事；后有要继位的太子你，他也不去依附。贤啊！这真是我守法的臣子。"于是就给执法官加了两级爵位。又打开后门让太子出去，告诫他说："以后不要再犯类似的错误了。"

能否做到法律面前人人平等，是法制建设的关键。这个宫廷执法官宁可得罪未来的君主也要依法办事，毫不顾及个人的地位与安危，这是需要极大的勇气的，但楚王的态度也很重要，如果他听从太子，惩罚执法官，以后谁还愿意严格执法呢？这里顺便提一下历史上广泛传颂的"强项令"，说的是东汉光武帝时董宣担任洛阳县令，光武帝的姐姐湖阳公主的家奴行凶杀人，董宣趁湖阳公主出行时宣布其家奴的罪行并加以格杀。公主去光武帝处哭诉，光武帝大怒，命令董宣给公主叩头谢罪。董宣不从，宫中太监按住他的脖子使劲往下压，董宣两手撑在地上，硬着脖子就是不肯把头叩下去。光武帝最终也无可奈何，称他为"强项令"（硬脖子的县令），后来还加以赏赐。

THE LAW ENFORCER AND THE CROWN PRINCE

King Zhuang of Chu stipulated the following rule concerning the outer court where state affairs were discussed: "Ministers, senior officials and princes shouldn't allow horse hooves to step onto the place where water drops down from the eaves when entering the court by carriages. If anyone breaks the rule, the law enforcer of the court is to cut off his carriage shaft and kill his driver." One day, when the crown prince entered the court, his horse stepped onto the place where water dropped down from the eaves. Therefore, the law enforcer of the court cut off the prince's carriage shaft and killed the prince's driver. The crown prince was enraged, so he took the incident to King Zhuang and said, "You must take revenge for me and kill that law enforcer." King Zhuang said, "No, I can't. Laws are used to honor the ancestral temple and to show respect for the state. Such being the case, a man like the law enforcer, who can establish the rule, obey the laws and respect the state, is a minister of the state. How can I kill him? Violating the law, making rules invalid and showing disrespect for the state are the behaviors showing that a minister dominates and offends the monarch. If a minister dominates the monarch, the monarch will lose his power and influence; if a minister offends the monarch, the position of the monarch will be threatened. If my power and influence are lost and my position is threatened, I won't keep my state safely. Then what can I leave to my posterity? What can I leave to you?" Then the crown prince turned around and left in a hurry. He went away to sleep outside in the open for three days and kept kowtowing to the north to plead to be given death penalty.

Another version of the story goes as follows. According to the law of the State of Chu, no one was allowed to ride a carriage to go to the second gate of the palace. Once the King of Chu urgently summoned the crown prince. It rained at that time, so there was a lot of water in the courtyard of the palace and it became very hard for one to walk through. Therefore, the crown prince was about to ride his carriage to the second gate. The law enforcer of the court said, "You mustn't ride the carriage to go to the second gate, for it is illegal to go to the second gate by carriage." The crown prince said, "The king summoned me urgently. You can't expect me to walk over when no water is left?" So he continued to drive forward. Then the law enforcer raised his weapon, thrust at the crown prince's horse, and destroyed his carriage. After the crown prince entered the palace, he complained tearfully to the King of Chu, "Since there was too much water in the yard, I drove my carriage to the second gate, but the law enforcer said that it was illegal. Then he raised his weapon to thrust at my horse and destroyed my carriage. You must kill him." The King of Chu said, "There is me, the old monarch, before him, but the law enforcer didn't violate the rules; there is you, the crown prince to succeed to the throne in the future, after him, but he didn't fawn on you. How virtuous he is! He is a real law-abiding subject." Therefore, the king promoted the law enforcer by two ranks and then opened the back door to let the crown prince go out, warning him, "Don't make such a mistake any more."

The key to the legal system is to ensure that everyone enjoys an equal footing before the law. This law enforcer in the court would rather offend the future monarch than violate the law, with no regard to his personal status or safety. To do this, one would need great courage, but the attitude of the King of Chu is also very significant. If he followed the crown prince's idea and punished the law enforcer, who would like to enforce the law strictly? Let's take a brief look at a famous story of "the Strong-Necked County Magistrate". It is about Dong Xuan, who acted as the county magistrate of Luoyang in the reign of Emperor Guangwu of the Eastern Han Dynasty. A servant of the emperor's sister, Princess Huyang, committed homicide, and Dong Xuan convicted and executed the servant while Princess Huyang went for an outing.

The princess complained to the emperor in tears, and the angry emperor ordered Dong Xuan to kowtow to the princess to offer an apology. Dong Xuan wouldn't give in, so the palace eunuchs pressed his neck down with force. But Dong Xuan kept his neck up with his hands pushing against the ground. He just wouldn't drop his head. At last, the emperor had to give up and called Dong Xuan "the Strong-Necked County Magistrate". The emperor even rewarded Dong Xuan handsomely afterwards.

53. 吴起立信

　　名将吴起在魏武侯时担任西河的地方长官——郡守。当时秦国有个侦查用的小哨亭靠近魏国边境，吴起很想攻占它，因为如果不除掉这个哨亭，就会对附近种田的魏国百姓构成很大的威胁。但要除掉它，似乎又不值得为这点小事专门动用军队。于是吴起就想了一个办法。他在北城门外竖起一根车辕，然后下命令说："有谁能把这根车辕搬到南门外的，就赏给他上等的田地和住宅。"开始没人信，都不去搬。后来，终于有人抱着不妨试试看的心理把车辕搬到了南门外，吴起立即按照先前所说的待遇赏赐了这个人。不久，吴起又在东门外放了一石红豆，并下令说："有谁能把这一石红豆挑到西门去的，也按前一次的标准赏赐。"所有的人都抢着去挑红豆。这时吴起见时机成熟了，就下达命令："明天将要攻打那个秦国的哨亭，有谁能先登上去的，就任命他做大夫，赏给他上等的田地和住宅。"命令一下，老百姓们都争先恐后，一个早上就把哨亭拿下了。

吴起是著名的法家代表人物，其守信在当时是很有名的。同属法家的商鞅也有过类似的"立信"举措。商鞅在秦国将要实行变法前，已经拟好了有关法令，但还没有公布，他怕公布了民众也不信，就在国都集市的南门外树立了一根三丈高的木头，并宣布有谁能将它搬到集市的北门外树立起来的，就奖给他十金。大家都很奇怪，不敢相信，没有人敢去搬。商鞅又重新下令，把赏金增加到五十金。有一个人去搬了，马上就给了他五十金，表明决不欺骗。然后商鞅颁布有关新法令，最终变法大获成功。由此可见，取得人民的信任，乃是执政者的一个基本条件。

WU QI ESTABLISHES CREDIT

The famous general Wu Qi once held the post of a local official in Xihe in the reign of Marquis Wu of Wei. At that time, a scouting outpost in the State of Qin was located near the border of the State of Wei. Wu Qi wanted to seize it, for if it was not removed, it would pose a great threat to the farmers of Wei who worked nearby. However, it seemed there wasn't the need to resort to the regular army for such a trivial matter. Therefore, Wu Qi got an idea. He erected a shaft outside the north gate and ordered, "If anyone carries this shaft to the outside of the south gate, I will reward him with fertile farmland and a nice house." At the beginning, people didn't believe it, so no one wanted to have a try. Later a man thought he had nothing to lose anyway and carried the shaft to the outside of the south gate. Wu Qi immediately gave him the reward as promised. Soon after that, Wu Qi put a hectoliter of red beans outside the east gate and ordered, "If anyone carries these beans to the west gate, he will get the same reward as last time." This time, everyone rushed to carry the beans. At this moment, Wu Qi thought the time was ripe, so he ordered, "Tomorrow we are going to attack that scouting outpost of Qin. Anyone climbing onto it first will be appointed a senior official and rewarded with fertile farmland and a fine house." Once the order was given, the people all rushed to attack, and the outpost was seized early in the morning.

Wu Qi, a representative figure of the Legalist school, was well-known for keeping his word at that time. Another representative of the Legalist school called Shang Yang also took such a measure to "establish credit". Before carrying out the reform in the State of Qin, Shang Yang had already drawn up the relevant decrees, which were not yet announced in case that the people wouldn't believe. Shang Yang erected a wooden pole ten meters tall outside the south gate of the market of the capital and declared that if anyone could carry it to the outside of the north gate and erect it there, he would be rewarded with ten gold coins. People were all surprised; unable to believe it, they didn't dare to have a try. Shang Yang then gave a new order increasing the reward to fifty gold coins. A man made it and was given fifty gold coins at once, which showed that Shang Yang didn't cheat the people. After that, Shang Yang issued the new decrees and eventually succeeded in his reform. From the above stories we can see that winning people's trust is key to government's success.

54. 吴起吮脓

　　吴起担任魏军将领时，有一次率军攻打中山国。士兵中有一个长了毒疮的人，吴起亲自跪着为他吸掉脓血。这个士兵的母亲看见后，却马上哭泣不止。有人劝她说："你的儿子只是一个普通的士兵，吴起将军却待他这么好，你还有什么可哭的？"这位母亲回答道："吴起将军过去用口吸过这孩子父亲的疮口，结果他父亲在战斗中勇猛冲杀，死于疆场。现在吴起将军又为我儿子吸脓，我不知道这孩子又会在哪里奋战而死了。现在我就是为这个而哭啊。"

　　吴起以将军的身份，不顾秽辱，亲自为士兵吸掉脓血以医治毒疮，本是值得肯定的，但士兵的母亲却觉得不以为然，认为吴起太"假"。用今天的话来说，就是"作秀"。所谓"爱兵如子"，实际上是有意收买人心，好让手下人死心塌地卖命的一种手段，所以是一种"巧诈"。韩非的看法是巧诈不如拙诚。相比之下，同样是以"爱兵如子"著称的汉代名将李广，就比吴起高明得多了。据史书记载，李广为人廉洁，常把自己的赏赐分给部下。他爱兵如子，凡事能身先士卒。他与士兵同吃同饮，行军遇到缺水断食之时，士兵不全喝到水，他不近水边；士兵不全吃遍，他不尝饭食。因此李广深得官兵爱戴，士兵甘愿为他出死力。关于李广，史书里全是正面评价，反映了人们对李广的普遍赞誉。

WU QI SUCKS PUS FOR HIS SOLDIER

As the general of Wei, Wu Qi once led troops to attack the State of Zhongshan. One of the soldiers got an inflaming wound, and Wu Qi knelt down to suck the pus from the wound for him. When the soldier's mother saw it, she started to cry without stop. Someone calmed her, "Your son is only an ordinary soldier, but General Wu Qi treats him so well. Why should you cry?" The mother answered, "General Wu Qi had sucked pus for the father of my son, and then the man fought bravely in battle and died on the battlefield. Now General Wu Qi sucked pus for my son. I have no idea where my son will die of fighting. That is why I am crying."

Being a general, Wu Qi could suck pus for a soldier to cure his inflammation in spite of the dirtiness. That was a noble act by itself. However, the soldier's mother disapproved of Wu Qi's behavior as she thought it was "hypocritical". Put in today's language, it can be said to be "making a show". The so-called scene of "loving his soldiers as one loves his children" is, in fact, a tactic for the general to win popular support, so that his subordinates will be willing to sacrifice their own lives for him. Therefore, this is a kind of "insincere cleverness". In Han Feizi's opinion, insincere cleverness is not as good as sincere clumsiness.

By contrast, General Li Guang of the Han Dynasty, also well-known for "loving his soldiers as one loves his children", is much wiser than Wu Qi. According to historical records, Li Guang was honest as a general, and he always distributed his own rewards among his subordinates. He loved his soldiers as he loved his children and always charged at the head of them in a battle. He ate and drank together with his soldiers. When there was a shortage of provisions on the march, he wouldn't have a drop of water if any of the soldiers didn't have water to drink, and he wouldn't have a taste of food if any of the soldiers didn't have food to eat. As a result, he won deep love and high esteem from his officers and soldiers, who were willing to die for him. The positive comments on Li Guang in historical records reflected the universal acclaim for the general at that time.

55. 吴起休妻

　　吴起有一次让他妻子织丝带。妻子织好后，吴起一量，幅度比要求的尺度窄。吴起让她改一下，妻子说："行。"等到织成，又量了量，结果还是不符合尺度，吴起非常生气。他妻子还强辩说："我开头就把经线确定好了，不可以更改了。"吴起为这事休掉了他的妻子。妻子回娘家后，让哥哥去找吴起替自己求情，请求能让她回去。她哥哥说："吴起是制定法令的人。他制定法令，是想用来为大国建功立业的。他必须首先在自己妻妾身上兑现，然后才能推行起来。你不要指望回去了。"吴起妻子的弟弟这时正受卫君重用，也去请求吴起，企图凭着国君器重的身份让吴起听从。吴起仍然不听，同时觉得在卫国也呆不下去了，便离开卫国到楚国去了。

　　吴起的做法乍看起来似乎有点小题大做，然而这个故事的寓意就在于要以小喻大，以家喻国。正人必先正己，这个"己"还包括统治者的家人。对于普通民众来说，制定法令、执行法令者的家人正不正，跟他自己正不正同等重要。如果制定、执行法令的人连他身边的人都管不好，法律就没有威严了。儒家讲"修身"而后"齐家"而后"治国"最终"平天下"，讲君主和卿大夫要为"给自己的妻子作榜样，推广到兄弟，进而治理好一家一国"，也是同样的道理。只不过儒家更多地强调正面的、积极亲身实行以作出表率，而法家更多地强调反面的、公平惩处违法行为以作出表率。

WU QI ABANDONS HIS WIFE

Wu Qi, the famous general, asked his wife to weave a silk ribbon. When his wife finished it, Wu Qi measured it and found that it was narrower than required. Wu Qi asked his wife to alter it, and his wife said, "All right." When it was finished again, Wu Qi measured it again and found that it was still not up to standard, so he was very angry. But his wife still argued strongly, "Since I have fixed the number of warps at the beginning, it can't be altered." Wu Qi then abandoned his wife for this. After coming back to her parents' home, Wu Qi's wife asked her elder brother to appeal to Wu Qi's mercy for her, so that she could be allowed to go back. Her elder brother said, "Wu Qi is the person who makes laws. He makes laws because he wants to use them to make great contributions and accomplish great tasks for the state. So he must practice his laws on his own wife and concubines before he can practice his laws in a larger scale." The wife's younger brother, now favored by the monarch of the State of Wei, also requested Wu Qi to let his wife back, thinking that an intimate relationship with the monarch might add weight to the request. But Wu Qi still wouldn't listen. At the same time, Wu Qi thought he couldn't stay in the State of Wei any longer, so he left the State of Wei for the State of Chu.

At first glance, Wu Qi seemed to be making a mountain out of a molehill. However, the value of this story lies in explaining a significant idea by means of a trivial matter, to explain a state affair with the business of an individual family. One must correct oneself if he wants to correct others, and this "oneself" also includes the family members in the case of a ruler. From the viewpoint of the ordinary people, the law-abidance of the family members of the law-makers and law-enforcers are as important as the law-abidance of the law-makers and law-enforcers themselves. If the law-makers and law-enforcers can't restrain their family members with laws, then the laws will certainly lose credit. According to the Confucian school, a gentleman begins by "cultivating himself in virtues", proceeds to "running his family", then to "ruling a state", and finally tries to "unite the world"; meanwhile, monarchs and ministers should "set an example for their wives and extend the example to their brothers, in order to successfully run their families and states." That is basically the same idea as advocated by Han Feizi and the Legalist school. The difference is that the Confucian school lays more emphasis on setting an example by actively taking personal actions, while the Legalist school lays more emphasis on setting an example by punishing illegal activities fairly.

56. 弥子瑕色衰爱弛

　　卫灵公有个男宠，叫弥子瑕。他年轻的时候英俊漂亮，很得卫灵公的宠爱。有一次弥子瑕的母亲生病了，有人抄近路连夜通知弥子瑕，弥子瑕就假托君命驾着卫灵公的马车赶回家去探视母亲。这在当时是很重的罪行，按卫国法令的规定，私自驾驭国君车子的，论罪要处以被砍脚的刖刑。但卫灵公听说此事后，却认为弥子瑕德行好，说："弥子瑕真是孝顺啊！为了母亲的缘故，忘了自己会犯受刖刑的罪。"又有一次，弥子瑕和卫灵公在果园游览，他摘了一个桃子，吃着觉得很甜，没有吃完，就把剩下的半个献给卫灵公吃。灵公又感叹："弥子瑕是多么爱我啊！有好吃的自己不舍得吃，还要留给我。"等到后来弥子瑕年老色衰了，灵公另有新欢，想起以前的事，非常生气，说："弥子瑕竟敢假托君命私自驾驭我的车子，又曾经把吃剩下的桃子给我吃！"于是治了弥子瑕的罪。虽然弥子瑕的行为和当初并没有两样，但先前称贤、后来获罪的原因，是卫君的爱憎有了变化。所以被君主宠爱时，才智就显得恰当而更受亲近；被君主憎恶时，才智就显得不恰当，遭到谴责而更被疏远。

　　韩非把这个故事归结为"所以谏说谈论的人不可不察看君主的爱憎，然后进言"。这个故事里卫灵公的"翻手为云、覆手为雨"令人心寒。同一件事情，高兴时就加以赞许，有一套说法；讨厌时就加以惩罚，又有一套理由。做臣下的真是难办。君臣利害各异，必然造成君主的多疑、喜怒无常，有时表现为宽容，有时表现为残暴，其心理活动往往呈现多变的复杂状态。对同样的事，君王作判断的标准随时在变化，而且其权力至高无上，没有人能够约束他。俗话说"伴君如伴虎"，就是这个道理。就弥子瑕而言，如果得意时不那么任性，失意时或许也就不至于这么凄惨吧。看来做人还是应该能够得意不忘形为好。

MI ZIXIA LOSES BEAUTY AS WELL AS THE DUKE'S FAVOR

Duke Ling of Wei had a gay pal named Mi Zixia. The boy was handsome when he was young, so Duke Ling of Wei was very fond of him. One time as Mi Zixia's mother was ill, someone took a shortcut to inform Mi Zixia of it. Then Mi Zixia faked Duke Ling's order and drove the duke's carriage to go home to see his mother. It was a very grave crime at that time, for according to the laws of the State of Wei, anyone who drove the monarch's carriage without permission would be punished by having his feet cut off. But when Duke Ling of Wei heard about it, he thought Mi Zixia was quite virtuous, "What a filial man Mi Zixia is! He forgot that he would receive the punishment of getting his feet cut off for the sake of his mother." Another time, when Mi Zixia and Duke Ling of Wei were taking a tour in an orchard, Mi Zixia picked a peach and ate it. As he found the peach very sweet, he gave the rest of the peach to Duke Ling before he finished eating it. Duke Ling of Wei sighed with content, "How deeply Mi Zixia loves me! When he has delicious food, he begrudges eating it himself and saves it for me." Later Mi Zixia lost his beauty when gaining in age, and Duke Ling had a new gay pal. Then Duke Ling thought of what happened before and became very angry. He said, "Mi Zixia even dared to fake my order and drive my carriage without my permission. He also dared to offer me the peach he had half eaten." Therefore, he punished Mi Zixia. Though Mi Zixia's actions were not different from before, he was praised as virtuous earlier and punished as a criminal later because Duke Ling had a change of mind. When he was favored by the monarch, his wisdom seemed to be proper, so he would become closer to the monarch; when he was hated by the monarch, his wisdom seemed to be improper, so he would be condemned and alienated.

Han Feizi sums up this story as follows: "Those who would like to offer counsel to the monarch should pay great attention to the monarch's love and hate before giving advice." The dramatic change of attitude of Duke Ling from love to apathy is like, to be put verbatim in a Chinese idiom, "Making cloud with palm up and rain with palm down." He would praise something with a set of excuses when he was happy, and impose punishment for exactly the same thing with another set of excuses when he was unhappy. That made the life hard for his subordinates. Since the ministers tended to have different interests than the monarch, the monarch usually became suspicious and unpredictable: he might seem generous at one moment and cruel at another moment, and his mind was dominated by caprice at all time. The standard by which the monarch made judgement was constantly changing, and the power by which monarch passed out his rule was supreme. Therefore, the risk of serving the monarch is best described in a Chinese saying: "Being in the king's company is like living with a tiger." As for Mi Zixia, if he didn't behave like a spoiled brat when he was in the duke's favor, he might not suffer a miserable fate when that favor had gone. The moral is that no one should lose his head in success.

57. 杀牛塞祷

秦昭襄王生病，百姓为他祈祷；病好后，百姓杀牛向神还愿。侍从官阎遏、公孙衍出门看见了，说："现在不是祭土地神和腊祭的时候，为什么要杀牛祭祀呢？"他们感到很奇怪，就询问百姓。百姓说："国君生病，我们为他祈祷；现在他病好了，我们杀牛向神还愿。"阎遏、公孙衍很高兴，晋见昭襄王拜贺道："您已经胜过尧、舜了。"昭襄王吃惊地问："此话怎讲？"他们回答说："尧和舜，还没有到百姓为他们祈祷的地步。现在大王生病，百姓用牛许愿；大王病愈，百姓杀牛还愿。所以我们私下认为大王是胜过尧和舜了。"于是昭襄王派人查问，看是哪个里（古代五家为邻，五邻为里）这样干的，要罚那个里的长官——里正和伍老各出两副盔甲。昭襄王说："罚他们每人出两副盔甲。没有命令而擅自祈祷，这是爱我。他们爱我，我如果也改变法令，用同样的心去爱他们，这样法就立不起来；法立不起来，是乱国亡身之道。不如每人罚他们两副盔甲，这事就算过去了，我再重新跟他们用法而不是用爱来治理好国家。"阎遏、公孙衍惭愧难当，不敢吭声。

过了几个月，昭襄王饮酒正痛快时，阎遏、公孙衍对昭襄王说："前段时间我们私下认为大王胜过尧和舜，并非胆敢故意讨好。尧和舜生病，百姓还不至于为他们祈祷；现在大王生病，百姓用牛许愿，大王病愈，百姓杀牛还愿。现在竟然罚那个里的里正和伍老各出两副盔甲，我们私下深感奇怪。"昭襄王说："你们为什么不懂这些呢？那些百姓能够为我所用，并不是因为我爱他们，他们就为我所用，而是因为我有权势，他们才为我所用。要是我放弃了权势和他们相互交结，那样的话，我偶然不爱他们，他们马上就不为我所用了。所以，要治国就应该摒弃仁爱的做法啊。"

韩非说："仁爱太多，法制就建立不起来；威严不足，领导者就会被属下侵害。"法令是无情的，在依法办事时，如果君主、执法者跟民众之间"仁爱"太多，就难免徇情枉法，不是什么好事。所以高明的领导者，往往避免在公事之外过多地与下属接触，这样才好什么事都"公事公办"，处理问题不受私人感情的左右。这里还提出了一个问题：什么是君主"爱"百姓的标准和方式？对此，各家有着不同的看法。法家的看法是，宽缓刑罚、对人民多加赏赐等都不是对人民真正的爱；建立君主的威严和法制的威严，哪怕一些做法显得无情，但最终能使国富兵强，百姓安居乐业，这才是君主对百姓真正根本的爱。

PEOPLE SACRIFICE CATTLE TO EXPRESS THEIR GRATITUDE TO GODS

King Zhaoxiang of Qin was ill, and the people all prayed for him. When he recovered, the people sacrificed cattle to fulfill their vows to gods. Chamberlains Yan E and Gongsun Yan went out and saw the rituals. They said, "Now it's not the time for offering sacrifices to the God of the Land or for the end of the year. Then why are they offering cattle as sacrifices?" Confused, they asked the people about it. The people said, "When our monarch was ill, we prayed for him. Now that he has recovered, we sacrifice cattle to fulfill our vows to gods." Yan E and Gongsun Yan were excited, and they went to see King Zhaoxiang to congratulate him, "You are a better monarch than Yao and Shun." (Yao and Shun are legendary emperors in the Chinese mythology.) King Zhaoxiang said in surprise, "What does that mean?" They answered, "Even Yao and Shun couldn't make the people pray for them. Now when you were ill, the people made vows to gods with cattle; when you recovered, they sacrificed cattle to fulfill their vows. Therefore, we privately thought that you are better than Yao and Shun." Then King Zhaoxiang sent men to find out which village did this and punished the officials there — the village head and the military head were to offer two suits of armor as punishment. King Zhaoxiang said, "Have them offer two suits of armor as punishment. They took the liberty to pray without order, although it appeared to be an act of showing love to me. If I also change the laws to love them with the same magnitude just because they love me, then no laws can be established. If laws cannot be established, we are bound to lose our state and our lives. It would be better to punish them by having each one offer two suits of armor, and then we can forget about this. I will try to run our state by rule of law again instead of by love." Yan E and Gongsun Yan felt ashamed, and they didn't dare to utter a single word. After several months, when King Zhaoxiang was drinking to his heart's content, Yan E and Gongsun Yan said to King Zhaoxiang, "A while ago, we privately thought that you were better than Yao and Shun. It was not that we dared to fawn on you in a deliberate way. When Yao and Shun were ill, the people didn't go so far as to pray for them. Now when you were ill, the people made vows to gods with cattle, and when you recovered, they sacrificed cattle to fulfill their vows. But you actually punished the responsible officials by having them offer two suits of armor each, which made us privately feel so surprised." King Zhaoxiang said, "Why don't you understand? The reason that those people serve me is not because I love them. They serve me because I have power. If I give up my power to make friends with them, they will not serve me when I don't love them occasionally. Therefore, to run the state, I have to give up the benevolent practice."

Han Feizi says, "If too much benevolence is shown, the rule of law can't be established; if his awe-inspiring dignity is not enough, the leader will be infringed upon by his subordinates." Laws are ruthless. When acting by law, if the monarch and the law enforcers show too much "benevolence" to the people, they can hardly avoid bending the law for the benefit of certain people — that is not a desirable situation. Therefore, a wise leader always avoids having too much personal involvement with his subordinates outside business, so that it is easier for him to "do official business according to the rules" and keep personal considerations out of his execution of public duty. Here also arises the question about how much and in what ways the monarch should "love" his people. As for this, different philosophical schools hold different ideas. According to the Legalist school, to relieve punishments and to grant more rewards to people are neither genuine love for them. The establishment of the dignity of the monarch and the rule of law is the real fundamental love the monarch should have for the people: although some practices may seem ruthless, they can eventually make the country prosperous and the army strong, and let the people live and work in peace and contentment.

58. 秦昭王拒绝开放五苑

秦昭王时，有一年遇到了严重的饥荒。应侯向昭王请求说："我们秦国有五处属于王家的苑囿，其中的草木植物，包括蔬菜、栎树果实、枣子、栗子等，足以养活百姓。请您开放这些苑囿，让百姓可以进去随意采摘，好挨过荒年。"秦昭王说："我们秦国的法令，是让百姓有功才受赏，有罪就要受罚。现在如果开放五苑的蔬菜瓜果，却是不论有功无功都要让百姓受到赏赐，这是使国家混乱的做法啊！开放五苑而使国家混乱，还不如烂掉那些瓜果蔬菜而使国家太平。"

关于秦昭王回答的另一种说法是："如果我命令开放五苑的瓜果蔬菜，倒也足以可以养活百姓，但却会使有功的人和无功的人相互争夺。与其让他们活着而使国家混乱，不如让他们死掉而使国家安定，你们还是放弃自己的主张吧！"

《韩非子》的"与其让他们活着而使国家混乱，不如让他们死掉而使国家安定"这话，常常被后人引用来作为法家"刻薄寡恩"的例子，备受指责。其实儒家也有类似的说法。《论语·颜渊》记载，有一次孔子的学生子贡向孔子请教怎样治理政事。孔子说："充足粮食，充足军备，老百姓对政府就有信心了。"子贡问："如果迫不得已，在粮食、军备和人民的信心三者之中一定要去掉一项，先去掉哪一项？"孔子说："去掉军备。"子贡又问："如果迫不得已，在粮食和人民的信心两者之中一定要去掉一项，先去掉哪一项？"孔子回答说："去掉粮食。没有粮食，不过导致部分百姓死亡的后果，但自古以来谁都免不了死亡；如果人民对政府缺乏信心，那国家就站立不起来了。"孔子与韩非的这类议论，都应该理解成一种将对某一标准的强调推到极端的说法，只是各自所强调的对象不同。比较起来，法家显得更加不近人情一点，因为它将赈灾救命与无功受赏混为一谈，把遇到天灾时政府应有的赈灾救命的职能和义务否定了。

KING ZHAO OF QIN REFUSES TO OPEN THE FIVE PARKS

One year during the reign of King Zhao of Qin, there was a great famine in the state. Marquis Ying begged King Zhao, "There are five parks in our state belonging to the royal family, where herbage plants, including vegetables, oak nuts, dates, chestnuts, etc., are enough to provide for the people. Please open these parks to the people and allow them to go inside and pick the vegetables and fruits freely, so that they may survive the famine." King Zhao of Qin said, "The law of the State of Qin is to allow the people to get rewards when they make contributions and to receive punishments when they have faults. If I open the five parks and allow them to pick the vegetables and fruits now, it is to give rewards to them regardless of their contributions or faults. That will plunge the state into chaos! If opening the five parks could bring about chaos to the state, it might be better to let the vegetables and fruits rot but keep the state in peace."

Another version of King Zhao's answer goes like this: "If I order to open the five parks, the vegetables and fruits might be enough to provide for the people, but those who have performed meritorious service will have to scramble for the rewarded food with those who haven't. It is better to let them die to keep the state in peace than let them live to plunge the state into chaos. You'd better give up your proposal."

Han Feizi provides an unlikely solution, namely, "It is better to let them die to keep the state in peace than let them live to plunge the state into chaos." That was often quoted as an example for the ideal of "treating the people harshly and ungenerously" advocated by the Legalist school and always attracted flak from other schools. In fact, the Confucian school also put forward a similar idea. According to the records in *The Analects*, Zigong, one of Confucius's disciples, asked Confucius about how to handle political affairs. Confucius said, "If there is enough food and armament, the people will have confidence in the government." Zigong asked, "If one of the three elements — food, armament and people's confidence — has to be forsaken under the pressure of circumstances, which one should go first?" Confucius said, "Armament should go." Zigong asked again, "If one of the two elements — food and people's confidence — has to be forsaken under the pressure of circumstances, which one should go first?" Confucius said, "Food should go. Without food, a portion of the population will die; yet, no one can escape death since ancient times. However, without people's confidence in the government, the state won't stand on its own." Arguments like these by both Confucius and Han Feizi can be understood as a proposition set in extreme conditions, although the Confucian school and the Legalist school do have a difference in emphasis. The Legalist school does seem a little "heartless" in this respect, as it confuses distress relief with unnecessary rewards and completely ignores the governmental responsibilities of providing distress relief to people during natural disasters.

59. 收藏旧裤子与一城换一囚

　　韩昭侯是战国初韩国的有为之君。一天，他的裤子有些破了，他让侍从马上把破裤子收藏起来。侍从对他说："君王您也太不仁爱了，连一条破旧的裤子都不肯赏赐给臣下们，反而要收藏起来。"昭侯说："这不是你所能理解得了的。我听说，明君连自己的一颦一笑都要加以珍惜，不能轻易表露；颦有颦的目的，笑有笑的目的。现在说的是裤子了，岂止是一颦一笑啊！和一颦一笑相比，裤子的价值可高多了，我又怎能轻易给人呢？我一定要等待有功的人赏赐给他，所以要收藏好——现在还没有给予的对象呢。"

　　卫嗣君在位时，有个囚犯逃往了魏国，到魏国后为魏襄王的王后治病，得到了很高的地位。卫嗣君听说了，就派人请求魏襄王允许用五十金赎回囚犯，以依法加以诛罚。使者往返五趟，魏王就是不给人。卫嗣君就请求用左氏城来交换囚犯。群臣近侍劝卫嗣君说："用一个大城邑去买一个囚犯，值得吗？"卫嗣君说："这不是你们所能理解的。治不在小，乱不在大。如果法令不设立，诛罚不兑现，即使有十个左氏城也没什么好处；如果法令设立，诛罚兑现，即使失去十个左氏城也没有什么损害。"魏王听说后说："卫君想治理好国家，我却不答应他的要求，不吉利。"于是用车子装了囚犯送到卫国，无代价地交付给卫嗣君。

　　韩非说的这两则故事其实是一个意思：没有合适正当理由的赏赐，即便所赐极小也不随便给予；按照法律当行的诛罚，哪怕付出再大的代价也要兑现。这样做，可能都会失去一些眼前的利益：韩昭侯使臣下觉得他太不仁爱了，卫嗣君用一个大城邑去买回一个用来加以诛罚的囚犯，更是大大地"划不来"。但是从长远来看，君主"信赏必罚"的建立，使臣下民众竭尽其能以求得应得的赏赐，不敢犯法以避免逃不掉的诛罚，对整个国家的好处可就无可估量了。

STORING UP A PAIR OF OLD TROUSERS AND EXCHANGING A CITY FOR A PRISONER

Marquis Zhao of Han was a capable monarch in the State of Han in the early Warring States Period. One day, a pair of his trousers got a little worn out, so he asked his attendant to store it up. The attendant said to him, "It is really not benevolent of Your Majesty to do so. You wouldn't even grant a pair of old trousers to your liegemen but store it up instead." Marquis Zhao said, "This is beyond you. Listen to me. A wise monarch would even cherish every twinkle and every smile, never expressing them lightly. A twinkle has its own aim; a smile has its own purpose. Now we are talking about a pair of trousers, not just a twinkle or a smile. The value of a pair of trousers is much greater. Then how can I give it to anyone easily? I must wait to give it to a person with outstanding merits as a reward. Therefore, it must be stored up well since there is not a person to receive it yet."

During the reign of Duke Si of Wei, a prisoner escaped to another state, the State of Wei. After arriving in the State of Wei, he gave medical treatment to the queen of King Xiang of Wei and was granted a high position. Hearing about it, Duke Si of Wei sent an envoy to ask King Xiang to ransom the prisoner with fifty gold, who was to be punished by law. The envoy went back and forth for five times, but King Xiang of Wei simply wouldn't agree. Then Duke Si of Wei asked to exchange the prisoner for Zuoshi City. The officials and ministers all dissuaded Duke Si of Wei, "Is it worthwhile to buy a prisoner with such a big city?" Duke Si of Wei said, "This is beyond you. Fair rule is a respectable achievement when it is still confined to a small area, and chaos is already a big problem before it reaches a big scale. If laws and decrees are not established and if punishment is not carried out, there won't be any good even with ten Zuoshi Cities; if laws and decrees are established and if punishment is carried out, there won't be any harm with the loss of ten Zuoshi Cities." Hearing about Duke Si's words, King Xiang of Wei said, "Duke Si of Wei wants to rule his state well, but I don't agree to his request. In that case, the bad omen falls on me." So the king had the prisoner sent back to Duke Si of Wei for free in a paddy wagon.

The two stories told by Han Feizi are essentially the two sides of one coin. Without a proper reason, no reward will be given easily even though it is extremely trivial; meanwhile, the punishment that should be carried out by law must be put into reality no matter what price is paid. To do this, some short-term profit might be lost: Marquis Zhao of Han made his liegemen feel that he was not benevolent, and Duke Si of Wei wanted to exchange a big city for a prisoner to get him punished by law, which was obviously a bad deal. But in the long run, the establishment of the monarch's rule that "due rewards and punishments will be meted out without fail" would certainly make the people try their utmost to get the rewards they deserve and not dare to break laws for fear of the unavoidable punishment. Such being the case, the state would enjoy benefits beyond measure.

60. 爱吃鱼的公仪休

公仪休是鲁国的丞相。他很爱吃鱼，全都城的人都争相买鱼进献给他，可公仪休一概不收。他的弟弟劝他说："你爱吃鱼，人家送给你，你却不收，这是为什么呢？"公仪休回答说："正因为爱吃鱼，我才不收。假如收了，一定就得在有些事上迁就那些送鱼的人；如果迁就他们，就将违背法令；违背法令，我就会被罢免相位。这样一来，我即使爱吃鱼，他们也不一定再给我送，而且我自己也没有足够的财力去买鱼吃了。假使不收鱼，就不会被免职，就算我比现在更爱吃鱼，我自己也能买得起啊。"《韩非子》总结说："公仪休这么做，是懂得依靠别人不如依靠自己，懂得靠别人相助不如自助的道理。"

公仪休当然不仅仅是为了天天吃鱼才不受贿，但他这么说却蕴含深意。一个官员可能没有什么大的毛病，既不贪财好色也不嗜赌，但他作为一个人，总难免有点什么特别的嗜好，这种嗜好哪怕很小很不起眼，也很容易成为他的弱点。别人可以通过投其所好逐步拉拢关系，使他最后丧失原则，走上徇私枉法的道路。有的人看不到自己的弱点，有的人知道自己的弱点却不能像公仪休那样时时保持警惕。于是，苍蝇就来叮有缝的蛋了。

GONGYI XIU LOVES EATING FISH

Gongyi Xiu was the prime minister of the State of Lu. As he loved eating fish, people all over the capital were eager to offer him fish, but Gongyi Xiu never accepted any of the offerings. His younger brother asked him, "You love eating fish, but why don't you accept the fish that others give you as a present?" Gongyi Xiu answered, "I don't accept the fish offered to me because I love eating fish. If I did accept the fish, I would have to give in to those who sent me fish for certain favors. If I gave in to them, I would violate the laws and decrees. If I violated the laws and decrees, I would be removed from the post as the prime minister. In that case, even if I loved eating fish, they might not send me fish any more, and I couldn't afford fish myself. If I don't accept their fish, I won't be removed from my post. Even if I should love eating fish more than I do now, I still can afford it myself." *Han Feizi* draws a conclusion like this, "The reason why Gongyi Xiu did so is that he understood that depending on oneself is better than depending on others and that helping oneself is better than getting help from others."

Of course, Gongyi Xiu rejected bribes because of greater concerns than merely a wish to eat fish every day. Yet, what he said is thought-provoking. An official may be straight enough to be free from any shortcomings, such as greed, lust or addiction to gambling. However, as a human being he may always have a certain hobby. However trivial or insignificant the hobby can be, it may still become his weak point, which someone with ulterior motives will try to exploit. Eventually the hobby will be the bane of the official and lead him into endless corruption. Some people can't see their weak points, and some people know their weak points but can't stay alert at all times as Gongyi Xiu did. Then, as a Chinese idiom goes, "The fly goes for the cracked egg."

61. 屦贱踊贵

　　齐景公去探视上大夫晏子，对晏子说："您的住宅太小了，又靠近集市，环境不好。请把您家搬到豫章的园林去吧。"晏子拜了两拜推辞说："我家里穷，靠去集市买东西吃，早晚都要赶集，不能离得太远。"景公笑着说："您家人熟悉市场行情，知道什么东西贵什么东西便宜吗？"当时景公施行的刑罚繁多，晏子就针对这一点回答道："断脚人穿的踊贵，常人穿的鞋子就很便宜。"景公不解地问："什么缘故呢？"晏子回答说："刑罚太多了。受刖刑而断脚的人多，他们穿的踊需求量大，所以就贵了，普通的鞋子反而就便宜了。"景公惊讶得脸色大变，说："这么说来，我大概太残暴了吧！"于是减去了五种刑罚。但韩非却不以为然，他说："晏子说踊贵，不是他的真心话，是想借此来劝说景公不要多用刑罚。这是他不懂治国之道的过错。刑法适当就不嫌多，刑罚不适当就不是少不少的问题了，换句话说也无所谓少了。晏子不以刑罚不当来作为进谏的理由，却以用刑太多来劝说景公，这是不懂法术的过错。……爱惜茅草便会损害庄稼，宽容盗贼便会伤害良民。现在减轻刑罚，实行宽惠，这是便宜了坏人而伤害了好人啊，这不是用来治国的办法。"

　　成语"屦贱踊贵"就出自这个故事，原指被砍脚的人很多，致使鞋价贱而踊价贵，后形容刑罚既重又滥，也比喻犯罪的人多。古代专制制度下君王享有至高无上的权力，臣子如果直言劝谏，往往谏不成反伤身，于是有无数的委婉之谏、比喻之谏流传下来。晏子在近乎闲聊的对话中使景公自动减少了刑罚，常被作为善谏的典型例子。但韩非的看法高于晏子，因为刑罚的好坏不在用刑的多少，而是用刑是否适当。当然了，用现在的标准来看，砍脚的确是一种不人道的刑罚。

THE SHOES FOR THE FEETLESS ARE MORE EXPENSIVE THAN NORMAL SHOES

Duke Jing of Qi visited Yanzi and suggested to the wise minister, "Your residence is too small and too close to the fair, so the environment is not good enough. Please move to the garden in Yuzhang." Yanzi bowed to the duke twice and declined, "My family is poor, so we have to depend on the fair for food. As we have to go to the fair in the morning and in the evening, we can't live too far away from it." Duke Jing said with a smile, "Since your family are familiar with market prices, do you know what is expensive and what is cheap?" Duke Jing imposed a great variety of punishments then, so Yanzi answered, "The shoes for those whose feet were cut off are expensive, while normal shoes are cheap." Duke Jing asked in bewilderment, "What's the reason for that?" Yanzi answered,

"Because there are far too many punishments for the people. Since there are too many people whose feet were cut off as punishment, there is a great demand for the kind of special shoes they wear. Therefore, those shoes are expensive while normal shoes are cheap." Duke Jing was so shocked that color drained from his face. Then he said, "Such being the case, I'm probably too cruel!" As a result, he abolished five kinds of punishments. Nevertheless, Han Feizi doesn't see eye to eye with Yanzi's counsel. He says, "When Yanzi said that the shoes for those whose feet were cut off as punishment were expensive, he was not telling the truth from his heart. He said so because he wanted to persuade Duke Jing to stop using too many punishments, which showed his lack of knowledge about how to run a state. If the punishments are reasonable, there can never be enough of them; if they are not reasonable, it is not a problem whether there should be more or fewer punishments. Yanzi didn't persuade Duke Jing to examine the appropriateness of the punishments, but to indiscriminately reduce the punishments instead — that was a mistake as he didn't understand the methods of governing a state. If one cherishes weeds, he will do harm to crops; if one is lenient towards robbers, he will do harm to good people. Now that the punishment was reduced, and generous and benevolent policies were put into effect, the state would suffer the consequences of benefiting the evil but harming the good. Therefore, that is not the way to run a state."

The idiom "The shoes for the feetless are more expensive than normal shoes" comes from this story and originally means that since too many people got their feet cut off, the shoes for these people became expensive while normal shoes were cheap. Later, this idiom expresses the idea that there are too many severe punishments or that there are too many people breaking the law. Under the autocratic monarchy of the ancient times, the monarch enjoyed supreme power. If the ministers dared make admonishments directly, they generally wouldn't succeed and might invite trouble for themselves. As a result, a lot of tactful and metaphorical admonishments for the monarchs were made successfully and passed down. Yanzi made Duke Jing reduce the punishment willingly in a casual talk, which became a good example for a successful admonishment. But Han Feizi thought deeper than Yanzi, for the desirability of a punishment lies not in its amount but in its appropriateness. Of course, cutting a man's feet off is an inhuman punishment by today's standards.

62. 子产察奸

　　子产是春秋时有名的贤臣，曾长期担任郑国的丞相。有一次，子产早晨乘车外出，经过东巷的大门时，听见有一个妇女在哭泣，从她哭泣中夹杂的诉说，知道她是在哭自己刚死去的丈夫。这时，子产按住车夫的手，示意停车，再仔细听听。过了一会儿，子产派官吏把那个妇女抓来审问，结果得知就是她亲手绞死了自己的丈夫。后来车夫向子产请教说："您是凭什么知道那妇女是凶手的呢？"子产说："她的哭声显得很恐惧。一般说来，大家对于亲爱的人，他刚生病时感到忧愁，临死时感到恐惧，已死后就感到悲哀。现在她哭已死去的丈夫，不是感到悲哀却是感到恐惧，所以我知道她一定有奸情。"当时许多人读了这个故事，都十分赞叹子产的智慧聪明，但韩非却不以为然。他说："子产治国，难道不是太多事了吗？奸情一定要等亲自听到和看到，然后才了解，那么郑国查到的奸情就太少了。不任用主管狱讼的官吏，不采用多方面考察验证的政治措施，不彰明法度，而依靠竭尽聪明、劳心费神去获知奸情，难道不是缺少治国的方法吗？况且世间事物众多，个人的智慧是有限的，寡不胜众，个人的智慧难以普遍地了解万物，所以要利用事物来治理事物。臣下多而君主少，少不胜多，君主难以普遍地了解每一个臣下，所以要依靠人来了解人。……《老子》说：'凭借个人智慧来治理国家，这是国家的灾难。'大概就是说的子产这种做法吧。"

这里，韩非清楚地说明了统治者不必"事必躬亲"的道理。在中国历史上，人们常把"事必躬亲"的官员视为勤政敬业的好官、清官。三国时期的诸葛亮，集军政大权于一身，大至军国事务，小至校对文书、检查账目、处罚士兵等，都亲自裁决，一一过问。《资治通鉴》中有这样一则记载：诸葛亮曾亲自校对登记册，主簿杨颙知道后劝他："治国和治家一样，都应该有规则和秩序，上下职务不能相互侵犯。"他打了个比方，有位主人派男仆从事耕地，女仆烧火做饭，鸡管报时，狗管看家防盗，牛负重载，马跑长途，他自己的任务就是查看监督。如果家里的各项工作都没有旷废，各种需要都能得到满足，他就从容地去休息了。忽然有一天早上，这位主人打算亲自去做所有的活儿，去干种种琐事，结果累得疲惫不堪，却一无所成。问题不在于他的智慧不如男女奴仆和鸡狗牛马，而在于"丢了当家做主的方法"。杨颙的比方和劝说，真可谓中肯之极。可惜诸葛亮并没有听进去，最后"出师未捷身先死"，因过度劳累而以身殉职。看起来，事必躬亲，终日忙碌，却常常得不到好的效果。

ZICHAN DETECTS THE PLOY OF A MURDER

Zichan was a well-known talented minister in the Spring and Autumn Period.

He acted as the prime minister of the State of Zheng for a long time. Once Zichan went out by carriage in the morning. When he passed by the gate of the East Neighborhood, he heard a woman crying. From her sobbing words he knew that she was crying for her newly deceased husband. At that moment, Zichan pressed the driver's hand, signalling to stop the carriage for him to listen more carefully. After a while, Zichan sent an official to take the woman for questioning. It turned out that the woman had strangled her husband. Later, the driver asked Zichan, "How can you know that the woman is the murderer?" Zichan said, "Her crying seemed to show that she was very frightened. Generally speaking, we feel worried when our beloved ones turn ill, feel frightened when they are about to die, and feel sad after their death. Now when she was crying for her deceased husband, she didn't feel sad but felt frightened, so I knew she must have committed adultery." When many people read about this story then, they all praised Zichan for his wisdom, but Han Feizi didn't give it high regard. He said, "If Zichan ran the state in this way, wasn't he too meddlesome? If the ploys of murder had to be disclosed after hearing and seeing them in person, then there would be too few cases found out in this way in the State of Zheng. He didn't appoint officials in charge of trials, didn't adopt political measures for investigation from various aspects, didn't make the laws clear to the people, but tried to solve murder cases by exhausting his wisdom and energy and racking his own brains. Wasn't he lacking in ways to run a state? Besides, there are too many things in the world, and an individual's wisdom is limited. As the few are no match for the many, an individual can't expect to rely on his wisdom to understand everything generally. Therefore one should learn to make use of things to run things. The ministers are many while the monarchs are few. Since the few are no match for the many, a monarch can hardly know every minister generally, so he should depend on people to know people … *Laozi* says, 'Running a state by an individual's wisdom is a disaster for that state.' It probably refers to such practice of Zichan."

Han Feizi clearly explains the idea that the ruler doesn't have to "take care of every single matter personally." In the Chinese history, people often regarded those officials who "took care of every single thing personally" as good, honest and upright ones who did public service with diligence and dedication. Zhuge Liang (181–234, famous strategist) in the Three Kingdoms Period enjoyed both political and military power and made every decision for everything by himself, from important state affairs to minor events such as proof-reading documents, checking accounts and punishing soldiers. In the book *Comprehensive Mirror to Aid in Government* there is such a story. Zhuge Liang once proof-read the register by himself. When the assistant magistrate, Yang Yu, knew it, he persuaded Zhuge Liang, "Running a state is like running a family, as both should follow regulations and orders, with the superior and the subordinate refraining from interfering with each other's duties." Yang Yu went on to make an analogy. A master asked his male servant to do farming, his female servant to cook meals, the rooster to crow, the dog to guard the house, the ox to carry heavy loads and the horse to go long journeys. The task for himself was to inspect and supervise them. If every work in his home was not neglected and all the needs could be satisfied, he then went to have a leisurely rest. One morning, this master suddenly wanted to do all the jobs and to deal with all the trifles by himself. Consequently, he was worn out but had nothing done. The problem is not that his wisdom couldn't match that of his servants and animals, but that he "lost the way to be the master of the house." Yang Yu's persuasion was made to the point, but it was a pity that Zhuge Liang didn't follow the good advice. Eventually Zhuge Liang "died before winning a single victory" — overworking himself and thus losing his life when still busy with his duty. It seems that to take care of every single thing personally or to be on the go all day usually does not turn out well.

63. 守株待兔

  宋国有个农夫，一天正在田里耕作，田中有一个树桩。这时有一只野兔大概受惊了，奔跑时慌不择路，不偏不倚一头撞在树桩上，碰断了脖子，死了。于是这个宋人美美地饱餐了一顿兔子肉。从此，他便放下手中的农具，不再种地，整天守在那树桩旁边，等待奇迹的出现，希望再次捡到死兔子。他当然不可能再得到兔子，结果田地也荒芜了，自己也成了宋国的一个笑话。对此，韩非感叹道："现在假使还要用先王的政治来治理当代的民众，那就无疑属于守株待兔了。"

  成语"守株待兔"就是从这个寓言故事来的，常比喻怀着侥幸心理希图不经过努力而得到成功，也比喻死守狭隘经验，不知变通。韩非用这则寓言来譬喻守旧者的愚蠢可笑。守旧人物首先是指死守旧制度、按旧办法治理国家的君主和大臣，他们无视礼崩乐坏的大趋势，更不想走变法图强之路，而是拘泥旧制，抱残守缺。然而，作为圣人则应该不期望照搬古法，不死守陈规旧俗，而是根据当前社会的实际情况，进而制定相应的政治措施。

农夫之所以荒了土地，为人所笑，乃是因为他混淆了偶然与必然，心存侥幸。在现实生活中，人人都可能碰上点好运气。这时，我们就应该想想事情的发生有什么必然性，这种必然性产生的条件是什么，人应该怎样按照必然性来支配自己的行动，不要闹出"守株待兔"那样的笑话。

STANDING BY A TREE STUMP WAITING FOR A HARE

There was a farmer in the State of Song. One day he was doing farm work in the field, where there was a tree stump. At that moment, a hare probably got frightened, so it fled on any path it could find without heeding which it chose. As a result, it banged its head right against the tree stump, broke its neck and died. Then this man of Song had a delicious meal of hare meat. From then on, he put down his farm tools and stopped doing farm work. He waited by the tree stump every day, in the hope that the miracle would happen again so that he could get another hare. Of course, he could no longer get any hare. At last, his field was overgrown with weeds, and he himself became a laughing stock in the State of Song. As for this, Han Feizi sighs, "Now if we still employed the ancient kings' methods to govern the people at the present time, we would undoubtedly become the man who stood by a tree stump waiting for a hare."

The idiom "Standing by a tree stump waiting for a hare" comes from this allegory. It describes the silliness of those who wish to win by a fluke without working hard. It also describes the silliness of those who stick to limited, outdated experience without making any adaptation to the present situation. Han Feizi uses this allegory to describe the absurdity of fogyism. The leading figures of fogyism in Han Feizi's mind are those monarchs and ministers who stuck to the old political systems and ran their states according to the old methods, completely oblivious of the social tendency of declining rites and rituals at the time; they would rather follow the outdated rules and regulations blindly than initiate reforms to strengthen their states. On the contrary, a wise man should not expect to copy the ancient ways or stick to old conventions; instead, he should help to devise new political measures based on the actual situations at the present time.

The reason why the farmer made his field lie waste and himself laughed at is that he confused an accidental phenomenon with a certainty and hoped to take unlikely chances. In the real life, everyone can get lucky now and then. At the lucky moment, we should consider why and in what circumstances the lucky event becomes possible, and in what ways we should coordinate our actions based on that possibility. Otherwise, we would certainly hold ourselves to ridicule by "standing by a tree stump waiting for a hare".

64. "直躬"与孝子

　　楚国有个被称作"直躬"的人,这并不是他的真实姓名,而是他的外号,取自当时人对他的评价,意思是说他"立身行事坦白直率"。有一次,"直躬"的父亲偷了人家的羊,他便到令尹那儿告发,令尹说:"杀掉他!"因为令尹认为这人对君主虽算正直,而对其父亲却属不孝,结果判了他死罪。由此看来,君主的忠臣倒成了父亲的逆子。鲁国有个人跟随君主去打仗,屡战屡逃。孔子向他询问原因,他说:"我家中有年老的父亲,我死后就没人养活他了,所以要在战场上逃跑。"孔子认为他是孝子,便推举他做了官。由此看来,父亲的孝子恰恰是君主的叛臣。所以令尹杀了"直躬",楚国的坏人坏事就没有人再向上告发了;孔子奖赏逃兵,鲁国人作战就会轻易地投降逃跑。

　　韩非对令尹、孝子和孔子都是持反对态度的,说他们把是非曲直都搞乱了,而对"直躬"的行为则很赞赏。令尹的判决来源于当时社会上流行的儒家所讲的"亲亲相隐"，即亲属间相互为对方隐瞒罪行的观念。《论语·子路》说，叶公告诉孔子说："我住的地方有个坦白直率的人，他父亲偷了羊，他便向官府告发。"孔子说："我们那里坦白直率的人跟你们的不同：父亲替儿子隐瞒，儿子替父亲隐瞒——直率就在这里面了。"孟子也说，假设舜的父亲杀了人，舜作为天子，应该命令执法官将自己的父亲抓起来。但舜作为儿子，他就应该背起父亲偷偷逃到海边没有人的地方住下，抛弃天下就如同抛弃不值钱的破鞋子一样。

"直躬"与孝子的故事，反映了历史上对"亲亲相隐"和"以法治国"两者关系是有不同看法的。在中国的历代法典中都有对"亲亲相隐"加以支持的有关规定，西方人也有类似的观念，古希腊有"容隐"、主张为亲属隐罪的观念，近现代以来包括英、法、德、美在内的一些西方国家的现行法律体系，也在限定范围内规定"近亲属有拒绝作证的权利"，并且还有对某些明知亲属犯罪而故意不告发、包庇藏匿、帮助脱逃、作伪证等行为"不处罚或减轻处罚"的规范。看来，怎样认识、发展中国传统文化中的"亲亲相隐"观念，是需要仔细斟酌的。

FILIAL LOYALTY VERSUS RULE OF LAW

In the State of Chu, there was a man called Straight Stature, which was not his real name but his nickname derived from people's evaluation of him that he "behaved frankly and straightforwardly". Once the father of Straight Stature stole a sheep, and Straight Stature went to the local magistrate to report it. The local magistrate said, "Kill him." The local magistrate finally passed out the death penalty for Straight Stature as he believed that Straight Stature kept loyal to the monarch but betrayed his own father. In that case, a monarch's loyal subject became a father's unfilial son. A man in the State of Lu followed the monarch to fight in war, but he escaped every time he fought a battle. Confucius asked him about the reason. He said, "I have an old father at home. If I die, there is no one to support him any longer, so I have to escape from the battle." Confucius thought he was a filial man and recommended him to be an official. Judging from this, the father's filial son was exactly a traitor to the monarch. Therefore, after the local magistrate killed Straight Stature, no one would report any evil person or matter to the government; after Confucius rewarded the deserter, the soldiers of Lu would easily surrender or escape.

Han Feizi disapproves of the local magistrate, the filial son and Confucius, saying that they confused right with wrong, but highly appreciates the behavior of Straight Stature. The death penalty for Straight Stature made by the local magistrate was based on the prevailing Confucian concept then that "relatives should cover each other", namely, relatives should conceal each other's crime. In *The Analects,* the Duke of Ye told Confucius, "A righteous man who lived in my neighbourhood reported his father's theft of a sheep to the local government." Confucius said, "The righteous people living in our place are different from those in your place. Fathers conceal their sons' crimes, and sons conceal their fathers' crimes as well — that is where righteousness resides." Mencius also said that if the father of Shun (a legendary emperor in the Chinese mythology) committed homicide, Shun should order the law enforcer to catch his father, but as a son, he should carry his father on his back and escape secretly to the uninhabited seaside, where he would settle down and live a secluded life, discarding the throne as if discarding worthless worn-out shoes.

The stories of Straight Stature and the filial son deserting from battle reflect the different views about the relationship between filial loyalty and rule of law. In the legal codes of the Chinese feudal dynasties, there are relevant stipulations supporting the idea that "relatives should cover each other". Similar ideas can be found in the West. In ancient Greece, there was the idea of "tolerance to concealment", which means that one is allowed to hide his relative's crimes. In the modern legal systems of some Western countries, such as the United Kingdom, Germany, France and the United States, there are relevant clauses stipulating that "a person has the right to reject testimony against his close relatives" under limited circumstances; in addition, there are clauses stipulating that "a person receives no or reduced penalty" if he knows about his close relative's crime but deliberately remains tacit, provides hiding place or means of escape for the suspect, or commits perjury. It seems that the old Chinese idea that "relatives should cover each other" is still viable in the present day and demands to be rediscovered and reassessed.

65. 以貌取人失之子羽，以言取人失之宰予

澹台子羽有着君子的仪表，孔子以为他是真君子，就收他为徒；同他相处时间长了，却发现他的品行和他的容貌很不相称。宰予说起话来非常文雅，孔子相信他是真文雅，就收他为徒；同他相处时间长了，却发现他的智力远不及他的口才。因此孔子感叹说："按照容貌取人吧，在子羽身上行不通；按照言谈取人吧，在宰予身上行不通。"

俗话说，"人不可貌相，海水不可斗量。"即使以孔子那样的聪明睿智，也还有看走眼的时候。韩非把这件事引申到君主任用人才上面去，指出："现在流行起来的巧辩大大超过了宰予，而当代君主听起话来又比孔子还要眩惑；因为喜欢他的言论，就去任用他这个人，这怎么能不出差错呢？"君主误用能言善辩之徒而造成恶果，最显著的两个例子莫过于孟卯和赵括了。魏国听信了孟卯的辩辞，结果造成在秦、魏华阳之战中孟卯所领魏军十三万全军覆没的惨祸；赵国听信了赵括的纸上谈兵，结果酿成长平之战被秦国坑杀四十余万士兵的灭顶之灾。这都是"以言取人"的惨痛教训。

要透过表面的容貌和语言去真正了解一个人，常常是很困难的。对此韩非提出的办法是用实践来检验。他说："只看人的相貌和衣着，只听他说话议论，孔子也难以断定其任职才能；让他在官位上试一试，考察他办事的成效，就是平常人也能分辨出愚智。"除了靠实践，还有一个办法就是靠时间。孔子同澹台子羽和宰予相处时间长了，自然就会对他们有进一步的、更合乎事实的认识，这就是俗话所说的"路遥知马力，日久见人心"。

JUDGING A PERSON BY HIS LOOKS OR HIS TALKS

Tantai Ziyu had gentlemanlike looks, so Confucius thought he was a real gentleman and took him as a disciple. But after spending some time with Ziyu, Confucius found that the disciple's conduct could not match his looks. Zaiyu was genteel in speech, so Confucius believed that he was really genteel and took him as a disciple. But after spending some time with Zaiyu, Confucius found that the disciple's wisdom could hardly match his eloquent speech. Therefore, Confucius sighed, "Judging a person by looks doesn't work with Ziyu; judging a person by talks doesn't work with Zaiyu."

As the saying goes, "As the sea cannot be measured with a bushel, people cannot be judged by their appearances." Even though Confucius was so wise and sensible, sometimes he might make wrong judgements. Han Feizi uses this story to explain by what standards monarchs should choose talented people for important posts. "The prevailing flowery speeches today have already surpassed the eloquent speech of Zaiyu, and the monarchs today are even more carried away by flowery speeches than Confucius by Zaiyu's speech. If a monarch employs a man simply because of the latter's eloquence, how can this not go wrong?" The best examples of the tragic results brought about by the monarch's wrong appointment of glib-tongued men are the cases of Meng Mao and Zhao Kuo. The State of Wei believed Meng Mao's argument and suffered the great disaster of losing all the Wei troops of a hundred and thirty thousand soldiers led by Meng Mao in the battle at Huayang between the State of Qin and the State of Wei. The State of Zhao relied on Zhao Kuo's armchair strategy and suffered the catastrophe that Zhao's troops of over four hundred thousand soldiers were buried alive by the Qin troops after the failure of the battle at Changping. These are bitter lessons resulting from "judging a person by his speech".

It is usually very difficult to truly know a person by his looks or talks. As for this, Han Feizi puts forward the way of judging a person by practice. He says, "Only by looking at one's looks and clothes or by listening to one's talks, even Confucius had difficulty judging a person's ability. To let him have a try in an official position and then examine what he has done, even an ordinary man can tell the foolish from the wise." Besides practice, another way is to test by time. After spending some time with Tantai Ziyu and Zaiyu, Confucius naturally had a better and more reasonable understanding of them. That is described in a Chinese saying, "The strength of a horse is tested with the distance travelled, and the heart of a person is seen with the passage of time."

66. 驭下之术（一）：心理威慑

　　庞敬是个县令，有一次，他任命了一位管理市场的人员——市者。在将派遣这个市者出发上任时，庞敬又特地召回另一位市场管理人员——公大夫来见自己。当市者和公大夫都在场后，他先把市者派走。后来公大夫又站了一会儿，庞敬其实并没有什么可告诫的，最后还是就这样让他走了。市者却以为县令庞敬后来对公大夫有所指示，而对自己不予信任，因此再不敢作奸犯科。

　　庞敬的行为，是一种典型的驭下之术。管理者使属下互不信任，互相监视，是古今常见的手段。但这也容易带来弊端，属下不能通力合作，由于内耗而降低办事效率。庞敬其实并没有让公大夫监视市者，但其行为给市者在心理上造成了威慑，起到了同样的效果，其手段更加高明。

THE ART OF MANAGEMENT (I): PSYCHOLOGICAL DETERRENCE

Pang Jing was a county magistrate. Once he appointed a market administrator called "the market manager". When he was about to send the market manager to take office, Pang Jing called back another market administrator called "the market lord" to see him. When the market manager and the market lord were both present, he first sent the market manager away. Then the market lord stood there for a while. Pang Jing didn't actually say anything before sending the market lord away at last. The market manager thought the county magistrate didn't trust him and had given some instructions to the market lord after he left, so he didn't dare to violate the law or take bribes.

Pang Jing's action is a good example of managing his subordinates. It is a common practice for the superior to make his subordinates watch each other in distrust. But this can also lead to some problems: the subordinates don't cooperate with each other whole-heartedly, and the work efficiency is decreased owing to internal friction. Pang Jing didn't actually asked the market lord to keep an eye on on the market manager, but he used an even smarter strategy by imposing some psychological deterrence on the market manager.

67. 驭下之术(二): 微服考察

　　宋国的太宰派遣年轻的侍仆到市场上去, 等他回来后问道: "你在市场上见到了些什么? "侍仆回答说: "没见到什么。"太宰说: "不会吧, 你总该见到了一些什么东西吧? "侍仆回答说: "市场南门外牛车很多, 仅能勉强通行。"太宰就告诫他说: "不准告诉别人我问你的话。"于是太宰召来市场官吏并责骂说: "市场门外为什么有那么多的牛屎? "市场官吏很奇怪太宰怎么知道得这么快, 于是开始惶恐小心地对待职守了。

　　战国时代韩国的国君韩昭侯, 有一次派人骑马去巡视县城。使者回报时, 昭侯问道: "你看见了些什么? "使者回答说: "没看见什么。"昭侯说: "你起码见到了一些什么东西吧? "使者回答说: "在南门外, 有条小黄牛正在大路左边吃禾苗。"昭侯听后, 对使者说: "不准泄露我问你的事。"接着昭侯就发布命令说: "现在正值禾苗生长的时候, 我们老早就定下命令，禁止牛马跑进百姓的农田里面破坏庄稼。但官吏们却不把这命令当回事，有很多牛马跑到农田里面去了。现在马上把这个数目报上来！有漏掉的，我将重重治罪。"于是很快地东、西、北三面的数目都报了上来。然而昭侯却说："不够吧，还有。"经官吏再去细查，才发现南门外的小黄牛。官吏们都认为昭侯明察，于是加倍惶恐小心地对待职守，再不敢为非歹了。

战国时卫国的君主卫嗣公，为了考察地方的官吏们是否尽到职责，就派人假扮成客商的模样，到某关口的集市上去。结果管理关市的官吏故意刁难这假扮的客商，他就用金子贿赂了官吏，于是官吏才放他过关。当然，这些事情也就全部被报告给卫嗣公了。后来，卫嗣公接见这位官吏时，一副轻描淡写的样子对他说道："某月某天某个时候，有个客商经过你管理的地方，给了你金子，你才放他走的。有这回事吧？"官吏听后非常恐惧，赶紧承认了这件事，认为嗣公具有明察秋毫的神奇本领。

卫嗣公的时候，有人受命在一个县令身边窥探。县令无意中掀起床上的褥子时，露出了下面垫着的很破旧的席子。窥探的人当然马上就报告了卫嗣公。卫嗣公随即派人送给这位县令新的席子，说："我听说你今天掀起褥子时，露出的席子很破旧，特此赏赐给你新的席子。"县令非常吃惊，认为卫嗣公真是个神明人物。

宋太宰、韩昭侯、卫嗣公派人微服考察，从而发现下边人的失职、渎职甚至为非作歹，这是统治者常用的一种"术"。通过各种方法的考察，在有关下属面前制造出其"无所不知"的假象，给属下以威慑，使臣下由神秘感而带来畏惧，从而不敢胡作非为。这种术最初还只是偶尔为之，没有形成制度，没有设立专门机构。后世集权统治下的特务制度就厉害多了。明朝时，皇帝的权力空前加强，为了加强对全国臣民的监视，明太祖朱元璋设立特务机构锦衣卫，特务遍布全国，监视大臣们的生活细节，直报朱元璋，以便随时清肃他想铲除的臣子。明成祖又设立东厂，明宪宗再设西厂，合称"厂卫"，由宦官统领，暗中监视察听官员们的一言一行。到了清代的雍正皇帝，由于他夺取了嫡系皇子的皇位，树敌遍布朝野，为既保绝对权力又保绝对安全，他深居大内，开创了几乎完全凭密折统治天下的密折政治。

THE ART OF MANAGEMENT (II): INSPECTIONS IN DISGUISE OR BY PROXY

The grand steward of the State of Song sent a young servant to go to the market. When the servant came back, the grand steward asked, "What did you see in the market?" The servant answered, "Nothing in particular." The grand steward said, "That is not possible. You should always see something." The servant answered, "There were many ox wagons outside the south gate of the market, and I could hardly pass through." The grand steward then warned the servant, "Don't tell others about what I asked you." After that he called in the officials in charge of the market and scolded them, "How come there is so much ox excrement outside the gate of the market?" The officials were so surprised that the grand steward got the news so quickly. Therefore, they started to feel afraid and became very careful about their duty.

Marquis Zhao of Han in the Warring States Period once sent a messenger to go on an inspection tour around a county by horse. When the messenger came back, Marquis Zhao asked, "What did you see?" The messenger said, "Nothing in particular." The marquis said, "You should have seen something at least." The messenger said, "There was a yellow calf eating the seedling of the crops on the left side of the road outside the south gate." Hearing this, Marquis Zhao said to the messenger, "Don't let out what I asked you." After that, Marquis Zhao issued an order: "Now it is at a time when the seedlings are growing. And we have already given the order before that oxen and horses should not run into farmlands and ruin the crops. But the officials didn't take this order seriously, and many cattle and horses went into the farmlands. Report the number of the stray oxen and horses at once! If any is left out, I will give out severe punishment." Therefore, the number from the east, the west and the north were all reported soon. However, Marquis Zhao said, "That is not enough. There should be more." Then the officials went to check carefully again and found the yellow calf outside the south gate at last. The officials all thought Marquis Zhao had keen observation, so they put more efforts into fulfilling their duties with great diligence and no longer dared to engage in corruption.

Duke Si of the State of Wei in the Warring States Period sent a man disguised as a merchant to the market of a certain customs station, in order to inspect if the local officials could fulfill their duty. It turned out that the official in charge of the market purposely make difficulties for the merchant in disguise and wouldn't let the merchant pass without taking a bribe of gold. Of course, all was soon reported to Duke Si of Wei. Later, when meeting this official, Duke Si of Wei said to him with a casual manner, "A merchant passed by your area and wasn't allowed to get by until he gave you some gold. Is that true?" Hearing this, the official was extremely frightened and admitted it at once, believing that Duke Si had uncanny ability to know the tiniest things.

During the reign of Duke Si of Wei, a man was asked to spy upon a county magistrate. When the county magistrate unwittingly lifted the mattress on his bed, a worn-out mat was revealed. The spying man reported it to Duke Si of Wei at once. Duke Si of Wei immediately ordered someone to send a new mat to this county magistrate, saying, "I heard that a worn-out mat was revealed when you lifted the mattress, so I specially grant this new mat to you." The county magistrate was very surprised and thought that Duke Si of Wei had godlike wisdom.

The grand steward of Song, Marquis Zhao of Han and Duke Si of Wei all sent out their men to make inspection tours in disguise and thus found out that the subordinates neglected their duty and even committed crimes. That is an "art" of personnel management used by ancient Chinese monarchs. By learning the specific situations through inspections in disguise or by proxy, the monarchs created an illusion of mysterious "omniscience" that instilled a sense of awe and fear in the minds of the subordinates and subjects, so that the latter believed that they were constantly watched and wouldn't dare to do bad things. This method was at first used occasionally, as there were no formal systems or special offices for that purpose. Later, the centralized governments of the feudal dynasties employed an imperial espionage system, which was much more thorough and effective. In the Ming Dynasty (1368 – 1644), the emperor enjoyed an unprecedented level of supreme power. Zhu Yuanzhang (1328 – 1398), or Emperor Taizu of the Ming Dynasty, founded a secret agency called "the Imperial Guards", which sent out spies all over the country to spy on every detail of the ministers and officials, so that the emperor could find out and eliminate his opposition at any time. Later, Emperor Chengzu of the Ming Dynasty founded "the East Depot" and Emperor Xianzong of the Ming Dynasty founded "the West Depot", both secret agencies. With the help of the so-called "Depots and Guards", a force of spies headed by the imperial eunuchs kept close surveillance of what the officials said and did. In the Qing Dynasty (1644 – 1911), since Emperor Yongzheng (1678 – 1735) seized the throne from the crown prince and made enemies all over the imperial court, he always stayed in the inner palace and ruled the country solely with the help of secrets reports in order to keep his throne safe.

68. 驭下之术(三)：无所不知

　　东周君丢了玉簪，让官吏们去找，三天都没能找到。东周君又派人寻找，结果在居民的房子中间找到了。东周君说："我的官吏都不做事。找根玉簪，三天都找不到；我派人寻找，不到一天就拿回来了。"于是官吏都震恐不已，认为君主神明。

　　东周君下令寻找弯曲的手杖，官吏找了几天没能找到。东周君私下派人再找，不到一天就找到了。东周君就对官吏说："我就知道你们不干事情。弯曲的手杖很容易找，但你们却没能找到；我派人寻找，不到一天就找到了。你们怎么能算忠诚啊！"官吏们于是都惶恐小心地对待职守，认为东周君神明。

　　西门豹做邺县令，假装丢失了车辖，命令官吏寻找，结果没能找到。西门豹再派专人寻找，结果在居民的房子中间找到了。

　　这些玉簪、手杖和车辖等东西，无疑都是东周君和西门豹预先命人藏好的。通过这种手段，能给臣下制造出君上很"神明"、无所不能的假象，从而使臣下对君上更加敬畏和死心塌地。韩非用这些事例来说明君主用来控制臣下的七种手段即"七术"中的第六种"挟智（知）"，意为"凭借利用已经知道的事情"。《韩非子》说："拿已知的事去问别人，那么不知道的事也就知道了。深入了解一件事，许多隐情就都能辨明了。"

THE ART OF MANAGEMENT (III): ALL-KNOWING WISDOM

The emperor of the Eastern Zhou Dynasty lost his jade hairpin, so he asked the officials to look for it. But they couldn't find it after three days. Then the emperor sent his men to look for it again, and finally found it in a place among civilian houses. The emperor said, "None of my officials performs his duties. I only asked them to look for a jade hairpin, but they didn't find it after three days. I asked my men to look for it and had it back within a day." Consequently, the officials were all overwhelmed, holding the emperor like a god.

The emperor of the Eastern Zhou Dynasty ordered the officials to look for a crooked walking stick, but they didn't find it after several days. The emperor then personally asked someone to look for it and got it back within a day. The emperor said to his officials, "I already know that none of you perform your duties. A crooked walking stick is easy to find, but you couldn't find it. I personally asked someone to look for it, and he found it within a day. How could you regard yourselves as loyal?" Then all the officials started to feel afraid and became very careful about their duties, believing that the emperor was an all-knowing god.

When Ximen Bao acted as the magistrate in the county of Ye, he pretended to have lost a linchpin and then asked the officials to look for it. Naturally the linchpin couldn't be found. Ximen Bao then sent a certain man to look for it again, and found it in a place among civilian houses at last.

The jade hairpin, the walking stick and the linchpin were undoubtedly hidden there at the order of the emperor and Ximen Bao beforehand. With this trick, they gave their subordinates an impression of "godlike all-knowing wisdom", which inspired the subordinates' diligence and devotion out of awe and fear. Han Feizi uses these instances to show the sixth of the "seven arts" that the monarch could employ in order to control his officials, namely, "holding wisdom", which means "making use of what is known". *Han Feizi* says, "If one asks others about what he has known, he will get to know what he hasn't known. If one looks into every matter in depth, many hidden things will be revealed."

69. 驭下之术（四）：引蛇出洞

韩昭侯包住手上留的长指甲，然后假装指甲掉了，很着急地到处寻找，于是近侍就割掉自己的指甲呈献给他。昭侯通过这件事来考察近侍是否忠诚。

子之做燕相，有一天坐在那里，子之撒谎说："咦，那跑出去的是什么？是白马吗？"侍从都说没看见。有一个人跑出去追赶，回来报告说："是白马。"子之通过这种方法去了解侍从中哪些人不诚实。

韩昭侯的故事也被用来说明君主用来控制臣下的七种手段中的第六种"挟智"。子之的故事则被韩非用来说明"七术"之第七种"倒言"。《韩非子》说："利用说反话、做反事来试探所怀疑的人和事，可能就会了解到实情。"君上有意"引蛇出洞"、"抛饵引鱼"，自己故意装糊涂而让下面的人猛表现自己，可以有效地试探出臣下是否忠诚老实。

THE ART OF MANAGEMENT (IV): DRAWING A SNAKE OUT OF ITS HOLE

Marquis Zhao of Han wrapped up his long fingernail and pretended to have lost it. Then he appeared to be very anxious to look for his fingernail. Therefore, a close attendant of Marquis Zhao cut his own fingernail and presented it to the marquis. Marquis Zhao used this trick to examine if his close attendants were loyal.

Zizhi was once the prime minister of the State of Yan. One day he sat there and lied, "Gee, what has just run out? Is it a white horse?" His attendants all said they hadn't seen it, but one man ran out to check and came back reporting, "It is a white horse." Zizhi used this trick to know who was dishonest among his attendants.

The story of Marquis Zhao of Han is also employed to show the sixth, "holding wisdom", of the "seven arts" the monarch could use to control his officials. Han Feizi uses the story of Zizhi to explain the seventh of the "seven arts", namely, "saying something opposite to the truth." *Han Feizi* says, "If one is suspicious about someone or something, he may try to beat around the bush by saying or doing what is opposite to the fact; in that way, one may get to know the actual situation." The monarch sometimes intentionally "draws the snake out of its hole" or "scatters bait to attract fish", with himself pretending to be confused so that his subordinates can behave themselves with great fervor. That can effectively help the monarch to detect whether his subordinates are loyal and honest.

70. 考察利害作明断

  战国韩昭侯的时候，有一次，厨师呈上饭食请他用膳，可昭侯却在已经煮熟的肉羹中发现了生的肝子，于是就召来厨师的助手，责骂他说："你为什么把生肝放到我的肉羹中？"厨师的助手叩头承认死罪，说："我私下想除掉那个主管大王膳食的厨师。"

  这个故事还有另一种说法是：韩昭侯有一次洗澡时，发现在热水中有小石子。昭侯问道："要是现在主管洗澡的官员被免职了，那么按规定有继任的人吗？"左右近侍回答说："有。"昭侯说："叫他来。"叫来后昭侯怒责他说："你为什么在热水里放小石子？"这个人没想到阴谋被识破，惶恐地认罪，回答说："如果主管洗澡的官员被免职，我就能够代替他，所以我在热水中放了小石子。"

  韩非用这个故事来说明君主常常会遇上的六种微妙的情况即"六微"之四"有反"。他说："事情发生了，如果有利可得，应当牢牢掌握它；如果有害，一定要从反面加以考察。因此明君考虑问题时，国家受害，就要察看谁能从中得到好处；臣下受害，就要考察与他利害相反的人。"表面看来，肉羹中有生肝和洗澡的热水里有小石子，这是主管膳食的厨师和主管洗澡的官员的失职，然而这两种情况都不合于常理，因为做坏事无利可得，昭侯所以不被表面简单的事实所迷惑，就是因为他认识到人与人之间利害关系的本质。

WEIGHING GAINS AND LOSSES TO MAKE A SOUND JUDGEMENT

During the reign of Marquis Zhao of Han in the Warring States Period, once a chef served food for the marquis, but the marquis found some raw liver in the already cooked meat broth. Then he called the chef's assistant over and scolded him, "Why did you put raw liver into my meat broth?" The chef's assistance kowtowed at once to admit his capital crime, "I privately wanted to get rid of the chef in charge of your meal."

There is another version of this story. When Marquis Zhao of Han had a bath, he found some small stones in the hot water. He then asked, "If the official in charge of bath is removed, is there anyone to take his place?" The attendants serving him said, "Yes, there is." The marquis said, "Call him in." When the man came, the marquis scolded him in anger, "Why did you put small stones in the hot water?" The man hadn't expected his scheme to be exposed, so he admitted his crime in a panic. He answered, "If the official in charge of bath is removed, I can take his place. So I put small stones in the hot water."

Han Feizi uses this story to explain the fourth of the six kinds of delicate situations that might face a monarch, namely, "six subtleties", called "weighing the opposite points of view." He says, "When something happens, if there is any benefit, one should grasp it tightly; if there is any harm, one should examine the matter from the opposite point of view. Therefore, when a wise monarch makes judgements, he should find out who is to get benefit if the state suffers from any loss; when his officials come to harm, he should examine those who may benefit from it." At first glance, the raw liver in the meat broth should be blamed on the chef in charge of the marquis's meal and the small stones in the hot water should be blamed on the official in charge of bath. However, such apparent attributions didn't make any sense, as the people responsible couldn't get any benefit from doing such wrongs. The reason why Marquis Zhao was not deceived by those frame-ups was that he understood the nature of the balance of gains and losses among the people.

71. 善于为自己辩护的厨师

　　晋文公有一次吃饭时，发现在厨师端上来的烤肉中有头发缠在上面。文公召来厨师，怒责他说："你想让我哽死啊，为什么把头发缠在烤肉上？"厨师叩头拜过两拜，请罪说："我有三条死罪：在磨刀石上磨刀，磨得像宝剑干将一样锋利，用来切肉，肉给切断了，但头发却不断，这是我的第一条罪状；拿起木棒穿透肉片却没有看见头发，这是我的第二条罪状；捧着烧得很旺的炉子，炭火都烧得通红，肉都熟了，头发却没有烧掉，这是我的第三条罪状。侍从中该没有暗中嫉恨我的人吧？"文公说："说得对。"就召来侍从讯问，果真是其中有人因嫉恨而陷害厨师，于是对他加以处罚。

　　这事的另一种说法是：晋平公请客喝酒，年轻的家臣端来烤肉，却有头发缠在肉上。平公催促下属去杀掉厨师，不得赦免。厨师大声呼叫："老天啊！我有三条罪状，死了也不知是犯的哪一条啊！"平公问：

"这话怎么说？"厨师回答说："我的刀很锋利，锋利得能斩断骨头，头发却斩不断，这是我的第一条死罪；用桑树烧成的木炭烤肉，肉烤熟了，该红的红了，该白的白了，头发却没有烧焦，这是我的第二条死罪；肉烤熟了，又眯着眼睛细看，头发缠在烤肉上，眼睛却看不见，这是我的第三条死罪。想来侍从中该有暗恨我的人吧？就这样把我杀掉不也太草率点了吗？"

这则故事里的厨师为自己脱罪之辞比前一则更加精彩。他不直接为自己辩解，不直接说自己无罪，厨师先顺着君主的意思表示自己有罪，再一一分析为什么说有罪，其荒谬不合常理之处自然就逐步显现出来，于是自然表明了自己是遭到了他人的陷害，最终再以反问暗示的方式指出谁是最大的嫌疑人。这个故事表现出的案件证据、逻辑关系等，对于审判案子的官员应该很有借鉴和学习价值，所以它甚至被作为经典案例编入了湖北江陵张家山出土的汉简法律文书《奏谳书》中。

THE WITTY CHEF IS GOOD AT DEFENDING HIMSELF

Duke Wen of Jin found a strand of hair on the roast meat served by his chef. Duke Wen called in the chef and scolded him in anger, "Do you want me to choke to death? Why did you wind hair around the roast meat?" The chef kowtowed twice and pleaded guilty with a speech, "I have committed three capital crimes. I ground the knife on the grindstone so that the knife was exceptionally sharp. However, I could cut off meat with it but couldn't cut off the hair with it. That was my first crime. I skewered the meat with a wooden stick, but I couldn't see the hair. That was my second crime. I made the stove burn so briskly that the charcoal fire became red-hot. However, when the meat was well-done, the hair wasn't burnt. That is my third crime. Isn't there anyone among the attendants who bears a secret grudge against me?" Duke Wen said, "You are right." Then he called in the attendants for questioning. It turned out one attendant framed up the chef out of hatred, so the duke punished him.

Another version of this story goes as follows. Duke Ping of Jin entertained some guests with drinks. When a young retainer brought the roast meat, some hair was found winding around it. Then Duke Ping ordered his subordinates to kill the chef without pardon. The chef cried out loudly, "Good heavens, I have three crimes, yet I won't know which crime I should die from." Duke Ping asked, "What do you mean?" The chef said, "My knife was very sharp, so sharp as to chop a bone in half, but it couldn't cut the hair in half. This is my first capital crime. I used charcoal made from mulberry trees to roast the meat, but when the meat was well-done, with some parts becoming red and some parts becoming white as they were supposed to be, the hair had somehow survived the fire. This is my second capital crime. When the meat was well-done, I strained my eyes to examine it carefully, but I couldn't see the hair winding around it. This is my third capital crime. Perchance there might be someone among the attendants who hates me secretly? Are you behaving too rashly if you kill me like this?"

This chef's defense for himself is even more brilliant than the one in the previous story. He didn't defend himself directly and didn't even say that he was innocent. He first said he was guilty in agreement with the duke's opinion and then analyzed one detail after another to show why he was guilty, actually revealing the absurdity of his "guilt" and little by little indicating that he was framed up by others. At last, he used a rhetorical question to suggest who was the most likely suspect. This story has great value in helping legal officials to understand the methods of using evidence and logic in dealing with lawsuits, so it was regarded as a classical case and was even included in the bamboo-slip legal document of the Han Dynasty called *Collection of Cases for Discussion*, which was unearthed in Zhangjia Mountain of Jiangling in Hubei.

72. 费无极用计杀郤宛

　　春秋晚期楚国的费无极一向是"令尹"（当时楚国的最高官员）子常最亲近信任的人，但后来郤宛侍奉令尹，做了令尹的助手"左尹"。令尹子常非常喜欢郤宛。费无极感到郤宛威胁到了自己的地位，就设计了一个阴谋。他先对令尹说："您很喜欢郤宛，为什么不到他家去喝一次酒呢？"令尹说："好啊。"就让费无极先到郤宛家去置办酒席。郤宛满心欢喜，问费无极说："令尹屈尊光临我家，不胜荣幸，我该用什么东西答谢呢？"费无极给他出主意说："令尹为人非常高傲，恐怕很难有什么看得上眼的东西。不过他非常喜欢兵器，您一定要在这一点上小心顺从他。先快点把家中的兵器多搬些出来陈列在厅堂下面和院子门口！令尹来了一定会顺便观赏，然后你就可以顺势将这些兵器作为礼物进献给他。"郤宛就照办了。结果令尹子常到了郤宛家，在门口一看就大吃一惊，瞪着那些兵器说："这是什么啊？怎么回事？"费无极假作慌张地说："您危险了，赶紧离开这里！看样子郄宛是不安好心啊，事情还不知会怎样呢！"令尹非常愤怒，马上发兵讨伐郄宛，杀了郄宛全家。

这可以说是一个典型的"借刀杀人"的诡计。此计看似设计周密、难以提防，但它完全是以两位受害人的互不沟通为前提的。如果令尹能够问一问郄宛，就算郄宛难以完全为自己解释，令尹恐怕也不会如此轻易地上当，成为被借之刀了。所以韩非一再强调君上对臣下的言论一定要加以验证，不能轻率地偏听偏信。

费无极是楚平王时声名狼藉的奸臣，是善于谗害同僚的阴谋家。他劝说平王娶了本该给太子建作妻子的秦女，将太子迁居城父，后来又进谗逼得太子出亡；伍奢向平王进谏，又因费无极进谗而使平王杀了伍奢父子。伍奢的另一个儿子伍子胥出奔吴国，向吴国借兵攻打楚国，使楚国遭到灭国之祸，平王也被伍子胥掘墓鞭尸。这段故事脍炙人口，是中国传统戏曲舞台上的常演剧目。

KILLING A RIVAL WITH A BORROWED KNIFE

Fei Wuji of the State of Chu had long been the most favored one of Zichang, the "chief minister" (the highest official in the State of Chu). However, Xi Wan began to serve as the assistant of the chief minister, "the left minister", and became a great favorite of Zichang. Fei Wuji felt that Xi Wan had posed a threat to his position, so he devised a conspiracy. He said to the chief minister Zichang, "Since you like Xi Wan, why don't you have a drink in his home?" The chief minister said, "All right." The chief minister asked Fei Wuji to go to Xi Wan's home to prepare a feast. Xi Wan was filled with joy and asked Fei Wuji, "It is my great honor that the chief minister condescends to come to my house. What can I offer to show my gratitude?" Fei Wuji advised, "The chief minister is very arrogant, so I am afraid that there won't be anything up to his taste. But he is extremely fond of weapons, so you must show obedience to him in this aspect. Please hurry up to gather as many weapons in your home as possible and display them in front of the hall by the gate of the yard. When the chief minister comes, he must conveniently have a look at them, and you can naturally offer him these weapons as gifts." Xi Wan did what he was told. As a result, when the chief minister came to Xi Wan's home, he was greatly shocked as he saw the display of weapons at the gate. He stared at the weapons and said, "What are these? What's the matter?" Fei Wuji pretended to be in a panic and said, "You are in danger now. Please leave here as quickly as possible! It seems that Xi Wan harbours no good intention. Who knows what will happen next?" The chief minister was very angry, so he sent his army to attack Xi Wan at once and eventually killed Xi Wan's whole family.

This is a good example of the scheme of "murdering a person with a borrowed knife." The scheme seemed to be carefully designed and hard to guard against, but it was entirely based on the prerequisite that the two victims had no communication between each other. If the chief minister could ask Xi Wan about it, he probably wouldn't be taken in so easily and become the borrowed knife after listening to Xi Wan's explanations. Therefore, Han Feizi repeatedly emphasizes that the monarch must examine the speeches of his officials and shouldn't listen only to one-sided views indiscreetly.

Fei Wuji was notorious for his treachery in framing up his peers in the reign of King Ping of Chu. He persuaded King Ping to marry a girl of Qin who was supposed to be the wife of the crown prince Jian. He also made the king move the crown prince to Chengfu and later forced the crown prince to escape into exile by slandering. A minister Wu She made admonishments to King Ping, but he and one of his sons were killed by the king due to Fei Wuji's slanderous words. Another son of Wu She, Wu Zixu, fled to the State of Wu to borrow troops to attack the State of Chu and triggered the downfall of the State of Chu. Eventually King Ping's body was dug out of his tomb and whipped by Wu Zixu. This story is so popular that it is often played on the stage of traditional Chinese operas.

73. 燕人受骗用屎浴身

　　燕国人李季喜欢出远门，经常不在家，他的妻子遂私下和某士通奸。有一次，李季突然出远门回来了，家里人事先都不知道。这时某士还在屋子里头，被堵了个正着。眼看事情就要败露，做妻子的非常害怕。她的女仆说："我有个办法：让这位公子光着身子，解开发结，径直走出门外，我们这些人都假装没看见。"于是那个奸夫听从她的计谋，光着身子，解开发结，快步跑出门外，一溜烟逃掉了。李季很奇怪地问："这是什么人？"家里所有的人都异口同声地说："没有人啊。"然后都拿一副很奇怪很无辜的眼神看着李季。结果李季自己倒心虚了，说："难道是我自己看见鬼了吗？"他妻子说："是啊，看来只能是这么回事了。""那怎么办呢？"妻子说："我听说，大白天遇到鬼是很不吉利的事情，只有用脏东西才能驱除脏东西，要用牲畜的屎来洗身才能去邪。"李季说："好吧。"于是家里人就拿牲畜的屎来给他洗了个"臭薰浴"。

　　这个燕国人并未中邪迷惑，却被小人蒙骗，用牲畜的屎来洗身，实在是让人哭笑不得。韩非用这个故事来说明"权势不可借"的道理。他的说法是："权力和威势不可以让给别人去用。君主失去一分权势，臣下就会把它当作百分去争。所以臣下得到君主的权势，力量就会强大起来；臣下力量强大起来了，朝廷内外就会被利用；朝廷内外一旦被利用，君主就会受到蒙蔽。"这个燕国人本是一家之主，就好比国君在一国中的地位。但妻子和某士通奸，那个奸夫俨然就成了实际上的一家之主，这个燕国人的权力和威势被奸夫借用去了，家里人都被奸夫利用，这个燕国人就只能任人摆布，任由家里人愚弄和欺骗了。

A BATH OF EXCREMENT

A man in the State of Yan called Li Ji liked to take long journeys, so he was often away from home. As a result, his wife had an affair with an esquire. Once Li Ji suddenly came back from a long journey, and nobody at home knew about it. At that moment, the esquire was still in the house, caught right on the spot. The adultery was about to be exposed, so Li Ji's wife was rather afraid. A maid said, "I've got an idea. Let this sir bare his body, untie his hair knot and walk straight out of the gate, and we all pretend not to see him." The esquire followed the advice. He walked quickly out of the gate with his body naked and his hair knot untied, and at last ran away swiftly. Li Ji asked in great surprise, "Who is that man?" The others all answered, "There is nobody." Then they all gave Li Ji a perplexed and innocent look. Li Ji felt unsure of himself and said, "Does it mean that I have seen a ghost?" His wife said, "Right. It seems that's the case." "What can I do?" His wife said, "I hear that it is ominous to see a ghost in the daytime. Dirty things can only be driven away with the help of equally dirty things, so you should bathe yourself with livestock excrement in order to get rid of the evil." Li Ji said, "All right." Then these people gave him a "smelly bath" with the dung of livestock.

The man of the State of Yan didn't get bewitched, but was deceived by those wicked people. It was rather pitiable for him to take a bath with the dung of livestock. Han Feizi uses this story to explain the idea that "one's power and influence can't be lent to others." He puts it like this: "Neither power nor influence can be lent to others. Once the monarch loses even one percent of his power and influence, his officials will regard it as a hundred percent and compete with each other to get it. When the officials get the monarch's power and influence, they will become stronger; when the officials become stronger, the imperial court, both inside and out, will be usurped; once the imperial court is usurped, the monarch would be deceived." This man of the State of Yan was actually the head of the family, a position just like that of the monarch in a state. But his wife committed adultery with an esquire, who then became the de facto head of the family. In this way, the power and influence of this man of Yan was lent to the esquire, who then enjoyed the loyalty of all people at home. Consequently, the man of Yan had to be manipulated by others, allowing himself to be fooled by those people at will.

74. 离间计

　　楚王派人到秦国去。派去的使者很能干，秦王很尊敬他。秦王说："敌国有贤人，就是我国的忧患。现在楚王的使者很能干，我很担心。"群臣劝谏说："凭大王的圣明和国家资财的丰富，而羡慕楚王手下的贤人，实在是没有多大必要啊。大王何不大力与这位使者结交，暗中加以笼络呢？您这样做了以后，这些情况一定会传回楚国去。等这位使者回到楚国，楚国国君以为他被外国利用，一定会处罚他。敌国就算有贤人，只要不被重用，也就没什么好担心的啦。"

　　孔子在鲁国执政，担任鲁国的司寇（相当于现在的司法部长），把鲁国治理得很好，达到了"路不拾遗"的程度。齐景公对此很忧虑，感到孔子留在鲁国做官对齐国不利。齐国大夫黎且对齐景公说："除去孔子，就像吹去毛发一样轻松容易。您何不一方面用厚禄高官招引孔子，同时又送给鲁哀公女子歌舞乐队来助长哀公的骄傲和虚荣心呢？哀公新得享乐，对政事一定懈怠，孔子一定会加以劝谏；他一劝谏，必定会遭到鲁哀公的厌恶，孔子自己也会失望，很容易就会跟鲁国断绝关系了。"景公说："很好。"就让黎且把四十八人的女子歌舞乐队送给哀公。哀公非常高兴，果然懒于治理政事。孔子劝谏，哀公不听，孔子就离开鲁国到楚国去了。

春秋时晋国的大臣叔向曾设计陷害周朝的贤人苌弘。有一次叔向出使周朝，预先伪造了一封书信，信中写道："苌弘致叔向：'你代我告诉晋君，我和他约定的时机已经到了，为什么还不快点带兵来攻打呢？'"随后叔向假装不小心把这封信遗失在周君的朝廷上，接着就急忙离去。周君看到了这封信，认为苌弘出卖周朝，就追究苌弘的罪责，最终杀掉了苌弘。

春秋时，郑桓公准备袭击郐国。他先打听到郐国的英雄豪杰、良臣智士的各种情况，把他们的名字全部记下，然后把郐国的良田写在他们名下，表示已经说好贿赂，又在他们名下写下官爵名称，表示已被收买。郑国假装在郐国都城的外城门外设了坛场，把有关记录埋在下面，再洒上鸡和猪的血来加以祭祀，搞得跟当时通行的结盟仪式一模一样。郐君当然很容易就发现了有关物证，于是认为国内将有大难，那些豪杰贤士已经与郑国结盟，将里通外国勾结作乱，郐君就把这些人全都杀掉了。这样一来，郑桓公再去偷袭郐国，很容易就攻取下来了。

春秋战国时期，各国君主对人才十分重视，求才若渴，秦国就是一例，最著名者如主持变法、使秦国国富兵强的商鞅是卫国人，集法家之大成者韩非是秦国不惜发兵攻打韩国才得到的。由此出发，韩非以大量生动的历史、传说故事告诫君主要提高警惕防范离间计。惑乱君主的视听，使之作出错误的判断，是实现离间计的途径；对敌国使用离间计，在国内要防止离间计，是帝王之术的一大手段。韩非讲的以上几个故事，都是以针对敌国贤人所使用的各种计谋为主题，反映了当时各国君主对于敌国贤人的态度：对于敌国的贤人，能够像由余（见下则故事）一样，想办法为我所用，是最好的；其次如晋人叔向陷害周人苌弘、郑桓公陷害邻国贤人那样，让他们被敌国除去；或如秦王离间楚国贤人一样，不让他在敌国受到重用；或如齐景公用计挑拨孔子与国君的关系，逼使其离开敌国。所以韩非提醒道，要防止"敌对的国家操纵本国储君和大臣的废立"。

A PLOT OF SOWING DISCORD

The King of Chu sent an envoy to the State of Qin. As the envoy was very talented, the King of Qin had great respect for him. The King of Qin said, "A talented man in the enemy state is a threat for my state. Now that the envoy of the King of Chu was very talented, I am very worried." The ministers persuaded the king, "There is really no need for you to admire the talented man working for the King of Chu since you possess great wisdom and national wealth. Why not try your best to make friends with this envoy and secretly win him over? When you do that, all the information will eventually make its way to the State of Chu. When this envoy returns, the King of Chu will believe that he has allied with other states and thus give him punishment. Even if there are talented men in the enemy state, there is nothing to worry about so long as they are not given important positions."

Once Confucius worked as the Minister of Law (the same as Attorney General in the present time) in the State of Lu. He ran the State of Lu so well that "no one picked up and pocketed anything left on the wayside." Duke Jing of Qi was very anxious about it and felt that it would pose a threat to the State of Qi if Confucius remained in office in the State of Lu. Li Qie, a senior official of the State of Qi, said to Duke Jing of Qi, "It is as easy as blowing away a piece of hair to get rid of Confucius. Why not appeal to Confucius with great wealth and power and at the same time send a band of women dancers, singers and musicians to Duke Ai of Lu to foster his pride and vanity? Once Duke Ai gets new enjoyment, he will surely relax his effort toward political affairs, and then Confucius will make admonishments. However, Confucius's admonishments will only lead to the duke's apathy and Confucius's disappointment. Then it will be very likely for Confucius to break away with the State of Lu." Duke Jing said, "Very good." Therefore, he asked Li Qie to send a band of 48 women dancers, singers and musicians to Duke Ai. Duke Ai was very pleased and became too lazy to deal with state affairs, as Li Qie had expected. Confucius admonished the duke, but the duke wouldn't listen, so Confucius left the State of Lu for the State of Chu.

In the Spring and Autumn Period, Shu Xiang, the minister of the State of Jin, once set up a plot against a talented man of the Zhou Dynasty named Chang Hong. Before going on a diplomatic mission to the Zhou Dynasty, Shu Xiang forged a letter saying, "Chang Hong salutes to Shu Xiang: 'Please tell the monarch of the State of Jin on my behalf that the time he and I agreed upon has been ripe. Why does he not hurry up to send troops to launch the attack?" Shu Xiang pretended to lose this letter in the palace of the emperor of the Zhou Dynasty carelessly and left in a hurry. The emperor read the letter and thought that Chang Hong had betrayed the Zhou Dynasty, so he convicted and killed Chang Hong.

In the Spring and Autumn Period, Duke Huan of Zheng prepared to launch an attack on the State of Kuai. He first inquired about the heroic generals and wise ministers in the State of Kuai and took down all their names. Then he allocated fertile farmlands of the State of Kuai under their names as "bribes", and wrote down titles of official positions under their names as "rewards". After that, the State of Zheng built an altar outside the outer gate of the capital of the State of Kuai, buried all the fabricated records under the alter, and offered sacrifices by spraying chicken and pig blood, as if holding a ceremony of alliance. The monarch of the State of Kuai, of course, easily found out the evidence and was alarmed that there would be a great disaster in his state, because he believed that those heroic generals and wise ministers had already formed an alliance with the State of Zheng and would conspire with the foreign state to rise in revolt from inside. Therefore, the monarch of Kuai killed all these men. Later, Duke Huan of Zheng launched a surprise attack on the State of Kuai and seized it very easily.

In the Spring and Autumn Period and the Warring States Period, the monarchs of various states all valued talented men and were eager to employ them. The State of Qin was one good example. Among the most well-known figures from outside Qin were Shang Yang, a man from the State of Wei who presided over the political reform and made the State of Qin wealthier and stronger, and Han Feizi, a leading philosopher of the Legalist school whom the State of Qin obtained at the price of dispatching troops to attack the State of Han. Starting from this point, Han Feizi uses a great many historical and legendary stories to warn the monarchs to raise their vigilance against the plot of sowing discord. The principal method of sowing discord is to confuse the monarchs so as to have them make wrong judgement. The monarchs should use such a plot against their enemy states and take precautions against such a plot in their own states. That was a great "art" of being a great monarch. All the above stories recounted by Han Feizi reflect a similar mentality of the monarchs towards the talented men in the enemy states: it would be best if the talented men could defect from the enemy state to this side, like Youyu (please see the next story); the second best option would be to deceive the enemy state to kill their talented men, like the case of Shu Xiang framing up Chang Hong and Duke Huan of Zheng framing up the heroic generals and wise ministers of the State of Kuai; other options would be preventing the talented men from being appointed important positions in the enemy state, as in the case of the King of Qin estranging the envoy of Chu from the King of Chu, or forcing the talented men to leave the enemy state, as in the case of Duke Jing of Qi sowing discord between Confucius and Duke Ai of Lu. Therefore, Han Feizi warns that the monarchs should be wary of "manipulations by enemy states on the appointment or dismissal of crown princes and ministers."

75. 秦穆公得由余

　　春秋时，西戎国王有次派由余对秦国进行国事访问。秦穆公接见由余后，问他说："我曾听说过治国之道，却没能亲眼看见，希望听您讲讲，古代君主得国失国常常是因为什么？"由余回答道："我曾经听说过，古代君主常常是因为俭朴而得国，因为奢侈而失国。"穆公感到很疑惑，由余随即长篇大论，对此作了一番详细的阐述，听得穆公连连点头称是，非常折服。由余退出后，秦穆公便把内史廖召来，询问他说："我听说，一国有圣人，对敌国来说就是忧患。现在由余就是圣人，我非常焦虑，应该怎么办？"内史廖回答说："我听说戎王占据的地方穷僻荒远，他没有听到过中原的音乐。您可以向戎王赠送女子歌舞乐队，用来迷惑戎王，扰乱其国政。然后替由余请假，阻隔由余的劝谏。他们君臣之间有了隔膜，以后就可以策划夺取戎地了。"穆公说："很好！"便派内史廖带十六人组成的女子歌舞乐队赠给戎王，顺便替由余请假迟归。戎王满口答应，见到女乐队十分高兴，搭幕帐，设酒宴，天天赏乐观舞。西戎本以畜牧业立国，民众逐水草而居，根据情况随时迁移牧场。但戎王迷恋女乐，一年到头也不往水草茂盛的地方迁移，结果牛马牲畜死亡过半，可以说失去了立国之本。后来由余回国，就去劝谏戎王。戎王听不进去，由余只好回到秦国。穆公亲自迎接由余并拜为上卿，详细询问戎国的军事力量和地理形势。穆公掌握了情况之后，便出兵攻打戎地，兼并十二国，开拓领土千余里。

《韩非子·十过》篇用这个故事来论述君主的十种过错之第六"耽溺女乐"，说明"耽溺女乐不顾国家政事，就会召来亡国之祸"的道理。同篇还记载了一个类似的故事：春秋时著名的音乐家师旷讲述前代历史事实，对晋平公详细阐述了君主沉溺于"靡靡之乐"足以造成亡国的道理。《庄子》中也有类似的故事：赵文王喜好剑术，击剑的人蜂拥而至，有剑客三千余人，他们在赵文王面前日夜比试剑术，死伤的剑客每年都有百余人，而赵文王喜好击剑的兴趣从来就不曾得到满足，致使国力衰退，赵国安全受到威胁。为劝说赵王，就有了庄子论剑的事情。需要指出的是，不管什么人，玩物丧志、沉迷于感官享乐之中，最终都得不到什么好结局。

DUKE MU OF QIN WINS THE LOYALTY OF YOUYU

In the Spring and Autumn Period, the King of Xirong (a nomadic tribe in the west) once sent Youyu to the State of Qin for a state visit. When meeting Youyu, Duke Mu of Qin asked him, "I have heard about the ways of running a state, but I've never seen them with my own eyes. I hope to listen to your explanation about the reasons why the ancient monarchs could keep or lose their states."

Youyu answered, "I have heard the ancient monarchs usually keep their states owing to their frugality, and they often lost their states due to extravagance." Duke Mu felt very puzzled, and then Youyu elaborated on this at great length, evoking such hearty admiration of Duke Mu that he kept nodding his head to show his agreement. After Youyu left, Duke Mu called in the royal secretary Liao and asked, "I hear that a wise man in a state is a worry for its enemy state. Now Youyu is a wise man, so I feel very worried. What should I do?" The royal secretary Liao answered, "I hear that the land occupied by the King of Xirong is both poor and remote, so he hasn't heard the music of the Central Plains. Your Majesty can send a band of women dancers, singers and musicians to the King of Xirong to confuse him and to disturb his mind in dealing with state affairs. Then you can ask for Youyu's leave to prevent him from going back to offer advice for his king. When there appears discord between Youyu and his king, we can plan to seize the territory of Xirong." Duke Mu said, "Very good." Then he sent the royal secretary Liao to bring a band of sixteen women dancers, singers and musicians as presents to the King of Xirong and ask for Youyu's leave at the same time. The King of Xirong agreed to Youyu's leave. Seeing the women's band, the king was very pleased, so he set up tents, prepared banquets, listened to the music and watched the dance every day. Xirong was a nomadic tribe that depended upon husbandry, and its people moved around as the season changed so as to be able to live where there was enough water and grass. But as the King of Xirong indulged himself in women and music, he wouldn't move to where there was abundant water and grass all the year round. As a result, over half of Xirong's cattle and horses died, and the tribe lost its livelihood. Later, when Youyu returned to Xirong, he went to persuade the king. As the king wouldn't listen, Youyu had to go back to the State of Qin. Duke Mu of Qin welcomed Youyu in person and appointed him as the senior minister. The duke also consulted Youyu on the military force and geography of Xirong. When Duke Mu obtained all the necessary information, he dispatched troops to attack

Xirong and expanded his territory significantly by annexing twelve states.

The story in the "Ten Faults" chapter of *Han Feizi* shows the sixth of a monarch's ten faults, "indulging himself in women and music", and explains that "if the monarch indulges himself in women and music and disregards state affairs, he will bring destruction to his state." There is also a similar story in the same chapter: Shi Kuang, a famous musician in the Spring and Autumn Period, explained to Duke Ping of Jin how a monarch would bring downfall to his state if he indulges himself in "demoralizing music". A story in *Zhuangzi* offers a similar moral: King Wen of Zhao was fond of sword play, so as many as 3,000 swordsmen came to curry the king's favor. The swordsmen dueled in front of the king every day and night, and over a hundred were injured or killed every year. Yet, the king's interest in sword play never waned, and the State of Zhao was weakened in its state power and military force. In order to admonish the king, Zhuangzi himself presented a fine speech about the sword play. All in all, indulgence in sensual pleasures won't yield any desirable results.

76. 刻在荆棘刺尖上的猕猴

　　燕国国王很喜欢精雕细刻、小巧玲珑的东西。有个卫国人说："我能在荆棘的刺尖上雕刻猕猴。"燕王很高兴，就用二十平方里土地的俸禄去供养他。随后燕王说："我想看看你雕刻在荆棘刺尖上的猕猴。"这个卫国人回答道："君王要想看到它，就必须先斋戒半年，在这期间不入后宫，不喝酒不吃肉；然后等到雨刚停、太阳刚出来时，在太阳照射不到的阴凉处再来观赏。只有这样，才能看清楚我在荆棘刺尖上刻的猕猴。"燕王因为那些条件都做不到，只好把这个卫国人一直供养着，但始终看不到他刻的猕猴。后来有个铁匠对燕王说："我听说，君主没有不喝酒不作乐的斋戒。现在这人知道君主不能长时间斋戒后再去观看那件没有用处的东西，所以定下了半年的斋戒期。这里头一定有鬼。我是做雕刻刀的工人，明白其中的道理。所有微小的东西一定要用雕刻刀来雕刻，被雕刻的东西一定会比雕刻刀大。现在的情形是，荆棘刺尖上容纳不下雕刻刀的刀锋，任何雕刻刀的刀锋都难以刻削荆棘刺的顶端。我作为一个铁匠，没有办法给那个卫国人制作雕刻刀。那所谓的猕猴肯定是不可能有的东西，大王一定要予以明察才是。大王不妨看看他的雕刻刀，能不能在荆棘刺尖上刻东西也就很清楚了。"燕王说："嗯，说得很对！"于是就问那个卫国人："你在荆棘刺尖上雕刻猕猴，是用什么工具来刻削的？"卫国人说："用雕刻刀。"燕王说："我想看看你的雕刻刀！"卫国人说："请您允许我回住处去取来。"卫国人这一去，就再也没敢回来。铁匠由此对燕王说："计谋是没有一定的标准加以衡量的。进言献计之人所说的话，多半是这种要在荆棘刺尖上雕刻猕猴之类的胡言乱语。"

韩非讲这个故事的目的，是要说明"君主听取意见，要把功效作为目的"的道理。君主不能被那些信口开河的臣下、辩士所迷惑，不管他们言语多么华丽，讲得多么天花乱坠，所声称的东西多么诱人和不可思议，君主始终要牢记把实际的功效作为检验的标准。这个声称能在荆棘刺尖上雕刻猕猴的卫国人，跟安徒生童话《皇帝的新衣》里的那两个骗子很相像。对于这一类违反常识的行动和言语，判断其真假的最好办法是像铁匠那样"回到常识"，用基本的逻辑和道理去推敲。

THE MACAQUE CARVED ON THE TIP OF A THORN

The King of Yan was fond of exquisitely and cleverly carved objects. A man from the State of Wei said, "I can carve a macaque on the tip of a thorn." The King of Yan was very pleased, so he provided the man with the salary from a land of twenty square *li*. Then the King of Yan requested, "I'd like to see the macaque you have carved on the tip of a thorn." This man from the State of Wei said, "If Your Majesty wants to see it, you have to go through a fast for half a year, during which you can't enter the ladies' chambers, or drink, or eat meat. You must wait until the moment when the rain has just stopped and the sun has just risen, and then you can see it in a shadowed place where the sun can't reach. Only in this way can you see clearly the macaque I have carved on the tip of the thorn." Since these requirements couldn't be met, the King of Yan had to go on providing for this man from Wei, without seeing the carved macaque at all. Later, a blacksmith said to the King of Yan, "I've never heard that monarchs observe long fasts that forbid drinking or merrymaking. Now this man knows that Your Majesty can't endure a long fast to see that useless thing, so he suggests a fast of half a year. There's some dirty work going on here. I make carving tools, so I understand how things work. All the minute objects must be made with carving tools, and the carved object has to be larger than the carving tool. The present situation is that the tip of a thorn can't hold the blade of a carving tool, and no carving tool can be applied to the tip of a thorn. As a blacksmith, I have no way to make a carving tool for that man from the State of Wei. The so-called macaque can't be possible, so Your Majesty must look into the whole matter. For example, Your Majesty might take a look at his carving tool. In that case, it will be clear whether he can carve anything on the tip of a thorn." The King of Yan said, "Yes, you are right." Then the king asked the man from Wei, "What do you use to carve the macaque on the tip of the thorn?" The man from Wei said, "A carving tool." The King of Yan said, "I'd like to have a look at your carving tool." The man from Wei said, "Please allow me to go back to my residence to get it." The man from Wei left, however, never to return. The blacksmith then said to the King of Yan, "Ruses always come up to defy established criteria. A panacea advice is often such nonsense as carving a macaque on the tip of a thorn."

Han Feizi tells this story to explain that "the monarch should judge advice by its effect." The monarch shouldn't be confused by those ministers or sophists who make wonderful speeches. No matter how beautiful their words are, no matter how extravagantly colorful their descriptions may sound, or no matter how appealing and incredible they claim the things to be, the monarch should always keep in mind that the advice's viability lies in its effect. The man from Wei who claimed to be able to carve a macaque on the tip of a thorn is similar to the two cheats in Andersen's fairy tale "The Emperor's New Clothes". As for such kind of abnormal actions and speeches, the best way to expose their falsehood is to "go back to the common sense" as the blacksmith did — putting the claims to the test of logic and reason.

77. 中山国是否可以攻打？

　　战国时候，赵武灵王有一次派李疵去打探中山国的情况，看可不可以攻打该国。李疵回来报告说："中山国可以攻打。您不赶紧攻打的话，就要落在齐国和燕国的后面了。"武灵王说："你根据什么说它可以攻打呢？"李疵回答说："中山国君亲近隐居而不出来做官的人。他亲自驱车拜访那些人并和他们同车出入，得到这样待遇的人有好几十个，中山国君以此来表彰显扬那些居住在小街小巷里不求闻达的读书人。他用平等的礼节来对待不做官的读书人，得到这样待遇的人有好几百个。"赵武灵王说："按你的话来判断，中山国君是个贤明的君主，怎么可以攻打他呢？"李疵说："不是这样的。喜欢显扬隐士并让他们参加朝会，战士们打仗时就会懈怠；君主尊重学者，文士高居朝廷，农夫就会懒于耕作。战士打仗时懈怠，兵力就削弱了；农夫懒于耕作，国家就贫穷了。兵力比敌人弱，国家内部又穷，这样怎么可能不衰亡呢？

照我这么说，攻打中山国难道不是可行的吗？"赵武灵王说："很好。"就起兵攻打，并灭亡了中山国。

战国时连年战乱，生民涂炭，不少贤士深感灰心失望，不愿入世而隐居，他们中有很多才能卓越的智者。各国竞相征召隐士让他们做官，尊重隐士成了风气。李疵的看法与此相左，但很受韩非的赞赏，韩非说，"那些隐居而从事私学的人，国家没有战争时不耕田出力，国家有难时又不披甲打仗。敬重这种人，就会使那些守法的民众不再努力从事耕战；不敬重这种人，他们就会危害君主的法制。国家安定，他们就尊贵显赫；国家遭到危难，他们就只会感到恐惧而无能为力——君主从这些隐居而从事私学的人那里能得到什么呢？"韩非的观点很清楚，亲近并重用隐士将导致民众不再努力从事耕战，国力大大削弱，极大地阻碍国家的发展。

CAN THE STATE OF ZHONGSHAN BE ATTACKED?

In the Warring States Period, King Wuling of Zhao once sent Li Ci to scout about the State of Zhongshan, in order to determine if it could be attacked. Li Ci came back and reported, "The State of Zhongshan can be attacked. If you don't launch the attack soon, either the State of Qi or the State of Yan will do so." King Wuling said, "What are your reasons to claim that it can be attacked?" Li Ci answered, "The monarch of Zhongshan likes those who live in recluse and refuse official posts. He goes to visit them by carriage himself and travels with them in his own carriage. There are dozens of people who have gotten such treatment. He uses this to praise the scholars who live in small streets or lanes without hoping to be officials. He treats like peers the scholars who are not in

the officialdom, and hundreds of people have gotten such treatment." King ·
Wuling of Zhao said, "According to what you said, the monarch of Zhongshan
is a wise one. How can we attack his state?" Li Ci said, "It's not that way. If the
monarch likes to praise men in recluse and asks them to take part in the royal
court meeting, the soldiers will suffer from low morale during battles; if the
monarch values scholars and lets them hold important positions in the royal
court, the farmers will become lazy when doing farm work. When the soldiers
have low morale during battles, the military power is weakened; when the farmers are lazy, the state becomes poor. When its military power is weaker than its
enemy and its coffers are empty, how will it not decline? According to what I
said, isn't it a good idea to attack the State of Zhongshan?" King Wuling said,
"Very good." Then he dispatched troops and conquered the State of Zhongshan.

During the Warring States Period, many talented people were disappointed
at the social chaos and poverty due to perennial warfare, so they shunned their
social responsibilities and lived in recluse. Some of those recluses boasted
great wisdom. All the states were eager to recruit those recluses into officialdom,
and respect for those recluses had been a popular trend at that time. However,
Li Ci held a different opinion that was appreciated by Han Feizi. According to
Han Feizi, "Those who live in recluse and engage in private studies neither do
farm work when the state is in peace nor put on armor to fight on the battlefield
when the state is at war. If those people are respected, the law-abiding public
will no longer want to work hard on the farmlands or on the battlefield; if those
people are not respected, they may pose a threat to the monarch's rule. When
the state is safe, they are in honorable positions; when the state is under attack,
they can do nothing but panic. What does a monarch get from those who live in
recluse and engage in private studies?" Han Feizi makes his point clear: unnecessary respect for the people living in recluse might discourage the general
public from doing their duties in farm work and military service, and possibly
lead to a setback in national development.

78. 齐景公弃车奔跑

　　春秋时的齐景公，有一次离开国都到渤海边游玩。驿使从国都赶来谒见说："上大夫晏子病得很重，快要死了，恐怕您赶不上见他最后一面了。"晏子是春秋时有名的贤臣，是齐景公最重要的辅佐大臣。所以景公闻讯非常着急，立刻起身准备出发赶回去。这时又有驿使到达告急，景公就更着急了，命令说："赶紧套上千里马拉的车，叫马车官韩枢驾车。"才跑了几百步，景公嫌韩枢赶马赶得不快，就夺过缰绳，亲自驾车。又跑了几百步，景公还是觉得慢，怪马不肯卖力往前跑，就干脆丢下车子，自己向前奔跑。凭千里马那样的好马和马车官韩枢那样高超的驾驭本领，而齐景公竟会认为不如自己下车跑得快！

　　这则故事刻画齐景公情急之下"不经过大脑"的行为非常生动。但韩非讲这个故事，其用意在于讽刺不懂"任势"的人。韩非说："如果不明确君臣名分，不要求臣下真心实意地效力，反要亲自出马管理臣下，那将会像齐景公不用车子而下去奔跑的事情一样愚蠢。"抛弃马车而自己徒步奔跑，现实生活中恐怕没有愚蠢到这种地步的人。但是众多放弃驭使臣下而事必躬亲的君主，和下车跑步的人实际却是十分相像的。

DUKE JING OF QI HOPS OFF HIS CARRIAGE TO RUN ON FOOT

Duke Jing of Qi in the Spring and Autumn Period once left the state capital to go sightseeing by the Bohai Sea. A courier came from the capital with sad news for the king, "Yanzi is critically ill. He's dying, and you probably can't make it to see him before he passes away." Yanzi was a famous wise minister in the Spring and Autumn Period and the most important counsellor of Duke Jing of Qi. The news brought great anxiety to the duke, and he decided to go back to the capital immediately. Then another courier came bearing still more urgent news of Yanzi's illness. Duke Jing became more anxious and ordered, "Ready the carriage pulled by the strongest horse and have the most skillful driver Han Shu drive it." After the carriage had just run a few hundred steps, Duke Jing thought that Han Shu didn't drive fast enough. So he took over the reins and drove himself. After another few hundred steps, Duke Jing thought that the horse didn't run fast enough. So he hopped off his carriage to run ahead. It was so odd for the good duke to believe that he could go faster by running on foot than traveling in his carriage, which was pulled by the strongest horse and driven by the most skillful driver Han Shu!

The story vividly depicts how Duke Jing of Qi takes silly actions without going through his brains in a desperate situation. However, Han Feizi relates to the story as a satire for those who are unable to "play out their roles". Han Feizi says, "If the monarch doesn't distinguish his own role from the ministers' roles, or if the monarch tells the ministers what to do without counting on their commitment to their duties, he is just as foolish as Duke Jing of Qi who hops off his carriage to run himself." There might not be such foolish people who prefer running on foot to traveling in a vehicle in real life. But the monarchs who give up controlling the ministers and attend to everything in person are actually similar to Duke Jing of Qi who hops off the carriage to run on foot.

79. 子皋断狱

　　孔子曾担任卫国的宰相，当时他的弟子子皋担任狱吏。任职期间，子皋依法砍掉了一个犯人的脚，按当时规定，被砍脚的犯人得去看守城门。后来有人在卫君面前中伤孔子说："孔子图谋作乱。"卫君打算捉拿孔子。孔子只好出逃，弟子们也都跟着孔子逃跑。结果子皋落在后面，到城门时眼看要被捉住了。这时那个断足守门人引着子皋逃到门边屋子里躲起来，最终官吏没有抓到子皋。到了半夜，追捕的事情终于平息下来了，看着难关就要过去，子皋就问那断足守门人："我不能破坏君主的法令，只得亲自判决砍掉了你的脚。现在正是你报仇的时候，为什么反而肯帮助我逃走呢？"那断足守门人说："我被砍掉脚，本来就是我罪有应得，这是没有办法的事情。但是当您按刑法给我定罪时，您反复权衡推敲法令条文，想尽办法为我说话，很想让我免罪，这些我心里都清楚。等到案子判定了，您心里十分不快，脸色上都表露出来了，这些我也清楚地看在眼里。您并不是徇私照顾我，而是本着与生俱来的仁爱之心才这样做的。这便是我心悦诚服并要报答您的原因。"

那个断足守门人可谓"仇将恩报"，由于"仇人"相救，子皋才得以死里逃生。韩非对这个故事总结说："以罪受诛，人不怨上。"由此可见公布成文法令和依法办事的重要性。有公开的法令在，犯人自己都可以判断自己是否有罪以及所判刑罚是否适当，避免执法官上下其手。执法官依法办事，犯人也就无话可说，只能认罪伏法。

ZIGAO PASSES VERDICTS

Confucius once acted as the prime minister of the State of Wei, during which his disciple Zigao worked as a prison officer. When in office, Zigao cut off a prisoner's feet as punishment according to law. The feetless prisoner was sent to keep the city gates in accordance with the rules then. Later someone defamed Confucius in the presence of the monarch of Wei, saying, "Confucius is plotting a revolt." The monarch of Wei intended to arrest Confucius, so Confucius had to escape, followed by his disciples. However, Zigao lagged behind and was about to be caught at the city gate. At that moment, that gate keeper whose feet were cut off led Zigao to hide in a house beside the gate, so Zigao was safe. At midnight, the commotion finally came to an end. Seeing that he was no longer in danger, Zigao asked the feetless gate keeper, "I can't violate the monarch's decrees, so I had to pass the verdict to cut your feet off. Now it's just the time for you to take revenge. Why do you help me to escape instead?" The gate keeper said, "I had my feet cut because I deserved it myself. No one could help with that. However, when you made the judgement on my case according to law, you repeatedly measured and weighed the decrees and stipulations, trying every means to speak for me. You really wanted to make me free of the punishment, which I knew clearly in my mind. When the judgement was made, you were so unhappy, which was all shown on your face. I saw this clearly with my own eyes. You didn't take care of me out of personal consideration, but out of the benevolence you were born with. This is why I have heartfelt admiration for you and want to pay back your kindness."

The feetless gate keeper actually "returns punishment with gratitude". Thanks to the help from someone who should have borne enmity against him, Zigao was able to escape a narrow death. Han Feizi summarizes the story with the following statement, "When a person is punished by law, he won't hold any grudge against the officials." This shows the importance of announcing statutes and acting in accordance with the law. With laws and decrees made known to everyone, even the prisoners themselves can judge whether they are guilty or not and whether the punishment is proper, while the law enforcers have no way of bending the laws at their will. When the law enforcers act according to the law, the criminals will have nothing to say but to plead guilty and await their verdicts.

80. "夔一足"

　　鲁哀公向孔子询问道："我听说古代有个'夔一足'，它果真只有一只脚吗？"孔子回答说："不是的，夔并非只有一只脚。因为夔这种野兽残暴凶狠，人们大多不喜欢它。虽说如此，它之所以还能避免被人伤害，是因为它守信用。人们都说：'单是有这一点，就足够了。''夔一足'不是'夔仅有一只脚'，而是'夔有这么一点就足够了'。"鲁哀公说："真是这样的话，有能守信用这么一点确实就足够了。"

　　关于这个故事还有另一种说法：鲁哀公向孔子询问道："我听说夔仅一足，可信吗？"孔子说："夔是人，怎么会仅有一只脚呢？他和别人没有什么差别，唯独能精通音律。尧说：'这种人有一个就足够了。'于是派他做主管音乐的官，所以君子说：'夔有一个就足够了。'并不是只有一只脚。"

　　这个故事还见载于《吕氏春秋·察传》等典籍中，"夔一足"应该是当时流行很广的传说。"夔"既是传说中的兽名，又相传是尧时的乐官。神话传说中的人或兽，本来就不是真实存在的，其形象往往具有常人觉得不可思议的神异性，这并不足为怪。"夔一足"也应该本来就是"夔只有一只脚"的意思。但孔子不谈论怪异、勇力、叛乱和鬼神，他对"夔一足"的解释，体现出了孔子客观理性的态度，反映出他要将神话传说加以合理化解释的努力。中国神话不像希腊神话那样系统，显得零碎，很重要的原因是神话转化成了历史，"夔一足"意义的变化，是对这一转变的印证。韩非引述这个故事，也为他"废先王之教"的论点提供了支持。

"KUI, THE ONE-LEGGED MONSTER"

Duke Ai of Lu asked Confucius, "I have heard that there was a 'one-legged monster' called Kui in ancient times. Did it really have one leg?" Confucius answered, "No, Kui didn't just have one leg. As Kui was a cruel and ferocious beast, people didn't like it. Nevertheless, it could avoid being hurt by people because it kept its word. People all said, 'This quality alone is enough.' 'Kui, the one-legged monster' doesn't mean 'Kui only has one leg', but means that 'Just one fine quality alone is enough for Kui.'" Duke Ai of Lu said, "If that is the case, the quality of keeping its word alone is indeed enough."

There was another version of this story. Duke Ai of Lu asked Confucius, "I have heard that Kui had only one leg. Is it true?" Confucius said, "Kui was human. How could he have only one leg? He was no different from others. He was just proficient with music. Yao said, 'One such person is enough.' Then the legendary emperor appointed Kui as the official in charge of music, so the gentlemen said, 'One such person like Kui is enough.' It's not that Kui had only one leg."

This story is also recorded in other works such as *Lü's Spring and Autumn Annals*. It is interesting in that it plays on a pun: the Chinese character *zu* means both "foot" and "enough", hence the popular legend of "Kui, the one-legged monster" at that time. "Kui" was both the name of a mythical beast and an official said to be in charge of music in Yao's time. The man or the beast depicted in the myth didn't exist in reality, so it was not surprising that it finally developed a mystical image which common people regarded as incredible. "Kui, the one-legged monster" originally should mean "Kui only had one leg." But Confucius didn't engage in talks about strange happenings, brute forces, rebellions and supernatural beings. His explanation of "Kui, the one-legged monster" shows his attitude toward objective rationality and reflects his efforts to give rationalized explanation to myths and legends. Chinese mythology is not as systematic as Greek mythology and may appear fragmented. An important reason for that is that Chinese mythology has been transformed into history. The change of the meaning of "Kui, the one-legged monster" is good proof for this transformation. Han Feizi quotes this story to support his idea of abolishing the out-dated doctrines of the ancient kings.

81. 自相矛盾

  楚国有个卖长矛和盾牌的人，有一天到市场上去叫卖。他先是向大家夸他的盾牌说："我的这个盾牌，是世界上最坚固的东西，没有什么东西能够刺穿它！"接着又夸他的长矛说："我的这个长矛，是世界上最锐利的东西，没有什么东西是它刺不穿的！"听到这话，围观的人群中马上就有人驳斥他说："那要是拿你的长矛来刺你的盾牌，结果会怎么样呢？到底是盾牌可以挡住长矛呢，还是长矛会把盾牌刺穿呢？"那卖长矛和盾牌的人顿时就张口结舌，说不出话来了。

  《韩非子》讲完这个故事后总结说："不能被刺穿的盾牌和没有什么刺不穿的长矛，在道理上是不可能同时存在的。"在《难一》篇中，韩非用这个故事作比喻，来说明"尧和舜不能同时称赞"。当时广为流传的历史故事说，在尧将帝位禅让给舜之前，舜曾经用自己的道德去感化人民，改变了历山农民相互侵占田界、黄河渔夫争夺水中高地的坏风气，一般人对此深信不疑。而韩非认为，如果尧确实为圣人明君，那么当时天下就不应该出现这样的坏风气，舜也就没有必要用道德去感化人民，否则就只能证明尧也有过失。"认为舜贤，就是否定尧的明察；认为尧圣，就是否定舜的德化——不可能二者都对。"同时，"贤治"和"势治"两者不能相容。因为按照贤治的原则，贤人是不受约束的；而按照势治的原则，君主的权势是没有什么管不了的，没有什么不能约束的。不受约束的贤治和没有什么不能约束的势治二者之间就构成了矛盾。韩非认为，答案只能有一个，那就是"任势"，使贤者服从权势才是顺理成章的。

不得不说，韩非这两处的论证，在逻辑上是非常有力的。后来发展起来的逻辑学，在形式逻辑中有一条"矛盾律"，"矛盾"一词就是从这里来的。"矛盾律"可以有多种不同的表述：作为事物的规律，它指的是任一事物不能同时既具有某属性又不具有某属性；作为思维规律，则是指在同一思维过程中，任一命题不能既真又不真，在同一时间、同一关系下对同一对象所作的相互对立的两个判断不能同时都真，其中必有一假。违反矛盾律的后果，就像这个卖矛和盾的商人一样，会"自己打自己的嘴巴"。后人根据这个故事，引申出"自相矛盾"这个成语，用来说明一个人夸大事实或做出前后不相符的事情，比喻语言、行动前后不一致或互相抵触；又引申出"以子之矛，攻子之盾"的成语，比喻用对方的言论、方法或缺点来反驳或攻击对方。

THE SELF-CONTRADICTION OF SPEAR AND SHIELD

Once there was a man selling spears and shields in the State of Chu. One day he went to the market to peddle his wares. He first bragged about his shield,

"This shield of mine is the most solid in the world that nothing can pierce it." He then bragged about his spear, "This spear of mine is the sharpest in the world that it can pierce through anything." Hearing his words, someone in the crowd refuted him at once, "What will happen if we thrust your spear at your shield? Will your shield be hard enough to withstand your spear or will your spear pierce into your shield?" The man selling spears and shields suddenly became dumbfounded, unable to utter a single word.

After telling this story, *Han Feizi* says in conclusion, "Logic dictates that the shield that can withstand anything and the spear that can pierce through anything can't exist at the same time." Han Feizi uses this story to explain that "Yao and Shun can't be both praised." According to the historical stories prevailing at that time, before Yao (a legendary emperor) passed the throne to Shun, Shun had guided the people toward a higher moral ground with his own examples and put an end to the immoral behaviors of the peasants in Lishan who encroached upon each other's fields and the fishermen on the Yellow River who fought with each other for the shoals in the river. People generally believed these without doubt, but Han Feizi thought that if Yao was indeed a wise monarch, there shouldn't have been such immoral behaviors in the country at that time and Shun wouldn't have to dedicate his efforts to improving people's moral well-being. The immoral behaviors in the country only proved that Yao was far from spotless in his rule. "To praise Shun as wise amounts to denying Yao's keen observation; to praise Yao as virtuous amounts to denying Shun's moralization. The two kinds of praise can't be both right." At the same time, "ruling by virtue" and "ruling by force" are not compatible with each other. According to the principle of ruling by virtue, virtuous people are not subject to control, but according to the principle of ruling by force, the monarch's supreme power enables him to control everything. Ruling by virtue which is not subject to control becomes contradictory with ruling by force which keeps everything under control. Han Feizi thinks there is only one answer, that is, "ruling by having everyone playing out his role", from which it logically follows that virtuous people should come under law.

Sound logic can be found in Han Feizi's stories "The Self-Contradiction of Spear and Shield" and "The Contradictory Praises for Yao and Shun". Actually the principle of contradiction in the formal logic is translated to "spear and shield" in Chinese. There are various iterations of the principle of contradiction. As a general rule, the principle of contradiction refers to the fact that any object cannot possess a certain attribute and deny that attribute at the same time. As a cognitive rule, the principle of contradiction refers to the fact that any proposition cannot be true and untrue at the same time in a certain process of inference; two opposite judgements of one object at the same time under the same situation cannot be both correct, as there must be an incorrect one among the two. Violation of the principle of contradiction only leads to absurdities like the case of the proverbial seller of spears and shields, "slapping himself right in the face". "The self-contradiction of spear and shield" has been widely used as a Chinese idiom to describe the incongruities in talks or behaviors, and the idiom "Your spear is used against your shield" describes a retort that applies the opponent's faulty arguments.